Praise for *Functional Programming with C#*

Simon is my go to for all things functional programming. This book perfectly reflects his knowledge, expertly guiding the reader through the topic.

—*Pete Gallagher, Microsoft Meetup Organizer and Development Manager at Avanade UK*

Functional Programming with C# takes a pragmatic view—building real solutions from functional aspects built into C# and techniques that bring even more functionality to C#.

—*Kathleen Dollard, Principal Program Manager, .NET, at Microsoft*

If you're diving into the world of functional programming and want to use C#, Simon Painter's book is a clear and helpful guide. He doesn't just throw around jargon or get lost in abstract concepts. Instead, Simon breaks down challenging topics into simple terms, making them easy to understand.

One of the standout features of the book is its examples. Simon offers great real-world examples that show the true benefits of functional programming in C#. These aren't just abstract ideas; they're practical tools and techniques you can use in your projects right away.

—*Chris Ayers, Senior Customer Engineer at Microsoft*

This book is an excellent guide on how to think functionally and better utilize the functional features of C# to write simpler, more robust code.

—*Ian Russell, Author of* Essential F#

Simon Painter makes functional programming easily accessible and applicable to C# developers new and experienced, even those as intransigent as myself, in *Functional Programming with C#*.

—*Jimmy Bogard, Independent Consultant*

Simon explains the benefits of functional programming succinctly, using helpful code samples to illustrate topics ranging from FP basics to more advanced features, as well as how to apply them in C#.

—*Isaac Abraham, Author of* F# in Action

As I was new to developing (+25y infra background), reading *Functional Programming with C#* was a hard nut to crack at first. When Simon described the concepts using a "baking cakes" analogy, it all started to make sense. Closing the book by building a Martian Trail game to the year 2147 was a great finish of the learning experience, and another analogy for the stretch of knowledge I picked up by going through this book.

—*Peter De Tender, Technical Trainer at Microsoft*

Functional Programming with C#

Create More Supportable, Robust,
and Testable Code

Simon J. Painter

Beijing · Boston · Farnham · Sebastopol · Tokyo  O'REILLY®

Functional Programming with C#

by Simon J. Painter

Published by O'Reilly Media, Inc., 1005 Gravenstein Highway North, Sebastopol, CA 95472.

O'Reilly books may be purchased for educational, business, or sales promotional use. Online editions are also available for most titles (*http://oreilly.com*). For more information, contact our corporate/institutional sales department: 800-998-9938 or *corporate@oreilly.com*.

Acquisitions Editor: Brian Guerin	**Indexer:** Sue Klefstad
Development Editor: Jill Leonard	**Interior Designer:** David Futato
Production Editor: Gregory Hyman	**Cover Designer:** Karen Montgomery
Copyeditor: Sharon Wilkey	**Illustrator:** Kate Dullea
Proofreader: Kim Cofer	

September 2023:   First Edition

Revision History for the First Edition

2023-09-12:   First Release

See *https://www.oreilly.com/catalog/errata.csp?isbn=9781492097075* for release details.

978-1-492-09707-5

[LSI]

To my wife, Sushma Mahadik. My Billi.

Also to my two daughters, Sophie and Katie. Your daddy loves you, girls.

Table of Contents

Part I. What Are We Already Doing?

Part II.   Into the Belly of the Functional

Part III.   And Out the Other Side

Preface

I attend developers' conferences as often as I'm able and have noticed a trend. Each year, there always seems to be more content about functional programming (FP), not less. Often an entire track is dedicated to it, and the other talks include FP content somewhere as a talking point.

FP is slowly but surely becoming a big deal. Why is that?

Because FP is one of the greatest innovations in the history of software development. It's also cool. Fun as well.

With the growth of concepts like containerization and serverless applications, FP isn't just a bit of fun for developers' free-time projects; it's not a fad that'll be forgotten in a few years. It has real benefit to bring to our stakeholders.

Further, in the .NET world, several additional factors are at play. Mads Torgerson, the C# lead designer, is himself a fan of FP, and one of the major driving forces behind the adoption of the functional paradigm into .NET. There's also F#, the .NET functional language. Because F# and C# share a common runtime, many functional features requested by the F# team often become available in C# in some form as well.

The big questions remain, though: What is FP? And will I need to learn an entire new programming language just to be able to use it? The good news is that if you're a .NET developer, you don't need to spend large chunks of your own time learning a new technology just to stay up-to-date. You don't even have to invest in another third-party library to add to your application's dependencies: FP is possible with out-of-the-box C# code, albeit with a little tinkering around.

This book introduces all the fundamental concepts of FP, demonstrates their benefits, and describes how they might be achieved in C#—not just for your own hobby programming, but with a real eye toward bringing immediate benefit to your work life as well.

These benefits include things such as the following:

- Code that is cleaner, tidier, and easier to read
- An easier-to-maintain codebase
- Applications that are significantly less likely to suffer from unhandled exceptions and their unpredictable consequences
- A codebase that's easier to write automated unit tests for

All this and more!

Who Should Read This Book?

This book is intended for developers—whether professional, student, or hobbyist—who already have a basic grounding in C#. You don't need to be an expert but do need to be familiar with the basics and feel comfortable putting together at least a relatively simply C# application.

Some more advanced .NET topics are covered, but I'll provide explanations when they come up.

This book has been written with a few categories of people in mind:

- Those of you who have learned the basics of C# but want to find ways to take your learning further via more advanced techniques for writing better, more robust code.
- .NET developers who have heard of FP and perhaps even know what it is, but want to know how to get started writing code that way in C#.
- F# developers looking for ways to keep using the functional toys you're used to.
- Those migrating to .NET from another functional, or functional-supporting, language (like Java).
- Anyone who really, truly loves coding. If you spend all day writing code in the office, then come home to write more for fun, this book is probably for you.

Why I Wrote This Book

I've been interested in programming for as long as I can remember. When I was a young boy, we had a ZX Spectrum, a British home computer developed by Sinclair Research in the early '80s. If anyone remembers the Commodore 64, it was a bit like that but far more primitive. It had just 15 colors and a screen resolution of 256 × 192.[1] I had the more advanced model with 48K of memory, though my Dad had the earlier machine, the ZX81, which had a single kilobyte of memory available (and rubber keys). It couldn't even have colored-in character sprites, just areas of the screen, so your game avatar would change color to that of whatever they were standing in front of. In short, it was pure awesome on toast.

One of the best things about it was its OS that effectively consisted of a text-based programming interface, and code was required to load a game (from a cassette tape, with the command LOAD ""), but magazines and books for kids were available with code you could enter yourself for games. It was from these that I developed my lasting obsession with the mysteries of computer code. Thanks so much, Usborne Publishing!

When I was around 14 years old or so, a computer-based careers advice program at school suggested I could think about taking up a career in software development. This is the first time I realized that you could take this silly hobby and turn it into something that you could actually make money from!

After university was over, it was time to get a proper job, and that was where I got my first exposure to C#. So the next step, I supposed, was to learn how to develop code *properly*. Easy, right? I'll be honest, nearly two decades on, I'm still trying to work that out.

One of the big turning points for me in my programming career was attending a developers' conference in Norway and finally starting to understand what this *functional programming* thing I'd been hearing about was actually about. Functional code is elegant, concise, and easy to read in a way that other forms of code just don't seem to be. As with any type of code, writing horrible-looking codebases is still possible, but the coding still fundamentally feels like it's finally being done *properly*, in a way that I've never really felt from other styles of coding. Hopefully, after reading this book, you'll not only agree but also be interested in searching out the many other avenues that exist out there for exploring it further.

Navigating This Book

This is how I've organized this book:

- Chapter 1 is the introduction and covers what you can do right now to start coding functionally in C#, without having to reference a single new NuGet package, use a third-party library, or hack around with the language. Nearly all

---

1 It had eight base colors and a bright version of each. One was black, though, and how on earth can you have bright black? So…15.

the examples in this chapter work with just about every version of C# since version 3. This chapter presents the very first steps into FP, all fairly easy code, which sets the groundwork for what's to come.

- Part I, "What Are We Already Doing?" (Chapters 2 through 4), is about ways to adopt a few functional ideas into your daily C# coding without needing to do anything that's fundamentally all that unfamiliar. Many of the code samples are straightforward, out-of-the-box C#. Try these chapters if you've never heard of FP before and want a nice, gentle introduction. Think of it as dipping your toes in the water to see if you're interested in going for a swim.

- Part II, "Into the Belly of the Functional" (Chapters 5 through 10), is where the gloves come off, and I start introducing some "proper" functional concepts. Don't panic, though; I'm going to be taking the gentle slope up to the summit, and will introduce ideas slowly and in easy-to-digest, bite-size pieces.

- Part III, "And Out the Other Side" (Chapters 11 through 14), wraps up and consolidates everything you've learned so far, as well as suggests where you might consider ways to continue learning further.

Feel free to dive in at the level you feel ready for. This isn't a novel;[2] read the chapters in the order that makes sense to you.

Conventions Used in This Book

The following typographical conventions are used in this book:

Italic
Indicates new terms, URLs, email addresses, filenames, and file extensions.

`Constant width`
Used for program listings, as well as within paragraphs to refer to program elements such as variable or function names, databases, data types, environment variables, statements, and keywords.

 This element signifies a general note.

---

2 But if this were a novel, you can guarantee it'd be a murder mystery, and the butler would have done it!

This element indicates a warning or caution.

Using Code Examples

Supplemental material (code examples, exercises, etc.) is available for download at *https://oreil.ly/functional-programming-with-csharp-code*.

If you have a technical question or a problem using the code examples, please send email to *bookquestions@oreilly.com*.

This book is here to help you get your job done. In general, if example code is offered with this book, you may use it in your programs and documentation. You do not need to contact us for permission unless you're reproducing a significant portion of the code. For example, writing a program that uses several chunks of code from this book does not require permission. Selling or distributing examples from O'Reilly books does require permission. Answering a question by citing this book and quoting example code does not require permission. Incorporating a significant amount of example code from this book into your product's documentation does require permission.

We appreciate, but generally do not require, attribution. An attribution usually includes the title, author, publisher, and ISBN. For example: "*Functional Programming with C#* by Simon J. Painter (O'Reilly). Copyright 2023 Simon J. Painter, 978-1-492-09707-5."

If you feel your use of code examples falls outside fair use or the permission given above, feel free to contact us at *permissions@oreilly.com*.

O'Reilly Online Learning

 For more than 40 years, *O'Reilly Media* has provided technology and business training, knowledge, and insight to help companies succeed.

Our unique network of experts and innovators share their knowledge and expertise through books, articles, and our online learning platform. O'Reilly's online learning platform gives you on-demand access to live training courses, in-depth learning paths, interactive coding environments, and a vast collection of text and video from O'Reilly and 200+ other publishers. For more information, visit *https://oreilly.com*.

How to Contact Us

Please address comments and questions concerning this book to the publisher:

O'Reilly Media, Inc.
1005 Gravenstein Highway North
Sebastopol, CA 95472
800-889-8969 (in the United States or Canada)
707-829-7019 (international or local)
707-829-0104 (fax)
support@oreilly.com
https://www.oreilly.com/about/contact.html

We have a web page for this book, where we list errata, examples, and any additional information. You can access this page at *https://oreil.ly/functional-programming-with-csharp*.

For news and information about our books and courses, visit *https://oreilly.com*.

Find us on LinkedIn: *https://linkedin.com/company/oreilly-media*

Follow us on Twitter: *https://twitter.com/oreillymedia*

Watch us on YouTube: *https://youtube.com/oreillymedia*

Acknowledgments

The very first person to thank is Kathleen Dollard. She gave a talk at the Norwegian Developers Conference (NDC) at Oslo some years ago called "Functional Techniques for C#." It was the first real exposure I'd ever had to FP, and it was a real eye-opener (*https://oreil.ly/nBpWu*).

The other guru I've followed on this trail is Enrico Buonanno, whose book *Functional Programming in C#* (Manning) was the first that allowed me to properly understand how some of the hard-to-grasp functional concepts worked. If you enjoy my book, please check out his next.

Ian Russell, Matthew Fletcher, Liam Riley, Max Dietze, Steve "Talks Code" Collins, Gerardo Lijs, Matt Eland, Rahul Nath, Siva Gudivada, Christian Horsdal, Martin Fuß, Dave McCollough, Sebastian Robbins, David Schaefer, Peter De Tender, Mark Seeman, Gerald Versluis, Alex Wild, Valadis Novakovits, Lackner Reinhard, Eric Lucas, Christopher Straten, Kathleen Dollard, and Scott Wlaschin read the early drafts and provided invaluable feedback. Thanks, folks!

Thanks also to my editor, Jill Leonard. She must have the patience of a saint to put up with me for a whole year!

CHAPTER 1
Introduction

If you've learned much programming before now—whether in C#, Microsoft Visual Basic, Python, or whatever—then chances are that what you learned was based around the programming paradigm that is currently the most dominant: object oriented. *Object-oriented programming* (OOP) has been around for quite a long time. The precise date is a matter of debate, but it was likely invented somewhere around the late '50s or early '60s.

Object-oriented coding is based around the idea of wrapping pieces of data—known as *properties*—and functionality into logical blocks of code called *classes*, which are used as a sort of template from which we instantiate *objects*. There's a lot more to it: inheritance, polymorphism, virtual and abstract methods—all sorts of stuff like that.

This is, however, not an OOP book. In fact, if you are already experienced with OOP, you'll probably get more from this book if you leave what you know already to one side.

In this book, I'll be describing a style of programming that serves as an alternative to OOP: functional programming (FP). FP, despite gaining some mainstream recognition in the last few years, is actually as old, if not older, than OOP. FP is based on mathematic principles developed between the late 1800s and 1950s, and has been a feature of some programming languages since the 1960s. I'll be showing you how to implement FP in C# without the necessity of learning a whole new programming language.

Before we get cracking with some code, I'd like to talk first about FP itself. What is it? Why should you be interested? When is it best used? These are all important questions.

What Is Functional Programming?

FP has a few basic concepts, many of which have fairly obscure names but are otherwise not terribly difficult to understand. I'll try to lay them out here as simply as I can.

Is It a Language, an API, or What?

FP isn't a language or a third-party plug-in library in NuGet; it's a *paradigm*. What do I mean by that? Although more formal definitions of paradigms exist, I think of it as a *style* of programming. Just as a guitar might be used to play many, often wildly different, styles of music, some programming languages offer support for different styles of working.

FP is also as old as OOP, if not older. I'll talk more about its origins in "Where Does Functional Programming Come From?" on page 14, but for now just be aware that it is nothing new, and the theory behind it predates not only OOP, but also the computing industry itself.

It's also worth noting that you can combine paradigms, like mixing rock and jazz. Not only can they combine, but sometimes you can use the best features of each to produce a better end result.

Programming paradigms come in many flavors,[1] but for the sake of simplicity, I'm going to talk about the two most common in modern programming:

Imperative
> This was the only type of programming paradigm for quite a long time. Procedural programming and OOP belong to this category. These styles of programming more directly instruct the executing environment of the steps that need to be executed in detail, i.e., which variable contains which intermediate steps and how the process is carried out step-by-step in minute detail. This is programming as it's usually taught in school or at work.

Declarative
> In this programming paradigm, we're less concerned with the precise details of how we accomplish our goal. Instead, the code more closely resembles a description of what is desired at the end of the process, and the details (such as the order of execution of the steps) are left more in the hands of the execution environment. This is the category FP belongs to. Structured Query Language

---

1 Including vanilla and my personal favorite, banana.

(SQL) also belongs here, so in some ways FP more closely resembles SQL than OOP. When writing SQL statements, you aren't concerned with the order of operations (it's not really `SELECT`, then `WHERE`, then `ORDER BY`), or with how exactly the data transformations are carried out in detail; you just write a script that effectively describes the desired output. These are some of the goals of functional C# as well, so those of you with a background working with Microsoft SQL Server or other relational databases might find some of the upcoming ideas easier to grasp than those who haven't.

Many more paradigms besides these exist, but they're well beyond the scope of this book. In fairness, most others are pretty obscure, so you're unlikely to run into them anytime soon.

The Properties of Functional Programming

This section covers each of the properties of FP and what they really mean to a developer.

Immutability

If something can *change*, it can also be said to *mutate*, like a Teenage Mutant Ninja Turtle.[2] Another way of saying that something can mutate is that it is *mutable*. If, on the other hand, something cannot change at all, it is *immutable*.

In programming, this refers to variables that have their value set upon being defined, and after that point, they may never be changed again. If a new value is required, a new variable should be created, based on the old one. This is how all variables are treated in functional code.

It's a slightly different way of working compared to imperative code, but it ends up producing programs that more closely resemble the step-by-step work we do in math to reach a solution. This approach encourages good structure and more predictable—and hence *more robust*—code.

`DateTime` and `String` are both immutable data structures in .NET. You may *think* you've altered them, but behind the scenes every alteration creates a new item on the stack. This is why most new developers get the talk about concatenating strings in `for` loops and why you should never, *ever* do it.

---

2 They were "hero turtles" when I was growing up in the United Kingdom in the '90s. I think the TV folks were trying to avoid the violent connotations of the word "ninja." They nevertheless still let us *see* our heroes regularly use sharp, bladed implements on their villains.

Higher-order functions

Higher-order functions are passed around as variables—either as local variables, parameters to a function, or return values from a function. The Func<T,TResult> or Action<T> delegate types are perfect examples.

In case you aren't familiar with these delegates, this is how they work in brief. They're both forms of functions stored as variables. They both take sets of generic types, which represent their parameters and return types, if any. The difference between Func and Action is that Action doesn't return any value—i.e., it's a void function that won't contain a return keyword. The last generic type listed in a Func is its return type.

Consider these functions:

```
// Given parameters 10 and 20, this would output the following string:
// "10 + 20 = 30"
public string ComposeMessage(int a, int b)
{
    return a + " + " + b + " = " + (a + b);
}

public void LogMessage(string a)
{
    this.Logger.LogInfo("message received: " + a);
}
```

They can be rewritten as delegate types like this:

```
Func<int, int, string> ComposeMessage =
    (a, b) => a + " + " + b + " = " + (a + b);

Action<string> LogMessage = a =>
  this.Logger.LogInfo($"message received: {a}");
```

These delegate types can be called exactly as if they were standard functions:

```
var message = ComposeMessage(10, 20);
LogMessage(message);
```

The big advantage of using these delegate types is that they're stored in variables that can be passed around the codebase. They can be included as parameters to other functions or as return types. Used properly, they're among the more powerful features of C#.

Using FP techniques, delegate types can be composed together to create larger, more complex functions from smaller, functional building blocks—like LEGO bricks being placed together to make a model *Millennium Falcon* or whatever you prefer. This is the real reason this paradigm is called *functional* programming: because we build our applications with *functions*, not, as the name suggests, that the code written in other paradigms doesn't function. Why would anyone ever use those paradigms if they didn't work?

In fact, here's a rule of thumb for you: if there's a question, FP's answer will almost certainly be "functions, functions, and more functions."

 Two kinds of callable code modules exist: functions and methods. Functions always return a value, but methods don't. In C#, functions return data of some kind, whereas methods have a return type of void. Because methods almost inevitably involve side effects, we should avoid any use of them in our code—except where unavoidable. Logging might be an example of method use that is not only unavoidable but also essential to good production code.

Expressions rather than statements

A couple of definitions are required here. *Expressions* are discrete units of code that evaluate to a value. What do I mean by that?

In their simplest form, these are expressions:

```
const int exp1 = 6;
const int exp2 = 6 * 10;
```

We can feed in values too, to form our expressions, so this is one as well:

```
public int addTen(int x) => x + 10;
```

This next one does carry out an operation—i.e., determine whether or not a condition is true—but it ultimately simply returns a value of type bool, so it's still an expression:

```
public bool IsTen(int x) => x == 10;
```

You can also consider ternary statements (the short form of an if statement) to be expressions if they're used purely for determining a value to return:

```
var randomNumber = this._rnd.Generate();
var message = randomNumber == 10
    ? "It was ten"
    : "it wasn't ten";
```

Another quick rule of thumb: if a line of code has a single equals sign, it's likely to be an expression, because it's assigning a value to something. That rule has some gray area. Calls to other functions could have all sorts of unforeseen consequences. It's not a bad rule to keep in mind, though.

Statements, on the other hand, are pieces of code that *don't* evaluate to data. These typically indicate an instruction to do something—either an instruction to the executing environment to change the order of execution via keywords like if, where, for, and foreach or calls to functions that don't return anything—and by implication instead carry out some sort of operation. Here's an example:

```
this._thingDoer.GoDoSomething();
```

A final rule of thumb is that if the code has *no* equals sign, it is *definitely* a statement.[3]

Expression-based programming

If it helps, think back to mathematics lessons from your school days. Remember those lines you used to have to write out to show your work when you were producing your final answer? Expression-based programming is like that.

Each line is a complete calculation and builds on one or more previous lines. By writing expression-based code, you're leaving your work behind, set in stone while the function runs. Among other benefits, the code is easier to debug, because you can look back at all the previous values and know they've not been changed by a previous iteration of a loop or anything like that.

This approach might seem like an impossibility, almost like being asked to program with your arms tied behind your back. It's entirely possible, though, and not even necessarily difficult. The tools have mostly been there for about a decade in C#, and plenty of more effective structures are available.

Here's an example of what I mean:

```
public decimal CalculateHypotenuse(decimal b, decimal c)
{
    var bSquared = b * b;
    var cSquared = c * c;
    var aSquared = bSquared + cSquared;
    var a = Math.Sqrt(aSquared);
    return a;
}
```

Now, strictly speaking, you could write that out as one long line, but it wouldn't look so nice and easy to read and understand, would it? You could also write this to save all the intermediate variables:

```
public decimal CalculateHypotenuse(decimal b, decimal c)
{
    var returnValue = b * b;
    returnValue += c * c;
    returnValue = Math.Sqrt(returnValue);
    return returnValue;
}
```

---

3 Credit must be given to functional programming supremo Mark Seemann (*https://blog.ploeh.dk*) for giving me these handy rules.

The issue here is that the code is a little harder to read without variable names, and all the intermediate values are lost—if there was a bug, we'd have to step through and examine returnValue at each stage. In the expression-based solution, all the work is kept where it is.

After a little experience working in this manner, going back to the old way will actually seem odd and even a little awkward and clunky.

Referential transparency

Referential transparency is a scary-sounding name for a simple concept. In FP, *pure functions* have the following properties:

- They make no changes to anything outside of the function. No state can be updated, no files stored, etc.
- Given the same set of parameter values, they will always return the exact same result. No. Matter. What. Regardless of what state the system is in.
- They don't have any unexpected side effects. Exceptions being thrown is included in that.

The term *referential transparency* comes from the idea that given the same input, the same output always results, so in a calculation you can essentially swap the function call with the final value, given those inputs. Consider this example:

```
var addTen = (int x) => x + 10;
var twenty = addTen(10);
```

The call to addTen() with a parameter of 10 will *always* evaluate to 20, with no exceptions. No possible side effects arise in a function this simple, either. Consequently, the reference to addTen(10) could in principle be exchanged for a constant value of 20 with no side effects. This is referential transparency.

Here are some pure functions:

```
public int Add(int a, int b) => a + b;

public string SayHello(string name) => "Hello " +
    (string.IsNullOrWhitespace(name)
        ? "I don't believe we've met.  Would you like a Jelly Baby?"
        : name);
```

No side effect can occur (I made sure a null check was included with the string), and nothing outside the function is altered; only a new value is generated and returned.

Here are impure versions of those same functions:

```
public void Add(int a) => this.total += a; // Alters state

public string SayHello() => "Hello " + this.Name;
// Reads from state instead of a parameter value
```

Both of these cases include a reference to properties of the current class that are beyond the scope of the function itself. The Add() function even modifies that state property. The SayHello() function has no null check either. All these factors mean we cannot consider these functions to be *pure*.

How about these?

```
public string SayHello() => "Hello " + this.GetName();

public string SayHello2(Customer c)
{
    c.SaidHelloTo = true;
    return "Hello " + (c?.Name ?? "Unknown Person");
}

public string SayHello3(string name) =>
    DateTime.Now + " - Hello " + (name ?? "Unknown Person");
```

None of these are likely to be pure.

SayHello() relies on a function outside itself. I don't actually know what GetName() does.[4] If it's simply returning a constant, we *can* consider SayHello() to be pure. If, on the other hand, it's doing a lookup in a database table, then any missing data or lost network packets could result in errors being thrown (all examples of unexpected side effects). If a function *had* to be used for retrieving the name, I'd consider rewriting this with a Func<T,TResult> delegate to inject the functionality safely into our SayHello() function.

SayHello2() modifies the object being passed in—a clear side effect from use of this function. Passing objects by reference and modifying them like this isn't all that unusual a practice in OOP, but it's absolutely not done in functional programming. I'd perhaps make this pure by separating out the update to the object properties and the processing of saying hello into two functions.

SayHello3() uses DateTime.Now, which returns a different value each and every time it's used. This is the absolute opposite of a pure function. One easy way to fix this is by adding a DateTime parameter to the function and passing in the value.

---

4 Because I made it up for this example.

Referential transparency is one of the features that massively increases the testability of functional code. It does mean that other techniques have to be used to track state, and I'll get into that in "Where Does Functional Programming Come From?" on page 14.

In addition, the amount of "purity" we can have in our application is limited, especially once we have to interact with the outside world, the user, or some third-party libraries that don't follow the functional paradigm. In C#, we're always going to have to make compromises here or there.

I usually like to wheel out a metaphor at this point. A shadow has two parts: the umbra and penumbra, as shown in Figure 1-1.[5] The *umbra* is the solid, dark part of a shadow (most of the shadow, in fact). The *penumbra* is the gray, fuzzy circle around the outside, the part where shadow and not-shadow meet and one fades into the other. In C# applications, I imagine that the pure area of the codebase is the umbra, and the areas of compromise are the penumbra. My task is to maximize the pure area and to minimize as much as humanly possible the nonpure area.

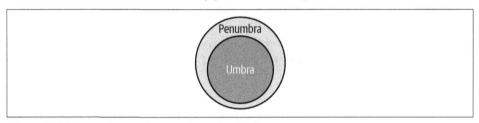

Figure 1-1. The umbra and penumbra of a shadow

If you want a more formal definition of this architectural pattern, Gary Bernhardt has given talks calling it Functional Core, Imperative Shell (*https://oreil.ly/-ooC4*).

Recursion

If you don't understand this, see "Recursion". Otherwise, see "Seriously, recursion".

Seriously, recursion

Recursion has been around for as long as programming, pretty much. It's a function that calls itself in order to effect an indefinite (but hopefully not infinite) loop. This should be familiar to anyone who has ever written code to traverse a folder structure or perhaps written an efficient sorting algorithm.

---

5 OK, artistic folks, I know there are actually about 12, but that's more than I need for this metaphor to work.

A recursive function typically comes in two parts:

A condition
> Used to determine whether the function should be called again or whether an end state has been reached (e.g., the value we're trying to calculate has been found, there are no subfolders to explore, etc.)

A return statement
> Either returns a final value or references the same function again, depending on the outcome of the end-state condition

Here is a very simple recursive Add():

```
public int AddUntil(int startValue, int endValue)
{
    if (startValue >= endValue)
        return startValue;
    else
        return AddUntil(startValue + 1, endValue);
}
```

> Never do this particular example in production code. I'm keeping it simple for the purposes of explanation.

Silly though this example is, note that I never change the value of either parameter integer. Each call to the recursive function uses parameter values based on the ones it itself receives. This is another example of *immutability*: I'm not changing values in a variable; I'm making a call to a function using an expression based on the values received.

Recursion is one of the methods FP uses as an alternative to statements like `while` and `foreach`. Some performance issues occur in C#, however. Chapter 9, on indefinite loops, includes a more detailed discussion on the use of recursion, but for now just use it cautiously and stick with me. All will become clear…

Pattern matching

In C#, *pattern matching* is basically the use of `switch` statements with "go-faster" stripes. F# takes the concept further, though. We've pretty much had pattern matching in C# for a few versions now. The `switch` expressions in C# 8 gave us C# developers our own native implementation of this concept, and the Microsoft team has been enhancing it regularly.

With this switching, you can change the path of execution on the type of the object under examination as well as its properties. This process can be used to reduce a large set of nested `if` statements like this:

```csharp
public int NumberOfDays(int month, bool isLeapYear)
{
    if(month == 2)
    {
        if(isLeapYear)
            return 29;
        else
            return 28;
    }
    if(month == 1 || month == 3 || month == 5 || month == 7 ||
        month == 8 || month == 10 || month == 12)
            return 31;
        else
            return 30;
}
```

into a few fairly concise lines, like this:

```csharp
public int NumberOfDays(int month, bool isLeapYear) =>
    (month, isLeapYear) switch
    {
        { month: 2, isLeapYear: true } => 29,
        { month: 2 } => 28,
        { month: 1 or 3 or 5 or 7 or 8 or 10 or 12 } => 31,
        _ => 30
    };
```

Pattern matching is an incredible, powerful feature and one of my favorite things.[6]

The next couple of chapters contain many examples of this, so skip ahead if you're interested in seeing more about what this is all about. Also, for those stuck using older versions of C#, there are ways of implementing this, and I'll show a few tips in "Pattern Matching for Old Versions of C#" on page 81.

Stateless

Object-oriented code typically has a set of state objects, which represent a process—either real or virtual. These state objects are updated periodically to keep in sync with whatever it is they represent. You might have code like this, for example, which represents data about my all-time favorite TV series, *Doctor Who*:

```csharp
public class DoctorWho
{
    public int NumberOfStories { get; set; }
```

---

6 For some reason, Julie Andrews won't return my calls to discuss an updated .NET version of her famous song.

```
    public int CurrentDoctor { get; set; }
    public string CurrentDoctorActor { get; set; }
    public int SeasonNumber { get; set; }
}

public class DoctorWhoRepository
{
    private DoctorWho State;

    public DoctorWhoRepository(DoctorWho initialState)
    {
        this.State = initialState;
    }

    public void AddNewSeason(int storiesInSeason)
    {
        this.State.NumberOfStories += storiesInSeason;
        this.State.SeasonNumber++;
    }

    public void RegenerateDoctor(string newActorName)
    {
        this.State.CurrentDoctor++;
        this.State.CurrentDoctorActor = newActorName;
    }
}
```

Well, forget ever doing that again if you want to do FP. There is no concept of a central state object, or of modifying its properties, as in the preceding code sample.

Seriously? Feels like purest craziness, doesn't it? Strictly, there *is* a state, but it's more of an emergent property of the system.

Anyone who has ever worked with React-Redux has already been exposed to the functional approach to state (which was, in turn, inspired by the FP language *Elm*). In Redux, the application state is an immutable object, which isn't updated, but instead a function is defined by the developer who takes the old state, a command, and any required parameters, and then returns a new state object based on the old one. This process became infinitely easier in C# with the introduction of record types in C# 9. I'll talk more on that in "Record Types" on page 67. For now, though, a simple version of how one of the repository functions might be refactored to work functionally looks like this:

```
public DoctorWho RegenerateDoctor(DoctorWho oldState, string newActorName)
{
    return new DoctorWho
    {
        NumberOfStories = oldState.NumberOfStories,
        CurrentDoctor = oldState.CurrentDoctor + 1,
        CurrentDoctorActor = newActorName,
```

```
        SeasonNumber = oldState.SeasonNumber
    };
}
```

The big advantage of this approach is predictability. In C#, objects are passed by reference—meaning that if you change the object *inside* the function, it's changed in the outside world as well! Therefore, if you've passed an object into a function as a parameter, you can't be sure it's unchanged, even though you didn't specifically assign a new value to it.

All changes made to objects in FP are always done via deliberate assignment of the value, so there is never any ambiguity over whether a change has been made.

That's enough about the properties of FP for now. Hopefully, you've got a good idea what it involves. Now I'm going to spend a bit of time being less intensely technical and consider FP from a wider perspective, as well as delve a little into FP's origins.

Baking Cakes

Let's look at a slightly higher level of description of the difference between the imperative and declarative paradigms. Here's how each would make cupcakes.[7]

An Imperative Cake

This isn't real C# code, just sort of .NET-themed pseudocode to give an impression of the imperative solution to this imaginary problem:

```
Oven.SetTemperatureInCentigrade(180);
for(int i=0; i < 3; i++)
{
    bowl.AddEgg();
    bool isEggBeaten = false;
    while(!isEggBeaten)
    {
        Bowl.BeatContents();
        isEggBeaten = Bowl.IsStirred();
    }
}
for(int i == 0; i < 12; i++)
{
    OvenTray.Add(paperCase[i]);
    OvenTray.AddToCase(bowl.TakeSpoonfullOfContents());
}
Oven.Add(OvenTray);
Thread.PauseMinutes(25);
Oven.ExtractAll();
```

---

7 With a little creative liberty taken.

For me, this represents typical convoluted imperative code: plenty of little short-lived variables cooked up to track state. The code is also very concerned with the precise order of things. It's more like instructions given to a robot with no intelligence at all, needing everything spelled out.

A Declarative Cake

Here's what an entirely imaginary bit of declarative code might look like to solve the same problem:

```
Oven.SetTemperatureInCentigrade(180);
var cakeBatter = EggBox.Take(3)
  .Each(e => Bowl.Add(e)
          .Then(b =>
              b.While(x => !x.IsStirred, x.BeatContents())
            )
          )
        .DivideInto(12)
    .Each(cb =>
      OvenTray.Add(PaperCaseBox.Take(1).Add(cb))
    );
```

That might look odd and unusual for now, if you're unfamiliar with FP, but over the course of this book, I'm going to explain how this all works, what the benefits are, and how you can implement all this yourself in C#.

What's worth noting, though, is that there are no state-tracking variables, no `if` or `while` statements. I'm not even sure what the order of operations would necessarily be, and it doesn't matter, because the system will work so that any necessary steps are completed at the point of need.

This is more like instructions for a slightly more intelligent robot, one that can think a little for itself. Instructions might sound something like "do this until such-and-such a state exists," which in procedural code would exist by combining a `while` loop and some state-tracking code lines.

Where Does Functional Programming Come From?

The first point I want to get out of the way is that despite what some people might think, FP is old. *Really* old (by computing standards, at least). It isn't like the latest trendy JavaScript framework—here this year, old news the next. It predates all modern programming languages and even computing itself to some extent. FP has been around for longer than any of us and is likely to be around long after we're all happily retired.

My slightly belabored point is that it's worth investing your time and energy to learn and understand FP. Even if one day you find yourself no longer working in C#, most other languages support functional concepts to a greater or lesser degree (JavaScript does to an extent that most languages can only dream of), so these skills will remain relevant throughout the rest of your career.

A quick caveat before I continue: I'm not a mathematician. I love mathematics, which was one of my favorite subjects throughout all of my education, but there eventually comes a level of higher, theoretical mathematics that leaves even me with glazed-over eyes and a mild headache. That said, I'll do my best to talk briefly about where exactly FP came from, which was, indeed, that very world of theoretical mathematics.

The first figure in the history of FP whom most people can name is usually Haskell Brooks Curry (1900–1982), an American mathematician who has no fewer than three programming languages named after him, as well as the functional concept of *currying* (you'll learn more in Chapter 8). His work was on *combinatory logic*, a mathematical concept that involves writing out functions in the form of lambda (or arrow) expressions and then combining them to create more-complex logic. This is the fundamental basis of FP. Curry wasn't the first to work on this, though; he was following on from papers and books written by these mathematical predecessors:

Alonzo Church (1903–1955, American)
Church coined the term *lambda expression*, which we use in C# and other languages to this day.

Moses Schönfinkel (1888–1942, Russian)
Schönfinkel wrote papers on combinatory logic that were a basis for Curry's work.

Friedrich Frege (1848–1925, German)
Arguably the first person to describe the concept we now know as currying. As important as it is to credit the correct people with discoveries, Freging doesn't quite have the same ring.[8]

---

8 For example, "I can't get this Freging code to work!"

The first FP languages were the following:

Information Processing Language (IPL)
> Developed in 1956 by Allen Newell (1927–1992, American), Cliff Shaw (1922–1991, American), and Herbert Simon (1916–2001, American).

LISt Processor (LISP)
> Developed in 1958 by John McCarthy (1927–2011, American). I hear that LISP still has its fans to this day and is still in production use in some businesses. I've never seen any direct evidence of this myself, however.

Interestingly, neither of these languages are what you would call "pure" functional. Like C#, Java, and numerous other languages, they adopted something of a hybrid approach, unlike the modern "pure" functional languages, like Haskell and Elm.

I don't want to dwell too long on the (admittedly, fascinating) history of FP, but it's hopefully obvious from what I have shown that it has a long and illustrious pedigree.

Who Else Does Functional Programming?

As I've already said, FP has been around for a while, and it's not just .NET developers who are showing an interest. Quite the opposite: many other languages have been offering functional paradigm support for a lot longer than .NET.

What do I mean by *support*? I mean that it offers the ability to implement code in the functional paradigm. This comes in roughly two flavors:

Pure functional languages
> Intended for the developer to write exclusively functional code. All variables are immutable, and the languages offer currying and higher-order functions out of the box. Some features of object orientation might be possible in these languages, but that's very much a secondary concern to the teams behind them.

Hybrid or multiparadigm languages
> These two terms can be used entirely interchangeably. They describe programming languages that offer features enabling code to be written in two or more paradigms—often two or more at the same time. Supported paradigms are typically functional and object oriented. A perfect implementation of any supported paradigms may not be available. It's not unusual for object orientation to be fully supported, but not to necessarily have all the features of the FP paradigm available to use.

Pure Functional Languages

Well over a dozen pure functional languages exist. Here is a brief look at the most popular ones in use today:

Haskell

Used extensively in the banking industry, Haskell is often recommended as a great starting place for anyone wanting to really get to grips with FP. This may well be the case, but honestly, I don't have the time or headspace to learn an entire programming language I never intend to use in my day job.

 If you're really interested in becoming an expert in the functional paradigm before working with it in C#, by all means go ahead and seek out Haskell content. A frequent recommendation is *Learn You a Haskell for Great Good!* by Miran Lipovača (No Starch Press).[9] I have never read this book myself, but friends of mine have and say it's great.

Elm

Elm seems to be gaining some traction these days, if for no other reason than the Elm system for performing updates in the UI has been picked up and implemented in quite a few other projects, including React.

Elixir

This general-purpose programming language is based on the same virtual machine that Erlang runs on. It's popular in industry and even has its own annual conferences.

PureScript

PureScript compiles to JavaScript, so it can be used to create functional frontend code, as well as server-side code and desktop applications in isometric programming environments—i.e., those like Node.js that allow the same language to be used on the client and server side.

Is It Worth Learning a Pure Functional Language First?

For the time being at least, OOP is the dominant paradigm for the vast majority of the software development world, and the functional paradigm is something that has to be learned afterward. I don't rule out that changing in the future, but for now at least, this is the situation we're in.

I have heard people argue the point that, coming from OOP, it would be best to learn FP in its pure form *first* and then come back to apply that learning in C#. If that's what you *want* to do, go for it. Have fun. I have no doubt that it's a worthwhile endeavor.

---

9 Available to read online for free (*https://oreil.ly/jE4nv*). Tell 'em I sent you.

To me, this perspective puts me in mind of those teachers we used to have here in the UK who insisted that children should learn Latin because, as the root of many European languages, knowledge of Latin can easily be transferred to French, Italian, Spanish, and so on.

I disagree with this somewhat.[10] Unlike Latin, pure functional languages aren't necessarily *difficult*, though they are very unlike object-oriented development. In fact, FP has fewer concepts to learn compared to OOP. This said, those who have spent their careers heavily involved in OOP will likely find it harder to adjust.

Latin and pure functional languages are similar, though, in that they represent a purer, ancestral form. They are both of only limited value outside of a small number of specialist interests.

Learning Latin is also almost entirely *useless* unless you're interested in subjects such as law, classical literature, or ancient history. It's far more useful to learn modern French or Italian. They're easier languages to learn by far, and you can use them *now* to visit lovely places and talk to the nice people who live there. There are some great French-language comics from Belgium too. Check 'em out. I'll wait.

In the same way, few places will ever actually use pure functional languages in production. You'd be spending a lot of time having to make a complete shift in the way you work and end up learning a language you'll probably never use outside of your own hobby code. I've been doing this job for a long time and have never encountered a company using anything more progressive in production than C#.

The lovely thing about C# is that is supports both object-oriented *and* functional code, so you can shift between them as you please. Use as many features from one paradigm or the other as you like without any penalty. The paradigms can sit fairly comfortably alongside each other in the same codebase, so it's an easy environment to transition from pure object oriented to functional at a pace that suits you, or vice versa. Mixing paradigms like this isn't possible in a pure functional language, even if a lot of functional features aren't possible in C#.

What About F#? Should I Be Learning F#?

What about F#? That's probably the most common question I get asked. It's not a pure functional language, but the needle is far closer to being a pure implementation of the paradigm than C#. It has a wide variety of functional features straight out of the box, as well as being easy to code in and producing applications that give a high level of performance in a production environment—why not use that?

---

10 Although I *am* learning Latin. *Insipiens sum. Huiusmodi res est ioci facio.*

I always like to check the available exits in the room before I answer this question. F# has a passionate user base, and they are probably all much smarter folks than me.[11] But...

It's not that F# isn't easy to learn. It is, from what I've seen, and most likely it's easier to learn than C# if you're entirely new to programming.

It's not that F# won't bring business benefits, because I honestly believe it will.

It's not that F# can't do absolutely everything any other language can do. It most certainly can. I've seen some impressive talks on how to make full-stack F# web applications.

Whether to learn F# is a professional decision. It isn't hard to find C# developers, at least in any country I've ever visited. If I were to put the names of every attendee of a big developers' conference in a hat and draw one at random, there's a better than even chance it would be someone who can write C# professionally. If a team decides to invest in a C# codebase, it's not going to be much of a struggle to keep the team populated with engineers who will be able to keep the code well maintained and the business relatively content.

Developers who know F#, on the other hand, are relatively rare. I don't know many. By adding F# into your codebase, you may be putting a dependency on the team to ensure that you always have enough people available who know it, or else take a risk that some areas of the code will be hard to maintain, because few people know how.

I should note that the risk isn't as high as introducing an entirely new technology, like, say, Node.js. F# is still a .NET language and compiles to the same Intermediate Language (IL). You can even easily reference F# projects from C# projects in the same solution. F# syntax would still be entirely unfamiliar to the majority of .NET developers, however.

It's my firm wish that this changes as time goes on. I've liked very much what I've seen of F#, and I'd love to do more of it. If my boss told me that a business decision had been made to adopt F#, I'd be the first to cheer!

The fact is, though, that scenario isn't very likely at present. Who knows what the future will bring. Maybe a future edition of this book will have to be heavily rewritten to accommodate all the love for F# that's suddenly sprung up, but for now I can't see that on the near horizon.

My recommendation is to try this book first. If you like what you see, F# might be the next place you go on your functional journey.

---

11 Especially F# guru Ian Russell, who helped with the F# content in this book. Thanks, Ian!

Multiparadigm Languages

It can probably be argued that all languages besides the pure functional languages are some form of hybrid. In other words, at least *some* aspects of the functional paradigm can be implemented. That's likely true, but I'm just going to look briefly at a few where FP can be implemented entirely, or mostly, and as a feature provided explicitly by the team behind it:

JavaScript

JavaScript is, of course, almost the Wild West of programming languages in the way that nearly anything can be done with it, and it does FP very well—arguably better than it does object orientation. Have a look for *JavaScript: The Good Parts* by Douglas Crockford (O'Reilly) and some of his online lectures (for example, "JavaScript: The Good Parts": *https://oreil.ly/rIDSN*) if you want insight into how to use JavaScript functionally and properly.

Python

Python has rapidly become a favorite programming language for the open source community, just over the last few years. It surprised me to find out it's been around since the late '80s! Python supports higher-order functions and has a few libraries available, such as *itertools* and *functools*, to allow further functional features to be implemented.

Java

The Java platform has the same level of support for functional features as .NET. Furthermore, spin-off projects such as Scala, Clojure, and Kotlin offer far more functional features than the Java language itself does.

F#

As I've discussed at length previously, F# is .NET's more purely functional-style language. It's also possible to have interoperability between C# and F# libraries, so you can have projects that utilize all the best features of both.

C#

Microsoft has slowly been adding support for FP ever since somewhere near the beginning. Arguably, the introduction of delegate covariance and anonymous methods in C# 2.0 all the way back in 2005 could be considered the very first item to support the functional paradigm. Things didn't really get going properly until the following year, when C# 3.0 introduced what I consider one of the most transformative features ever added to C#: LINQ.

LINQ is deeply rooted in the functional paradigm and is one of our best tools for getting started writing functional-style code in C# (have a look at Chapter 2 for a deeper discussion). In fact, it's a stated goal of the C# team that each version of C# released should contain further support for FP than the one before it. A number of factors are driving this decision, but among them is F#, which often requests new functional features from the .NET runtime folks that C# ends up benefiting from too.

The Benefits of Functional Programming

I hope that you picked up this book because you're already sold on FP and want to get started right away. This section might be useful for team discussions about whether to use it at work.

Concise

While not a feature of FP, my favorite of the many benefits is just how concise and elegant it looks, compared to object-oriented or imperative code.

Other styles of code are much more concerned with the low-level details of *how* to do something, to the point that sometimes an awful lot of code-staring is needed just to work out what that something even *is*. Functional programming is oriented more toward describing *what* is needed. The details of precisely which variables are updated, how and when, to achieve that goal are less of our concern.

Some developers I've spoken to about this have disliked the idea of being less involved with the lower levels of data processing, but I'm personally happier to let the execution environment take care of that. Then I have one thing fewer that I need to be concerned with.

It feels like a minor thing, but I honestly love the concision of functional code compared to the imperative alternatives. The job of a developer is a difficult one,[12] and we often inherit complex codebases that we need to get to grips with quickly. The longer and harder it is for you to work out what a function actually does, the more money the business is losing by paying you to do that, rather than writing new code. Functional code often reads in a way that describes—in something approaching natural language—what is being accomplished. It also makes it easier to find bugs, which again saves time and money for the business.

---

12 At least that's what we tell our managers.

Testable

One thing a lot of people describe as their favorite feature of FP is how incredibly testable it is. It really is. If your codebase isn't testable to something close to 100%, there's a chance you didn't follow the paradigm correctly.

Test-driven development (TDD) and behavior-driven development (BDD) are important professional practices. These programming techniques involve writing automated unit tests for the production code *first*, and then writing the real code required to allow the test to pass. This approach tends to result in better-designed, more robust code. FP enables these practices neatly. This, in turn, results in a better codebase and fewer bugs in production.

Robust

It's also not just the testability that results in a more robust codebase. FP comprises structures that actively prevent errors from occurring in the first place.

Alternatively, these structures prevent any unexpected behavior further on, making it easier to report the issue accurately. There is no concept of *null* in FP. That alone saves an incredible number of possible errors, as well as reducing the number of automated tests that need to be written.

Predictable

Functional code starts at the beginning of the code block and works its way to the end—exclusively in order. That's something you can't say of procedural code, with its loops and branching `if` statements. FP has only a single, easy-to-follow flow of code.

When done properly, FP doesn't even have any `try/catch` blocks, which I've often found to be some of the worst offenders when it comes to code with an unpredictable order of operations. If the `try` isn't small in scope and tightly coupled to the `catch`, sometimes it can be the code equivalent of throwing a rock blindly up into the air. Who knows where it'll land and who or what might catch it? Who can say what unexpected behavior might arise from such a break in the flow of the program?

Improperly designed `try/catch` blocks have been the cause of many instances of unexpected behavior in production that I've observed over my career, and it's a problem that simply doesn't exist in the functional paradigm. Improper error handling is still possible in functional code, but the very nature of FP discourages it.

Better Support for Concurrency

Two recent developments in the world of software development have become important in the last few years:

Containerization

Provided by products such as Docker and Kubernetes, among others, containerization is the idea that instead of running on a traditional server—virtual or otherwise—the application runs on something like a mini virtual machine (VM), which is generated by a script at deployment time. It isn't quite the same (no hardware emulation occurs), but from a user perspective, the result feels roughly the same. It solves the "it worked on my machine" problem that is sadly all too familiar to many developers. Many companies have software infrastructure that stacks up many instances of the same application in an array of containers, all processing the same source of input—whether that be a queue, user requests, or whatever. The environment that hosts them can even be configured to scale up or down the number of active containers, depending on demand.

Serverless

This option might be familiar to .NET developers as Azure Functions or Amazon Web Services (AWS) Lambda. This is code that isn't deployed to a traditional web server, such as Internet Information Services (IIS), but rather as a single function that exists in isolation out on a cloud-hosting environment. This approach allows the same sorts of automatic scaling as is possible with containers, but also micro-level optimizations: more money can be spent on more critical functions, and less money on functions requiring more time to render the output.

Both of these technologies use concurrent processing a great deal (i.e., multiple instances of the same functionality working at the same time on the same input source). It's like .NET's async features but applied to a much larger scope.

The problem with any sort of asynchronous operations tends to occur with shared resources, whether that's in-memory state or a literal shared physical or software-based external resource. FP operates without state, so no state can be shared among threads, containers, or serverless functions.

When implemented correctly, the functional paradigm makes it much easier to implement these much-in-demand technological features, but without giving rise to any unexpected behavior in production.

Reduced Code Noise

Audio processing uses a concept called the *signal-to-noise ratio*. This is a measure of the clarity of a recording, based on the ratio of the volume level of the signal (the thing you want to listen to) to the noise (any hiss, crackle, or rumble in the background).

In coding, the *signal* is the business logic of a code block—the goal it is actually trying to accomplish. The signal is the *what* of the code.

The *noise* is all the boilerplate code that must be written to accomplish the goal. The noise includes the `for` loop definition, `if` statements, that sort of thing.

Compared to procedural code, neat, concise FP has significantly less boilerplate and so has a much better signal-to-noise ratio. This isn't just a benefit to developers. Robust, easier-to-maintain codebases means the business needs to spend less money on maintenance and enhancements.

The Best Places to Use Functional Programming

FP can do absolutely anything that any other paradigm can, but in certain areas it's strongest and most beneficial—and in other areas it might be necessary to compromise and incorporate some object-orientation features, or slightly bend the rules of the functional paradigm. In .NET, at least, compromises must be made because base classes and add-on libraries tend to be written following the object-oriented paradigm. This compromise doesn't apply to pure functional languages.

FP is good when the code has a high degree of predictability—for example, data processing modules, or functions that convert data from one form to another. Business logic classes that handle data from the user or database and then pass it on to be rendered elsewhere are another example. Stuff like that.

The stateless nature of FP makes it a great enabler of concurrent systems—like heavily asynchronous codebases, or places where several processors are listening concurrently to the same input queue. When no shared state exists, it's just about impossible to get resource contention issues. If your team is looking into using serverless applications, such as Azure Functions, then FP enables that nicely for most of the same reasons.

FP is worth considering for highly business-critical systems because the paradigm facilitates producing code that's less error prone and more robust than applications coded with the object-oriented paradigm. If it's incredibly important that the system should stay up, and not have a crash and burn (i.e., terminate unexpectedly) in the event of an unhandled exception or invalid input, then FP might be the best choice.

Where You Should Consider Using Other Paradigms

You don't ever have to consider using other paradigms, of course. Functional can do anything, but looking around for other paradigms might be worthwhile in a few areas—purely in a C# context. And it's also worth mentioning again that C# is a hybrid language, so many paradigms can quite happily sit side by side, next to each other, depending on the needs of the developer. I know which I prefer, of course!

Interactions with external entities is one area for consideration: for example, I/O, user input, third-party applications, and web APIs. There's no way to make those pure functions (i.e., without side effects), so compromise is necessary. The same goes for third-party modules imported from NuGet packages. Even a few older Microsoft libraries are simply impossible to work with functionally. This is still true in .NET Core. Have a look at the `SmtpClient` or `MailMessage` classes in .NET if you want to see a concrete example.

In the C# world, if performance is your project's only, overwhelming concern—trumping all others, even readability and modularity—then following the functional paradigm might not be the best idea. Nothing is inherently poor in the performance of functional C# code, but it's not necessarily going to be the most utterly high-performing solution either.

I would argue that the benefits of FP far outweigh any minor loss of performance. These days, chucking a bit more hardware (virtual or physical, as appropriate) at the app is usually easy and is likely to be an order of magnitude cheaper than the cost of additional developer time that would otherwise be required to develop, test, debug, and maintain a codebase written in imperative-style code. This changes if, for example, you're working on code to be placed on a mobile device, where performance is critical because memory is limited and can't be updated.

How Far Can We Take This?

Unfortunately, it simply isn't possible to implement the entirety of the functional paradigm in C#. There are all sorts of reasons for that, including the need for backward compatibility in the language and limitations imposed on what remains a strongly typed language.

The intention of this book isn't to show you how all of it can be done, but rather to show the boundaries between what is and isn't possible. I'll also be discussing what's practical, especially with an eye to those of you maintaining a production codebase. This is ultimately a practical, pragmatic guide to functional coding styles.

~~Monads~~ Actually, Don't Worry About This Yet

Monads are often thought to be the functional horror story. Look on Wikipedia for definitions, and you'll be presented with a strange letter soup containing Fs, Gs, arrows, and more brackets than you'll find under the shelves of your local library. Even now, I find these formal definitions utterly illegible. At the end of the day, I'm an engineer, not a mathematician.

Douglas Crockford once said that the curse of the monad is that the moment you gain the ability to understand it, you lose the ability to explain it. So I won't. Monads might make their presence known somewhere in this book, however—especially at unlikely times.

Don't worry; it'll be fine. We'll work though it all together. Trust me…

Summary

In this first exciting installment of *Functional Programming with C#*, our mighty, awe-inspiring hero—you—bravely learned just what exactly FP is and why it's worth learning. You received an initial, brief introduction to the important features of the functional paradigm:

- Immutability
- Higher-order functions
- Preference for expressions over statements
- Referential transparency
- Recursion
- Pattern matching
- Stateless

You read about the areas FP is best used in and the relative merits of using the paradigm in its pure form. You also looked at the many benefits of writing applications by using the functional paradigm.

In the next thrilling episode, you'll learn what you can do in C# right here, right now. No new third-party libraries or Microsoft Visual Studio extension is required—just some honest-to-goodness out-of-the-box C# and a little ingenuity.

Turn the page to hear all about it. Same .NET time. Same .NET channel.[13]

---

13 Or book, if we're being picky.

What Are We Already Doing?

Believe it or not, there's a good chance you've been doing functional coding to a greater or lesser extent if you've been coding with .NET for any amount of time.

This first part of the book is all about showing you just how much of your everyday code is—or could easily be—functional. All of this without installing a single library beyond those provided by Microsoft. No tricky theory either.

Think of this part as the shores of your journey to the misty, dark, mysterious depths of FP. You're still on dry land, and everything should feel vaguely familiar.

In Part II, we'll start looking more into functional concepts. If you're finding Part I too easy as you're reading, feel free to skip ahead to Part II.

CHAPTER 2

What Can We Do Already?

Some of the code and concepts discussed in this chapter may seem trivial to some, but bear with me. I don't want to introduce too much too soon. More experienced developers might like to skip ahead to Chapter 3, in which I talk about the more recent developments in C# for functional programmers, or Chapter 4, where I demonstrate some novel ways to use features you might already be familiar with to achieve some functional features.

This chapter presents the FP features that are possible in just about every C# codebase in use in production today. I'm going to assume at least .NET Framework 3.5, and with some minor alterations, all the code samples provided in this chapter will work in that environment. Even if you work in a more recent version of .NET but are unfamiliar with FP, I still recommend reading this chapter, as it should give you a decent starting point in programming with the functional paradigm.

Those of you familiar with functional code, who just want to see what's available in the latest versions of .NET, might benefit from skipping ahead to the next chapter.

Getting Started

FP is easy, really it is! Despite what many people think, it's easier to learn than OOP. FP has fewer new concepts to learn.

If you don't believe me, try explaining polymorphism to a nontechnical member of your family! Those of us who are comfortable with object orientation have often been doing it so long that we've forgotten how hard it may have been to get our heads around it at the beginning.

FP isn't hard to understand at all, just different. I've spoken to plenty of students coming out of higher education who embrace it with enthusiasm. So, if *they* can manage it…

The myth does seem to persist, though, that getting into FP requires learning a whole load of stuff first. But what if I told you that if you've been doing C# for any length of time, you've already most likely been writing functional code for a while? In the next section, I'll show you what I mean.

Writing Your First Functional Code

Before we start with some functional code, let's look at a bit of nonfunctional. This is a style you most likely learned somewhere near the beginning of your C# career.

A Nonfunctional Film Query

In this quick, made-up example, we're getting a list of all films from an imaginary data store and creating a new list, copied from the first, but only those items in the Action genre:[1]

```
public IEnumerable<Film> GetFilmsByGenre(string genre)
{
    var allFilms = GetAllFilms();
    var chosenFilms = new List<Film>();

    foreach (var f in allFilms)
    {
        if (f.Genre == genre)
        {
            chosenFilms.Add((f));
        }
    }
    return chosenFilms;
}

var actionFilms = GetFilmsByGenre("Action");
```

What's wrong with this code? At the very least, it's not elegant. We've written a lot to do something fairly simple.

We've also instantiated a new object that's going to stay in scope for as long as this function is running. If there's nothing more to the whole function than this, we don't have much to worry about. But what if this were just a short excerpt from a long function? In that instance, the allFilms and actionFilms variables would both remain in scope, and thus in memory all that time, even if they aren't in use.

---

[1] I'm more of an SF (or sci-fi, if you prefer) fan, truth be told.

Copies of all the data may not necessarily be held within the item that's being replicated, depending on whether it's a class, a struct, or something else. At the very least, though, a duplicate set of references is being held unnecessarily in memory for as long as both items are in scope. That's still more memory than we strictly need to hold.

We're also forcing the order of operations. We've specified when to loop, when to add—both where and when each step should be carried out. If any intermediate steps in the data transformations needed to be carried out, we'd be specifying them too and holding them in yet more potentially long-life variables.

We could solve a few problems with a `yield` return like this:

```
public IEnumerable<Film> GetFilmsByGenre(string genre)
{
    var allFilms = GetAllFilms();

    foreach (var f in allFilms)
    {
        if (f.Genre == genre)
        {
            yield return f;
        }
    }
}

var actionFilms = GetFilmsByGenre("Action");
```

This hasn't done more than shave a few lines off, however.

What if there were a more optimal order of operations than the one we've decided on? What if a later bit of code actually meant that we don't end up returning the contents of `actionFilms`? We'd have done the work unnecessarily.

This is the eternal problem of procedural code. Everything has to be spelled out. One of the major aims of FP is to move away from all that. Stop being so specific about every little thing. Relax a little and embrace declarative code.

A Functional Film Query

So what would the preceding code sample look like written in a functional style? I hope many of you might already guess at how we could rewrite it:

```
public IEnumerable<Film> GetFilmsByGenre(
    IEnumerable<Film> source,
    string genre) =>
    source.Where(x => x.Genre == genre);

var allFilms = GetAllFilms();
var actionFilms = GetFilmsByGenre(allFilms, "Action");
```

You might at this point be saying, "Isn't that just LINQ?" And yes, yes, it is. I'll let you in on a little secret—LINQ follows the functional paradigm.

Just quickly, for anyone not yet familiar with the awesomeness of LINQ, it's a library that's been part of C# since the early days. LINQ provides a rich set of functions for filtering, altering, and extending collections of data. Functions like `Select()`, `Where()`, and `All()` are from LINQ and are commonly used around the world.

Think back for a moment to the list of features of FP and see how many LINQ implements:

Higher-order functions
> The lambda expressions passed to LINQ functions are all functions being passed in as parameter variables.

Immutability
> LINQ doesn't change the source array; it returns a new enumerable based on the old one.

Expressions instead of statements
> We've eliminated the use of a `foreach` and an `if`.

Referential transparency
> The preceding lambda expression does conform to referential transparency (i.e., no side effects), though nothing enforces that. We could easily have referenced a string variable outside the lambda. By requiring the source data to be passed in as a parameter, we're also making it easier to test without requiring the creation and setup of a mock of some kind to represent the data store connection. Everything the function needs is provided by its own parameters.

The iteration could well be done by recursion too, for all I know, but I have no idea what the source code of the `Where()` function looks like. In the absence of evidence to the contrary, I'm just going to go on believing that it does.

This tiny one-line code sample is a perfect example of the functional approach in many ways. We're passing around functions to perform operations against a collection of data, creating a new collection based on the old one. What we've ended up with by following the functional paradigm is something more concise, easier to read, and therefore far easier to maintain.

Focusing on Results-Oriented Programming

A common feature of functional code is that it focuses much more heavily on the end result rather than on the process of getting there. An entirely procedural approach to building a complex object would be to instantiate it empty at the beginning of the code block, and then fill in each property as we go along:

```
var sourceData = GetSourceData();
var obj = new ComplexCustomObject();

obj.PropertyA = sourceData.Something + sourceData.SomethingElse;
obj.PropertyB = sourceData.Ping * sourceData.Pong;

if(sourceData.AlternateTuesday)
{
    obj.PropertyC = sourceData.CaptainKirk;
    obj.PropertyD = sourceData.MrSpock;
}
else
{
    obj.PropertyC = sourceData.CaptainPicard;
    obj.PropertyD = sourceData.NumberOne;
}

return obj;
```

The problem with this approach is that it's open to abuse. This silly little imaginary code block is short and easy to maintain. What often happens with production code, however, is that the code can end up becoming incredibly long, with multiple data sources that all have to be preprocessed, joined, and reprocessed. We can end up with long blocks of `if` statements nested in `if` statements, to the point that the code starts resembling the shape of a family tree.

For each nested `if` statement, the complexity effectively doubles. This is especially true if multiple `return` statements are scattered around the codebase. The risk increases of inadvertently ending up with a `null` or other unexpected value if the increasingly complex codebase isn't thought through in detail. FP discourages structures like this and isn't prone to this level of complexity, or to the potential unexpected consequences.

Our preceding code sample defines `PropertyC` and `PropertyD` in two places. The code is not too hard to work with here, but I've seen examples that define the same property in around half a dozen places across multiple classes and subclasses.[2] I don't know whether you've ever had to work with code like this, but it has happened to me an awful lot.

These sorts of large, unwieldy codebases get harder to work with over time. With each addition, the speed at which the developers can do the work goes down, and the business leaders can end up getting frustrated because they don't understand why their "simple" update is taking so long.

---

2 And in one example, a couple of definitions were also outside the codebase in database stored procedures.

Functional code should ideally be written into small, concise blocks, focusing entirely on the end product. The expressions it prefers are modeled on the individual steps required to solve a mathematical problem, so you really want to write functional code like small formulas, each precisely defining a value and all the variables that make it up. There shouldn't be any hunting up and down the codebase to work out where a value comes from.

Here's an example:

```
function ComplexCustomObject MakeObject(SourceData source) =>
    new ComplexCustomObject
    {
        PropertyA = source.Something + source.SomethingElse,
        PropertyB = source.Ping * source.Pong,
        PropertyC = source.AlternateTuesday
            ? source.CaptainKirk
            : source.CaptainPicard,
        PropertyD = source.AlternateTuesday
            ? source.MrSpock,
            : source.NumberOne
    };
```

I know we're repeating the `AlternateTuesday` flag, but now all the variables that determine a returned property are defined in a single place. This approach makes the code much simpler to work with in the future.

If a property is so complicated that it will need either multiple lines of code or a series of LINQ operations that take up a lot of space, I'd create a break-out function to contain that complex logic. I'd still have my central, result-based return at the heart of it all, though.

Understanding Enumerables

I sometimes think enumerables are one of the most underused and least understood features of C#. An *enumerable* is the most abstract representation of a collection of data—so abstract that it doesn't contain any data itself, but just a description held in memory of how to go about getting the data. An enumerable doesn't even know the number of items available until it iterates through everything—all it knows is where the current item is and how to iterate to the next.

This process is called *lazy evaluation*, or *deferred execution*. Being lazy is a good thing in development. Don't let anyone tell you otherwise.[3]

---

3 Except your employer. They pay your bills. They hopefully send you birthday cards once a year too, if they're nice.

In fact, we can even write our own customized behavior for an enumerable. Under the surface is an object called an *enumerator*. By interacting with that, we can either get the current item or iterate on to the next. We can't use the enumerable or the enumerator to determine the length of the list, and the iteration works in only a single direction.

Have a look at the following code sample. First, a set of simple logging functions pop a message in a `List` of strings:

```
private IList<string> c = new List<string>();


public int DoSomethingOne(int x)
{
    c.Add(DateTime.Now + " - DoSomethingOne (" + x + ")");
    return x;
}

public int DoSomethingTwo(int x)
{
    c.Add(DateTime.Now + " - DoSomethingTwo (" + x + ")");
    return x;
}

public int DoSomethingThree(int x)
{
    c.Add(DateTime.Now + " - DoSomethingThree (" + x + ")");
    return x;
}
```

Then a bit of code calls each of those `DoSomething()` functions in turn with different data:

```
var input = new[]
{
    75,
    22,
    36
};

var output = input.Select(x => DoSomethingOne(x))
    .Select(x => DoSomethingTwo(x))
    .Select(x => DoSomethingThree(x))
    .ToArray();
```

What do you think the order of operations is? You might think that the runtime would take the original input array, apply `DoSomethingOne()` to all three elements to create a second array, then again with all three elements into `DoSomethingTwo()`, and so on.

If we were to examine the content of that List of strings, we'd find something like this:

```
18/08/1982 11:24:00 - DoSomethingOne(75)
18/08/1982 11:24:01 - DoSomethingTwo(75)
18/08/1982 11:24:02 - DoSomethingThree(75)
18/08/1982 11:24:03 - DoSomethingOne(22)
18/08/1982 11:24:04 - DoSomethingTwo(22)
18/08/1982 11:24:05 - DoSomethingThree(22)
18/08/1982 11:24:06 - DoSomethingOne(36)
18/08/1982 11:24:07 - DoSomethingTwo(36)
18/08/1982 11:24:08 - DoSomethingThree(36)
```

It's almost the exact same as we might get if we were running this through a for or foreach loop, but we've effectively handed over control of the order of operations to the runtime. We're not concerned with the nitty-gritty of temporary holding variables, what goes where and when. Instead we're just describing the operations we want and expecting a single answer back at the end.

The resulting list of strings might not always look exactly like this; it depends on what the code that interacts with the enumerable (via LINQ or a foreach) looks like. But the intent always remains that enumerables actually produce their data only at the precise moment it's needed. It doesn't matter where they're defined; it's when they're *used* that makes a difference.

By using enumerables instead of solid arrays, we've managed to implement some of the behaviors we need to write declarative code.

Incredibly, the preceding logfile would still look the same if we were to rewrite the code like this:

```
var input = new[]
{
    1,
    2,
    3
};

var temp1 = input.Select(x => DoSomethingOne(x));
var temp2 = input.Select(x => DoSomethingTwo(x));
var finalAnswer = input.Select(x => DoSomethingThree(x));
```

temp1, temp2, and finalAnswer are all enumerables, and none of them will contain any data until iterated.

Here's an experiment to try. Write some code like this sample. Don't copy it exactly, maybe something simpler like a series of selects amending an integer value somehow. Put in a break point and move the operation pointer on until the final answer has been passed, then hover over `finalAnswer` in Visual Studio. You'll most likely find that it can't display any data to you, even though the line has been passed. That's because the enumerable hasn't performed any of the operations yet.

Things would change if we did something like this:

```
var input = new[]
{
    1,
    2,
    3
};

var temp1 = input.Select(x => DoSomethingOne(x)).ToArray();
var temp2 = input.Select(x => DoSomethingTwo(x)).ToArray();
var finalAnswer = input.Select(x => DoSomethingThree(x)).ToArray();
```

Because we're specifically now calling `ToArray()` to force an enumeration of each intermediate step, then we really will call `DoSomethingOne()` for each item in input before moving on to the next stop.

The logfile will look something like this now:

```
18/08/1982 11:24:00 - DoSomethingOne(75)
18/08/1982 11:24:01 - DoSomethingOne(22)
18/08/1982 11:24:02 - DoSomethingOne(36)
18/08/1982 11:24:03 - DoSomethingTwo(75)
18/08/1982 11:24:04 - DoSomethingTwo(22)
18/08/1982 11:24:05 - DoSomethingTwo(36)
18/08/1982 11:24:06 - DoSomethingThree(75)
18/08/1982 11:24:07 - DoSomethingThree(22)
18/08/1982 11:24:08 - DoSomethingThree(36)
```

For this reason, I nearly always advocate for waiting as long as possible before using `ToArray()` or `ToList()`,[4] because this way we can leave the operations unperformed for as long as possible. And potentially, the operations may never be performed if later logic prevents the enumeration from occurring at all.

Exceptions exist for performance or for avoiding multiple iterations. While the enumerable remains un-enumerated, it doesn't have any data, but the operation itself remains in memory. If you pile too many enumerables on top of one another—especially if you start performing recursive operations—you might find that you fill up far too much memory and performance takes a hit, and possibly even end up with a stack overflow.

---

4 As a functional programmer and a believer in exposing the most abstract interface possible, I *never* use `ToList()`. I always use `ToArray()`, even if `ToList()` is ever so slightly faster.

Preferring Expressions to Statements

In the rest of this chapter, I'm going to give more examples of how you can use LINQ more effectively to avoid the need for statements like if, where, and for, or to mutate state (i.e., change the value of a variable). In some situations, it won't be possible to replace these statements with out-of-the-box C#. But that's what the rest of this book is for.

The Humble Select

If you've read this far in the book, you're most likely aware of Select() statements and how to use them. However, most people I speak to don't seem to be aware of a few of their features, and they're all things that can be used to make code a little more functional.

The first feature is something I've already shown in the previous section: we can chain them. We can either create a series of Select() function calls—literally one after the other, or in a single code line—or we can store the results of each Select() in a different local variable. Functionally, these two approaches are identical. It doesn't even matter if we call ToArray() after each one. So long as we don't modify any resulting arrays or the object contained within them, we're following the functional paradigm.

The important approach to get away from is the imperative practice of defining a List, looping through the source objects with a foreach, and then adding each new item to the List. This is long-winded, harder to read, and honestly quite tedious. Why do things the hard way? Just use a nice, simple Select() statement.

Iterator value is required

So what if we're Selecting an enumerable into a new form and need the iterator as part of the transformation? Say we have something like this:

```
var films = GetAllFilmsForDirector("Jean-Pierre Jeunet")
    .OrderByDescending(x => x.BoxOfficeRevenue);

var i = 1;

Console.WriteLine("The films of visionary French director");
Console.WriteLine("Jean-Pierre Jeunet in descending order");
Console.WriteLine("of financial success are as follows:");
```

```
foreach (var f in films)
{
    Console.WriteLine($"{i} - {f.Title}");
    i++;
}

Console.WriteLine("But his best by far is Amelie");
```

We can use a feature of Select() statements that surprisingly few people know about: they have an override that allows access to the iterator as part of the Select(). All we have to do is provide a lambda expression with two parameters, the second being an integer that represents the index position of the current item.

This is how our functional version of the code looks:

```
var films = GetAllFilmsForDirector("Jean-Pierre Jeunet")
    .OrderByDescending(x => x.BoxOfficeRevenue);

Console.WriteLine("The films of visionary French director");
Console.WriteLine("Jean-Pierre Jeunet in descending order");
Console.WriteLine("of financial success are as follows:");

var formattedFilms = films.Select((x, i) => $"{i} - {x.Title}");
Console.WriteLine(string.Join(Environment.NewLine, formattedFilms));

Console.WriteLine("But his best by far is Amelie");
```

Using these techniques, nearly no circumstance could exist where you need to use foreach loop with a List. Thanks to C#'s support for the functional paradigm, declarative methods are nearly always available to solve problems.

The two techniques for getting the i index position variable are a great example of imperative versus declarative code. The imperative, object-oriented approach has the developer manually creating a variable to hold the value of i, and also explicitly set the place for the variable to be incremented. The declarative code isn't concerned with where the variable is defined or with how each index value is determined.

 Notice that we use string.Join to link the strings together. This is not only another one of those hidden gems of the C# language, but also an example of *aggregation*—that is, converting a list of things into a single thing. That's what we'll walk through in the next few sections.

No starting array

The last trick for getting the value of i for each iteration is great if there's an array—or collection of another kind—available in the first place. What if there isn't an array? What if we need to arbitrarily iterate for a set number of times?

For these somewhat rare situations, we need a good, old-fashioned for loop instead of a foreach. How do we create an array from nothing? Our two best friends in this case are two static methods: Enumerable.Range and Enumerable.Repeat.

Range creates an array from a starting integer value and requires us to tell it the number of elements our array should have. It then creates an array of integers based on those specifications. Here's an example:

```
var a = Enumerable.Range(8, 5);
var s = string.Join(", ", a);
// s = "8, 9, 10, 11, 12"
// That's 5 elements, each 1 higher than the last,
// starting with 8.
```

Having whipped up an array, we can then apply LINQ operations to get our final result. Let's imagine I am preparing a description of the 9 times table for one of my daughters:[5]

```
var nineTimesTable = Enumerable.Range(1,10)
    .Select(x => x + " times 9 is " + (x * 9));

var message = string.Join("\r\n", nineTimesTable);
```

Here's another example: what if we want to get all the values from a grid, where x and y values are required to get each value. Imagine there's a grid repository that we can use to get values.

Imagining that the grid is a 5 × 5, this is how we'd get every value:

```
var coords = Enumerable.Range(1, 5)
    .SelectMany(x => Enumerable.Range(1, 5)
        .Select(y => (X: x, Y: y))
);

var values = coords.Select(x => this.gridRepo.GetVal(x.Item1,x.Item2);
```

The first line is generating an array of integers with the values [1, 2, 3, 4, 5]. We then use another Select() to convert each of these integers into another array using another call to Enumerable.Range. We now have an array of five elements, each of which is itself an array of five integers. Using a Select() on that nested array, we convert each of those subelements into a tuple that takes one value from the parent

---

5 No, Sophie. It's not good enough to just use your fingers!

array (x) and one from the subarray (y). SelectMany() is used to flatten the whole thing out to a simple list of all the possible coordinates, which would look something like this: (1, 1), (1, 2), (1, 3), (1, 4), (1, 5), (2, 1), (2, 2)...and so on.

Values can be obtained by Selecting this array of coordinates into a set of calls to the repository's GetVal() function, passing in the values of X and Y from the tuple of coordinates created on the previous line.

In another situation, we might need the same starting value in each case, but need to transform it in different ways, depending on the position within the array. This is where Enumerable.Repeat comes in. Enumerable.Repeat creates an array—referenced as an enumerable—of the requested size where every element has the same user-supplied value.

We can't use Enumerable.Range to count backward. Say we want to do the previous example, but start at (5,5) and move backward to (1,1). Here's an example of how to do it:

```
var gridCoords = Enumerable.Repeat(5, 5).Select((x, i) => x - i)
    .SelectMany(x => Enumerable.Repeat(5, 5)
        .Select((y, i) => (x, y - i))
);

var values = coords.Select(x => this.gridRepo.GetVal(x.Item1,x.Item2);
```

This looks a lot more complicated but isn't really. What we've done is to swap out the Enumerable.Range call for a two-step operation.

First, a call to Enumerable.Repeat is repeating the integer value of 5 five times. This results in an array like this: [5, 5, 5, 5, 5].

We then select using the overloaded version of Select() that includes the value of i, and deduct that i value from the current value in the array. Therefore, in the first iteration, the return value is the current value from the array (5) minus the previous value (0 from the first iteration, in this case); this gives back simply 5. In the next iteration, the value of i is 1, so 5 – 1 means 4 is returned. And so on.

At the end, we get back an array that looks something like this: (5, 5), (5, 4), (5, 3), (5, 2), (5, 1), (4, 5), (4, 4)...etc.

We can take this further still, but for this chapter we're sticking to the relatively simple cases, ones that don't require hacking around with C#. This is all out-of-the-box functionality that anyone can use right away.

Many to One: The Subtle Art of Aggregation

We've looked at loops for converting one thing into another, X items in → X new items out. Now I'd like to cover another use case for loops: reducing many items into a single value.

This could be making a total count; calculating averages, means, or other statistical data; or other more complex aggregations. In procedural code, we'd have a loop and a state-tracking value, and inside the loop we'd update the state constantly, based on each item from our array. Here's a simple example of what I'm talking about:

```
var total = 0;
foreach(var x in listOfIntegers)
{
    total += x;
}
```

LINQ has a built-in method for doing this:

```
var total = listOfIntegers.Sum();
```

We really shouldn't ever need to do this sort of operation longhand. Even if we're creating the sum of a particular property from an array of objects, LINQ still has us covered:

```
var films = GetAllFilmsForDirector("Alfred Hitchcock");
var totalRevenue = films.Sum(x => x.BoxOfficeRevenue);
```

Another function for calculating means in the same manner is called `Average()`. There's nothing for calculating median, so far as I'm aware.

We could calculate the median with a quick bit of functional-style code, however. It would look like this:

```
var numbers = new []
{
    83,
    27,
    11,
    98
};

bool IsEvenNumber(int number) => number % 2 == 0;

var sortedList = numbers.OrderBy(x => x).ToArray();
var sortedListCount = sortedList.Count();

var median = IsEvenNumber(sortedList.Count())
    ? sortedList.Skip((sortedListCount/2)-1).Take(2).Average()
    : sortedList.Skip((sortedListCount) / 2).First();

// median = 55.
```

More complex aggregations are required sometimes. What if we want, for example, a sum of two values from an enumerable of complex objects? Procedural code might look like this:

```
var films = GetAllFilmsForDirector("Christopher Nolan");

var totalBudget = 0.0M;
var totalRevenue = 0.0M;

foreach (var f in films)
{
    totalBudget += f.Budget;
    totalRevenue += f.BoxOfficeRevenue;
}
```

We could use two separate Sum() function calls, but then we'd be iterating twice through the enumerable, hardly an efficient way to get our information. Instead, we can use another strangely little-known feature of LINQ: the Aggregate() function. This consists of the following components:

Seed
A starting value for the final value.

Aggregator function
This has two parameters: the current item from the enumerable we're aggregating down, and the current running total.

The seed doesn't have to be a primitive type, like an integer; it can just as easily be a complex object. To rewrite the preceding code sample in a functional style, however, we just need a simple tuple:

```
var films = GetAllFilmsForDirector("Christopher Nolan");

var (totalBudget, totalRevenue) = films.Aggregate(
    (Budget: 0.0M, Revenue: 0.0M),
    (runningTotals, x) => (
            runningTotals.Budget + x.Budget,
            runningTotals.Revenue + x.BoxOfficeRevenue
        )
);
```

In the right place, Aggregate() is an incredibly powerful feature of C#, and one worth taking the time to explore and understand properly. It's also an example of another concept important to FP: recursion.

Customized Iteration Behavior

Recursion sits behind a lot of functional methods of iteration. For the benefit of anyone who doesn't know, recursion is a programming technique that involves a function that calls itself repeatedly until a certain condition is met.

Recursion is a powerful technique but has some limitations to bear in mind in C#. The most important two are as follows:

- If developed improperly, code using recursion can lead to infinite loops, which will run until the user terminates the application or all available space on the stack is consumed. As Treguard, the legendary dungeon master of the popular British fantasy RPG game show *Knightmare* would put it: "Oooh, nasty."[6]
- In C#, recursion tends to consume a lot of memory compared to other forms of iteration. There are ways around this, but that's a topic for another chapter.

I have a lot more to say about recursion, and we'll get to that shortly, but for the purposes of this chapter, I'll give the simplest example I can think of.

Let's say we want to iterate through an enumerable but don't know for how long. We have a list of delta values for an integer (i.e., the number to add or subtract each time) and want to find the number of steps required to get from the starting value (whatever that might be) to 0.

We could quite easily get the final value with an `Aggregate()` call, but we don't want the final value. We're interested in all the intermediate values and want to stop prematurely at some point mid-iteration. This is a simple arithmetic operation, but if complex objects were involved in a real-world scenario, performance might significantly improve because of the ability to terminate the process early.

In procedural code, we'd probably write something like this:

```
var deltas = GetDeltas().ToArray();
var startingValue = 10;
var currentValue = startingValue;
var i = -1;

foreach(var d in deltas)
{
    if(currentValue == 0)
    {
        break;
    }
    i++;
    currentValue = startingValue + d;

}

return i;
```

---

6 Check out the man himself on YouTube (*https://oreil.ly/86Bq7*).

In this example, we're returning -1 to say that the starting value is already the one we're looking for; otherwise, we're returning the zero-based index of the array that resulted in 0 being reached.

This is how we'd do it recursively:

```
var deltas = GetDeltas().ToArray();

int GetFirstPositionWithValueZero(int currentValue, int i = -1) =>
    currentValue == 0
        ? i
        : GetFirstPositionWithValueZero(currentValue + deltas[i], i + 1);

return GetFirstPositionWithValueZero(10);
```

This is functional now, but it's not really ideal. Nested functions have their place, but I don't personally find this code as readable as it could be. The code is delightfully recursive, but it could be made clearer.

The other major problem is that this won't scale up well if the list of deltas is large. I'll show you what I mean.

Let's imagine that the deltas have only three values: 2, -12, and 9. We'd expect the answer to come back as 1, because the second position (i.e., index = 1) of the array results in 0 (10 + 2 – 12). We would also expect that the 9 will never be evaluated. That's the efficiency saving we're looking for from our code here.

What is actually happening with the recursive code, though?

First, it calls `GetFirstPositionWithValueZero()` with a current value of 10 (i.e., the starting value), and i is given the default of -1.

The body of the function is a ternary `if` statement. If 0 has been reached, the function returns i; otherwise, the code calls the function again but with updated values for currentValue and i. This is what'll happen with the first delta (i.e., i = 0, current Value = 2), so `GetFirstPositionWithValueZero()` is called again with currentValue now updated to 12, and i as 0.

The new value is not 0, so the second call to `GetFirstPositionWithValueZero()` will call itself again, this time with the current value updated with deltas[1] and i incremented to 1. Because deltas[1] is -12, the third call results in a 0, which means that i can simply be returned.

Here's the problem, though. The third call gets an answer, but the first two calls are still open in memory and stored on the stack. The third call returns 1, which is passed up a level to the second call to `GetFirstPositionWithValueZero()`, which now also returns 1, and so on—until finally the original first call to `GetFirstPositionWith ValueZero()` returns the 1.

If you want to see that a little graphically, imagine it looking something like this:

```
GetFirstPositionWithValueZero(10, -1)
    GetFirstPositionWithValueZero(12, 0)
        GetFirstPositionWithValueZero(0, 1)
        return 1;
    return 1;
return 1;
```

That's fine with three items in our array, but what if there are hundreds? Recursion, as I've said, is a powerful tool, but it comes with a cost in C#. Purer functional languages (including F#) have a feature called *tail call optimized recursion* that allows the use of recursion without this memory usage problem.

Tail recursion is an important concept, and one I'm going to return to in Chapter 9, so I'm not going to dwell on it in any further detail here. As it stands, out-of-the-box C# doesn't permit tail recursion, even though it's available in the .NET common language runtime (CLR). We can try a few tricks to make it available to us, but they're a little too complex for this chapter, so I'll talk about them in Chapter 9 instead (be there, or be square). For now, consider recursion as it's described here, and keep in mind that you might want to be careful about where and when you use it.

Making Your Code Immutable

There's more to FP in C# than just LINQ. Another important feature I'd like to discuss is *immutability* (i.e., a variable may not change value once declared). To what extent is immutability possible in C#?

First, C# 8 and upward provide some newer developments with regards to immutability. See Chapter 3 for that. For this chapter, I'm restricting myself to what is true of just about any version of .NET.

To begin, let's consider this little C# snippet:

```
public class ClassA
{
    public string PropA { get; set; }
    public int PropB { get; set; }
    public DateTime PropC { get; set; }
    public IEnumerable<double> PropD { get; set; }
    public IList<string> PropE { get; set; }
}
```

Is this immutable? It very much is not. Any of those properties can be replaced with new values via the setter. The `IList` also provides a set of functions that allows its underlying array to be added to or removed from.

We could make the setters private, meaning we'd have to instantiate the class via a detailed constructor:

```csharp
public class ClassA
{
    public string PropA { get; private set; }
    public int PropB { get; private set; }
    public DateTime PropC { get; private set; }
    public IEnumerable<double> PropD { get; private set; }
    public IList<string> PropE { get; private set; }

    public ClassA(
        string propA,
        int propB, DateTime propC,
        IEnumerable<double> propD,
        IList<string> propE)
    {
        this.PropA = propA;
        this.PropB = propB;
        this.PropC = propC;
        this.PropD = propD;
        this.PropE = propE;
    }

}
```

Is it immutable now? No, honestly it's not. It's true that we can't outright replace any of the properties with new objects outside ClassA, which is great. The properties can be replaced inside the class, but the developer can ensure that no such code is ever added. We should hopefully have some sort of code review system to ensure that as well.

PropA and PropC are fine; strings and DateTime are both immutable in C#. The int value of PropB is fine too; ints don't have anything we can change except their value. Several problems still remain, however.

PropE is a List, which can still have values added, removed, and replaced, even though we can't replace the entire object. If we didn't need to hold a mutable copy of PropE, we could easily replace it with an IEnumerable or IReadOnlyList.

The IEnumerable<double> value of PropD seems fine at first glance, but what if it was passed to the constructor as a List<double>, which is still referenced by that type in the outside world? It would still be possible to alter its contents that way.

There's also the possibility of introducing something like this:

```csharp
public class ClassA
{
    public string PropA { get; private set; }
    public int PropB { get; private set; }
    public DateTime PropC { get; private set; }
```

```
public IEnumerable<double> PropD { get; private set; }
public IList<string> PropE { get; private set; }
public SubClassB PropF { get; private set; }

public ClassA(
    string propA,
    int propB, DateTime propC,
    IEnumerable<double> propD,
    IList<string> propE,
    SubClassB propF)
{
    this.PropA = propA;
    this.PropB = propB;
    this.PropC = propC;
    this.PropD = propD;
    this.PropE = propE;
    this.PropF = propF
}

}
```

All properties of `PropF` are also potentially going to be mutable, unless this same structure with private setters is followed there too.

What about classes from outside our codebase? What about Microsoft classes or those from a third-party NuGet package? There's no way to enforce immutability.

Unfortunately, C# doesn't provide any way to enforce universal immutability, not even in its most recent versions. Having a native C# method of ensuring immutability by default would be lovely, but there isn't one—and isn't ever likely to be for reasons of backward compatibility. My own solution is that when coding, I simply *pretend* that immutability exists in the project and never change any object. Nothing in C# provides any level of enforcement whatsoever, so you'd simply have to make a decision for yourself, or within your team, to act as if it does.

Putting It All Together: A Complete Functional Flow

I've talked a lot about simple techniques we can use to make our code more functional right away. Now, I'd like to show a complete, if minute, application written to demonstrate an end-to-end functional process.

We're going to write a simple CSV parser. In this example, we want to read in the complete text of a CSV file containing data about the first few series of *Doctor Who*.[7] We want to read the data, parse it into a plain old C# object (POCO, a class

---

7 For those of you unacquainted, this is a British SF series that has been running on and off since 1963. It is, in my opinion, the greatest TV series ever made. I'm not taking any arguments on that.

---

containing only data and no logic), and then aggregate it into a report that counts the number of episodes, and the number of episodes known to be lost for each season.[8] I'm simplifying CSV parsing for the purposes of this example; don't worry about quotes around string fields, commas in field values, or any values requiring additional parsing. Third-party libraries are available for all of that! I'm just proving a point.

This complete process represents a nice, typical functional flow. Take a single item, break it into a list, apply list operations, and then aggregate back down into a single value again.

Table 2-1 shows the structure of our CSV file.

Table 2-1. CSV file structure

Index	Field name	Description
[0]	Season Number	Integer value between 1 and 39. I'm running the risk of dating this book now, but there are 39 seasons to date.
[1]	Story Name	A string field I don't care about.
[2]	Writer	Ditto.
[3]	Director	Ditto.
[4]	Number of Episodes	Until 1989, all *Doctor Who* stories were multipart serials comprising 1 to 14 episodes.
[5]	Number of Missing Episodes	The number of episodes of this serial not known to exist. Any nonzero number is too many for me, but such is life.

We want to end up with a report that has just these fields:

- Season Number
- Total Episodes
- Total Missing Episodes
- Percentage Missing

Let's get rolling with some code:

```
var text = File.ReadAllText(filePath);

// Split the string containing the whole contents of the
// file into an array, where each line of the original file
// (i.e., each record) is an array element
var splitLines = text.Split(Environment.NewLine);
```

---

8 Sad to say, the BBC junked many episodes of the series in the 1970s. If you have any of those, please do hand them back.

```
// Split each line into an array of fields, splitting the
// source array by the ',' character.  Convert to Array
// for each access.
var splitLinesAndFields = splitLines.Select(x => x.Split(",").ToArray());

// Convert each string array of fields into a data class.
// parse any nonstring fields into the correct type.
// Not strictly necessary, based on the final aggregation
// that follows, but I believe in leaving behind easily
// extendible code
var parsedData = splitLinesAndFields.Select(x => new Story
{
    SeasonNumber = int.Parse(x[0]),
    StoryName = x[1],
    Writer = x[2],
    Director = x[3],
    NumberOfEpisodes = int.Parse(x[4]),
    NumberOfMissingEpisodes = int.Parse(x[5])
});

// group by SeasonNumber, this gives us an array of Story
// objects for each season of the TV series
var groupedBySeason = parsedData.GroupBy(x => SeasonNumber);

// Use a 3-field tuple as the aggregate state:
// S (int) = the season number.  Not required for
//                   the aggregation, but we need a way
//                   to pin each set of aggregated totals
//                   to a season
// NumEps (int) = the total number of episodes in all
//                   serials in the season
// NumMisEps (int) = The total number of missing episodes
//                   from the season
var aggregatedReportLines = groupedBySeason.Select(x =>
    x.Aggregate((S: x.Key, NumEps: 0, NumMisEps: 0),
        (acc, val) => (acc.S,
            acc.NumEps + val.NumberOfEpisodes,
            acc.NumMisEps + val.NumberOfMissingEpisodes)
    )
);

// convert the tuple-based results set to a proper
// object and add in the calculated field PercentageMissing
// not strictly necessary, but makes for more readable
// and extendible code
var report = aggregatedReportLines.Select(x => new ReportLine
{
    SeasonNumber = x.S,
    NumberOfEpisodes = x.NumEps,
    NumberOfMIssingEpisodes = x.NumMisEps,
    PercentageMissing = (x.NumMisEps/x.NumEps)*100
});
```

```
// format the report lines to a list of strings
var reportTextLines = report.Select(x =>
    $"{x.SeasonNumber}\t {x.NumberOfEpisodes}\t" +
    $"{x.NumberofMissingEpisodes}\t{x.PercentageMissing}");

// join the lines into a large single string with New Line
// characters between each line
var reportBody = string.Join(Environment.NewLine, reportTextLines);
var reportHeader = "Season\tNo Episodes\tNo MissingEps\tPercentage Missing";

// the final report consists of the header, a new line, then the reportbody
var finalReport = $"{reportHeader}{Environment.NewLine}{reportTextLines}";
```

In case you're curious, the results would look something like this (the \t characters are tabs, which make the output a bit more readable):

Season	No Episodes	No Missing Eps	Percentage Missing,
1	42	9	21.4
2	39	2	5.1
3	45	28	62.2
4	43	33	76.7
5	40	18	45
6	44	8	18.2
7	25	0	0
8	25	0	0
9	26	0	0

. . .

We could have made the code sample more concise and written just about all of this together in one long, continuous fluent expression like this:

```
var reportTextLines = File.ReadAllText(filePath)
    .Split(Environment.NewLine)
    .Select(x => x.Split(",").ToArray())
    .GroupBy(x => x[0])
    .Select(x =>
x.Aggregate((S: x.Key, NumEps: 0, NumMisEps: 0),
    (acc, val) => (acc.S,
        acc.NumEps + int.Parse(va[4]),
        acc.NumMisEps + int.Parse(val[5]))
    )
)
.Select(x => $"{x.S}, {x.NumEps},{x.NumMisEps},{(x.NumMisEps/x.NumEps)*100}");


var reportBody = string.Join(Environment.NewLine, reportTextLines);
var reportHeader = "Season,No Episodes,No MissingEps,Percentage Missing";

var finalReport = $"{reportHeader}{Environment.NewLine}{reportHeader}";
```

Nothing is wrong with this sort of approach, but I like splitting it into individual lines for a couple of reasons:

- The variable names provide some insight into what our code is doing. We're sort of semi-enforcing a form of code commenting.

- It's possible to inspect the intermediate variables, to see what's in them at each step. This makes debugging easier, because as I said in the previous chapter—it's like being able to look back on your work in a mathematics problem, to see at which step you went wrong.

The two approaches don't have any ultimate functional difference, nothing that would be noticed by the end user, so which style you adopt is more a matter of personal taste. Write in whatever way seems best to you. Do try to keep the code readable and easy for everyone to follow.

Taking It Further: Develop Your Functional Skills

Here's a challenge for you. If some or all of the techniques described to you here are new, go off and have fun with them for a bit. Challenge yourself to writing code with the following rules:

- Treat all variables as immutable: do not change any variable value after it's set. Basically, treat everything as if it were a constant.

- None of the following statements are permitted: if, for, foreach, while. An if statement is acceptable only in a ternary expression—i.e., the single-line expression in the style someBoolean ? valueOne : valueTwo.

- Where possible, write as many functions as small, concise arrow functions (aka lambda expressions).

Either do this as part of your production code or go out and look for a code challenge site. Try Advent of Code (*https://oreil.ly/_yysc*) or Project Euler (*https://oreil.ly/k8tLX*), something you can get your teeth into.

If you don't want to go through the bother of creating an entire solution for these exercises in Visual Studio, LINQPad (*https://www.linqpad.net*) can always provide a quick and easy way to rattle off some C# code.

After you have the hang of this, you'll be ready to move on to the next step. I hope you're having fun so far!

Summary

In this chapter, we looked at a variety of simple LINQ-based techniques for writing functional-style code immediately in any C# codebase using at least .NET Framework 3.5, because these features are evergreen and have been in place for all those years in every subsequent version of .NET without needing to be updated or replaced.

We discussed the more advanced features of `Select()` statements, some of the less well-known features of LINQ, and methods for aggregating and recursion.

In the next chapter, we'll look at some of the most recent developments in C# that can be used in more up-to-date codebases.

CHAPTER 3

Functional Coding in C# 7 and Beyond

I'm not sure when exactly the decision was made to make C# a hybrid object-oriented/functional language. The first foundation work was laid in C# 3. That was when features like lambda expressions and anonymous types were introduced, which later went on to form parts of LINQ in .NET 3.5.

After that, though, there wasn't much new in terms of functional features for quite some time. In fact, it wasn't really until the release of C# 7 in 2017 that FP seemed to become relevant again to the C# team. From C# 7 onward, every version of C# has contained something new and exciting to do more functional-style coding, a trend that doesn't currently show any signs of stopping!

Chapter 2 introduced functional features that could be implemented in just about any C# codebase likely to still be in use out in the wild. In this chapter, we're going to throw away that assumption and look at all the features you can use if your codebase is allowed to use any of the latest features—or at least those released since C# 7.

Tuples

Tuples were introduced in C# 7. NuGet packages do exist to allow some of the older versions of C# to use them too. They're basically a way to throw together a quick-and-dirty collection of properties, without having to create and maintain a class.

If we have a few properties we want to hold onto for a minute in one place and then dispose of immediately, tuples are great for that.

If we have multiple objects we want to pass between `Select()` statements, or multiple items we want to pass in or out of one, then we can use a tuple.

This is an example of the sort of thing we might consider using tuples for:

```
var filmIds = new[]
{
    4665,
    6718,
    7101
};

// Turns each int element of the filmIds array
// into a tuple containing the film and cast list
// as separate properties

var filmsWithCast = filmIds.Select(x => (
    film: GetFilm(x),
    castList: GetCastList(x)
));


// 'x' here is a tuple, and it's now being converted to a string

var renderedFilmDetails = filmsWithCast.Select(x =>
    "Title: " + x.film.Title +
    "Director: " + x.film.Director +
    "Cast: " + string.Join(", ", x.castList));
```

In this example, we use a tuple to pair up data from two lookup functions for each given film ID, meaning we can run a subsequent `Select()` to simplify the pair of objects into a single return value.

Pattern Matching

Switch statements have been around for longer than just about any developers still working today. They have their uses, but they're quite limited in what can be done with them. FP has taken that concept and moved it up a few levels. That's what pattern matching is.

C# 7 started to introduce this feature to the C# language. Later versions have subsequently enhanced pattern matching multiple times, and yet more features will likely be added in the future.

Pattern matching is an amazing way to save yourself an awful lot of work. To illustrate what I mean, I'll show you a bit of procedural code and then how pattern matching is implemented in a few versions of C#.

Procedural Bank Accounts

Let's imagine one of the classic object-oriented worked examples: bank accounts. We're going to create a set of bank account types, each with different rules for calculating the amount of interest. These aren't really based on real banking; they're straight out of my imagination.

These are our rules:

- A standard bank account calculates interest by multiplying the balance by the interest rate for the account.
- A premium bank account with a balance of $10,000 or less is a standard bank account.
- A premium bank account with a balance over $10,000 applies an interest rate augmented by a bonus additional rate.
- A millionaire's bank account contains so much money it's larger than the largest value a decimal can hold. (It's a really, really big number—around 8×10^{28}—so they must be very wealthy indeed. Do you think they'd be willing to lend me a little, if I were to ask? I could use a new pair of shoes.) An overflow balance property is used to add in all the millionaire's money that is over the max decimal value and that can't be stored in the standard balance property as for those of us unlucky enough *not* to be multibillionaires. The millionaire's interest is calculated based on both balances.
- A Monopoly player's bank account gets an extra $200 for passing Go. I'm not implementing the "Go Directly to Jail" logic, as there are only so many hours in a day.

These are our classes:

```
public class StandardBankAccount
{
    public decimal Balance { get; set; }
    public decimal InterestRate { get; set; }
}

public class PremiumBankAccount : StandardBankAccount
{
    public decimal BonusInterestRate { get; set; }
}

public class MillionairesBankAccount : StandardBankAccount
{
    public decimal OverflowBalance { get; set; }
}

public class MonopolyPlayersBankAccount : StandardBankAccount
{
    public decimal PassingGoBonus { get; set; }
}
```

The procedural approach to implementing the CalculateInterest() feature for bank accounts—or, as I think of it, the longhand approach—could look like this:

```
public decimal CalculateNewBalance(StandardBankAccount sba)
{
    // If real type of object is PremiumBankAccount
    if (sba.GetType() == typeof(PremiumBankAccount))
    {
        // cast to correct type so we can access the Bonus interest
        var pba = (PremiumBankAccount)sba;
        if (pba.Balance > 10000)
        {
            return pba.Balance * (pba.InterestRate + pba.BonusInterestRate);
        }
    }

    // if real type of object is a Millionaire's bank account
    if(sba.GetType() == typeof(MillionairesBankAccount))
    {
        // cast to the correct type so we can get access to the overflow
        var mba = (MillionairesBankAccount)sba;
        return (mba.Balance * mba.InterestRate) +
            (mba.OverflowBalance * mba.InterestRate)
    }

    // if real type of object is a Monopoly Player's bank account
    if(sba.GetType() == typeof(MonopolyPlayersBankAccount))
    {
        // cast to the correct type so we can get access to the bonus
        var mba = (MonopolyPlayersBankAccount)sba;
        return (mba.Balance * mba.InterestRate) +
            mba.PassingGoBonus
    }

    // no special rules apply
    return sba.Balance * sba.InterestRate;
}
```

As is typical with procedural code, this code isn't concise, and understanding its intent might take a little bit of reading. It's also wide open to abuse if many more new rules are added after the system goes into production.

The object-oriented approach would be to use either an interface or polymorphism— i.e., create an abstract base class with a virtual method for the CalculateNew Balance() function. The issue is that the logic is now split over many places, rather than being contained in a single, easy-to-read function. In the sections that follow, I'll show how each subsequent version of C# handled this problem.

Pattern Matching in C# 7

C# 7 gave us two ways of solving this problem. The first was the new is operator—a much more convenient way of checking types than had previously been available. An is operator can also be used to automatically cast the source variable to the correct type.

Your updated source would look something like this:

```
public decimal CalculateNewBalance(StandardBankAccount sba)
{
    // If real type of object is PremiumBankAccount
    if (sba is PremiumBankAccount pba)
    {
        if (pba.Balance > 10000)
        {
            return pba.Balance * (pba.InterestRate + pba.BonusInterestRate);
        }
    }

    // if real type of object is a Millionaire's bank account
    if(sba is MillionairesBankAccount mba)
    {
        return (mba.Balance * mba.InterestRate) +
            (mba.OverflowBalance * mba.InterestRate);
    }

    // if real type of object is a Monopoly Player's bank account
    if(sba is MonopolyPlayersBankAccount mba)
    {
        return (mba.Balance * mba.InterestRate) +
            mba.PassingGoBonus;
    }
    // no special rules apply
    return sba.Balance * sba.InterestRate;
}
```

Note that in this code sample, with the is operator, we can also automatically wrap the source variable into a new local variable of the correct type. This isn't bad: it's a little more elegant, and we've saved ourselves a few redundant lines. But we could do better, and that's where another feature of C# 7, type switching, comes in:

```
public decimal CalculateNewBalance(StandardBankAccount sba)
{
    switch (sba)
    {
        case PremiumBankAccount pba when pba.Balance > 10000:
            return pba.Balance * (pba.InterestRate + pba.BonusInterestRate);
        case MillionairesBankAccount mba:
            return (mba.Balance * mba.InterestRate) +
                    (mba.OverflowBalance & mba.InterestRate);
        case MonopolyPlayersBankAccount mba:
```

```
            return (mba.Balance * mba.InterestRate) + PassingGoBonus;
        default:
            return sba.Balance * sba.InterestRate;
    }
}
```

Pretty cool, right? Pattern matching seems to be one of the most developed features of C# in recent years. As I'm about to show, every major version of C# since has continued to add to it.

Pattern Matching in C# 8

Things moved up a notch in C# 8, which uses pretty much the same concept but with a new, updated matching syntax that more closely matches JavaScript Object Notation (JSON) or a C# object initializer expression. Any number of clauses to properties or subproperties of the object under examination can be put inside the curly braces, and the default case is now represented by the _ discard character:

```
public decimal CalculateNewBalance(StandardBankAccount sba) =>
    sba switch
    {
        PremiumBankAccount { Balance: > 10000 } pba => pba.Balance *
            (pba.InterestRate + pba.BonusInterestRate),
        MillionairesBankAccount mba => (mba.Balance * mba.InterestRate) +
            (mba.OverflowBalance & mba.InterestRate);
        MonopolyPlayersBankAccount mba =>
            (mba.Balance * mba.InterestRate) + PassingGoBonus;
        _ => sba.Balance * sba.InterestRate
    };
}
```

Also, switch can now *also* be an expression, which you can use as the body of a small, single-purpose function with surprisingly rich functionality. This means it can also be stored in a Func delegate for potential passing around as a higher-order function.

The next example uses an old childhood game: Scissors, Paper, Stone (known in the United States as *Rock, Paper, Scissors* and in Japan as *Janken*). I've created a Func delegate for this with the following rules:

- Both players choosing the same thing is a draw.
- Scissors beats Paper.
- Paper beats Stone.
- Stone beats Scissors.

This function is specifically determining the result from *my* perspective against my imaginary adversary, so *me* choosing Scissors and beating my opponent's choice of Paper would be considered a win, because *I* won, even if my opponent would consider it a loss:

```
public enum SPS
{
    Scissor,
    Paper,
    Stone
}

public enum GameResult
{
    Win,
    Lose,
    Draw
}

var calculateMatchResult = (SPS myMove, SPS theirMove) =>
    (myMove, theirMove) switch
    {
        _ when myMove == theirMove => GameResult.Draw,
        ( SPS.Scissor, SPS.Paper) => GameResult.Win,
        ( SPS.Paper, SPS.Stone ) => GameResult.Win,
        (SPS.Stone, SPS.Scissor) => GameResult.Win,
        _ => GameResult.Lose
    };
```

Having stored the logic that determines the winner of a given game in a Func<SPS,SPS> typed variable, I can pass it around to wherever needs it.

This can be as a parameter to a function, so that the functionality can be injected at runtime:

```
public string formatGames(
    IEnumerable<(SPS,SPS)> game,
    Func<SPS,SPS,Result) calc) =>

string.Join("\r\n",
    game.Select((x, i) => "Game " + i + ": " +
        calc(x.Item1,x.Item2).ToString());
```

If I wanted to test the logic of this function without putting the actual logic into it, I could easily inject my own Func from a test method instead, so I wouldn't have to care what the real logic is—that can be tested in a dedicated test elsewhere. This approach is another small way to make the structure even more useful.

Pattern Matching in C# 9

Nothing major was added in C# 9 but a couple of nice little features. The and and not keywords from is expressions now work inside the curly braces of one of the patterns in the list, and it's no longer necessary to have a local variable for a cast type if its properties aren't needed.

Although not groundbreaking, this does continue to reduce the amount of necessary boilerplate code and gives us an extra few pieces of more expressive syntax.

I've added a few more rules into the next example using these features. Now we have two categories of PremiumBankAccount with different levels of special interest rates[1] and another type for a closed account, which shouldn't generate any interest:

```
public decimal CalculateNewBalance(StandardBankAccount sba) =>
    sba switch
    {
        PremiumBankAccount { Balance: > 10000 and <= 20000 } pba => pba.Balance *
            (pba.InterestRate + pba.BonusInterestRate),
        PremiumBankAccount { Balance: > 20000 } pba => pba.Balance *
            (pba.InterestRate + pba.BonusInterestRate * 1.25M),
        MillionairesBankAccount mba => (mba.Balance * mba.InterestRate) +
            (mba.OverflowBalance + mba.InterestRate),
        MonopolyPlayersBankAccount {CurrSquare: not "InJail" } mba =>
            (mba.Balance * mba.InterestRate) + mba.PassingGoBonus;
        ClosedBankAccount => 0,
        _ => sba.Balance * sba.InterestRate
    };
}
```

Not bad, is it?

Pattern Matching in C# 10

Like C# 9, C# 10 added another nice time-and-boilerplate-saving feature. Here's the simple syntax for comparing the properties of subobjects belonging to the type being examined:

```
public decimal CalculateNewBalance(StandardBankAccount sba) =>
    sba switch
    {
        PremiumBankAccount { Balance: > 10000 and <= 20000 } pba =>
            pba.Balance * (pba.InterestRate + pba.BonusInterestRate),
        MillionairesBankAccount mba =>
            (mba.Balance * mba.InterestRate) +
                (mba.OverflowBalance + mba.InterestRate),
        MonopolyPlayersBankAccount {CurrSquare: not "InJail" } mba =>
```

---

1 Which, frankly, no bank would ever offer.

```
              (mba.Balance * mba.InterestRate) + PassingGoBonus,
      MonopolyPlayersBankAccount {Player.FirstName: "Simon" } mba =>
              (mba.Balance * mba.InterestRate) + (mba.PassingGoBonus / 2),
      ClosedBankAccount => 0,
      _ => sba.Balance * sba.InterestRate
   };
```

In this slightly silly example, it's now possible to exclude all Simons from earning so much money in Monopoly when passing Go. Poor, old me.

I'd suggest taking another moment at this point to examine the function in the preceding example. Think just how much code would have to be written if it weren't done as a pattern-matching expression! As it is, the function *technically* comprises just a single line of code. One...really long...line of code, with a whole ton of newlines to make it readable. Still, the point stands.

Pattern Matching in C# 11

C# 11 contains a new pattern-matching feature that probably has a somewhat limited scope of usage but will be devastatingly useful when something fits into that scope. The .NET team has added the ability to match based on the contents of an enumerable and even to deconstruct its elements into separate variables.

Let's imagine we are creating a simple text-based adventure game. These were a big thing when I was young—adventure games you played by typing in commands. Imagine something like *Monkey Island*, but with no graphics, just text. You had to use your imagination a lot more back then.

The first task is to take the input from the user and decide what they're trying to do. In English, commands just about universally have their relevant verbs as the first word of the sentence: GO WEST, KILL THE GOBLIN, EAT THE SUSPICIOUS-LOOKING MUSHROOM. The relevant verbs here are GO, KILL, and EAT, respectively.

Here's how we'd use C# 11 pattern matching:

```
var verb = input.Split(" ") switch
{
    ["GO", "TO",.. var rest] => this.actions.GoTo(rest),
    ["GO", .. var rest] => this.actions.GoTo(rest),
    ["EAT", .. var rest] => this.actions.Eat(rest),
    ["KILL", .. var rest] => this.actions.Kill(rest)
};
```

The two dots (..) in this switch expression mean, "I don't care what else is in the array; ignore it." We put a variable after the two dots to contain everything else in the array besides those bits that're specifically matched for.

In this example, if we were to enter the text GO WEST, the GoTo() action would be called with a single-element array ["WEST"] as a parameter, because GO is part of the match.

Here's another neat way of using this C# 11 feature. Imagine we're processing people's names into data structures and we want three of them to be FirstName, LastName, and an array, MiddleNames (I have only one middle name, but plenty of folks have many):

```
public class Person
{
    public string FirstName { get; set; }
    public IEnumerable<string> MiddleNames { get; set; }
    public string LastName { get; set; }
}

// The real name of Doctor Who actor Sylvester McCoy
var input = "Percy James Patrick Kent-Smith".Split(" ");

var sylv = new Person
{
    FirstName = input.First(),
    MiddleNames = input is [_, .. var mns, _] ? mns : Enumerable.Empty<string>(),
    LastName = input.Last()
};
```

In this example, the Person class is instantiated with the following:

```
FirstName = "Percy",
LastName = "Kent-Smith",
MiddleNames = [ "James", "Patrick" ]
```

I'm not sure I'll find many uses for this, but it'll probably get me excited when I do. It's a powerful feature.

Read-Only Structs

I'm not going to discuss structs a great deal here, as other excellent books talk about the features of C# in far more detail.[2] What's great about structs from a C# perspective is that they're passed between functions by value, not reference—i.e., a copy is passed in, leaving the original untouched. The old OOP technique of passing an object into a function for it to be modified there, away from the function that instantiated it, is anathema to a functional programmer. We instantiate an object based on a class and never change it again.

---

2 For a start, you could check out *C# 10 in a Nutshell* by Joseph Albahari (O'Reilly).

Structs have been around for an awfully long time, and although they're passed by value, they can still have their properties modified, so they aren't immutable as such. At least until C# 7.2.

Now, it's possible to add a `readonly` modifier to a struct definition, which will enforce all properties of the struct as read-only at design time. Any attempt to add a setter to a property will result in a compiler error.

Since all properties are enforced as read-only, in C# 7.2 itself, all properties need to be included in the constructor to be set. The code would look like this:

```
public readonly struct Movie
{
    public string Title { get; private set; };
    public string Directory { get; private set; };
    public IEnumerable<string> Cast { get; private set; };


    public Movie(string title, string directory, IEnumerable<string> cast)
    {
        this.Title = title;
        this.Directory = directory;
        this.Cast = cast;
    }
}

var bladeRunner = new Movie(
        "Blade Runner",
        "Ridley Scott",
        new []
        {
            "Harrison Ford",
            "Sean Young"
        }
);
```

This is still a little clunky, forcing us to update the constructor with every property as they're added to the struct, but it's still better than nothing.

It's also worth discussing this case, where I've added in a `List` to the struct:

```
public readonly struct Movie
{
    public readonly string Title;
    public readonly string Directory;
    public readonly IList<string> Cast;
```

```
        public Movie(string title, string directory, IList<string> cast)
        {
            this.Title = title;
            this.Directory = directory;
            this.Cast = cast;
        }
    }

    var bladeRunner = new Movie(
        "Blade Runner",
        "Ridley Scott",
        new []
        {
            "Harrison Ford",
            "Sean Young"
        }
    );

    bladeRunner.Cast.Add(("Edward James Olmos"));
```

This will compile, and the application will run, but an error will be thrown when the Add function is called. It's nice that the read-only nature of the struct is being enforced, but I'm not a fan of having to worry about another potential unhandled exception.

Still, it's a good thing that the developer can now add the readonly modifier to clarify intent. This modifier will prevent any easily avoidable mutability from being added to the struct—even if it does mean that there has to be another layer of error handling.

Init-Only Setters

C# 9 introduced a new kind of auto-property type. We already had Get and Set, but now there's also Init.

If you have a class property with Get and Set attached to it, the property can be retrieved or replaced at any time. If instead it has Get and Init, the property can have its value set when the object it's part of is instantiated, but can't then be changed again.

Therefore, our read-only structs (and, indeed all our classes too) can now have a slightly nicer syntax to be instantiated and then exist in a read-only state:

```
    public readonly struct Movie
    {
        public string Title { get; init; }
        public string Director { get; init;  }
        public IEnumerable<string> Cast { get; init; }
    }
```

```
var bladeRunner = new Movie
    {
        Title = "Blade Runner",
        Director = "Ridley Scott",
        Cast = new []
        {
            "Harrison Ford",
            "Sean Young"
        }
    };
```

This means we don't have to maintain a convoluted constructor (i.e., one with a parameter for every single property—and there could be dozens of them), along with the properties themselves, which has removed a potential source of annoying boilerplate code. We still have the issue with exceptions being thrown when attempting to modify lists and subobjects, though.

Record Types

In C# 9, one of my favorite features since pattern matching was added: record types. If you haven't had a chance to play with these yet, do yourself a favor and do so as soon as possible. Record types are fantastic.

On the face of it, they look about the same as a struct. In C# 9, a record type is based on a class, and as such is passed around by reference.

As of C# 10 and onward, that's no longer the case, and records are treated more like structs, meaning they can be passed by value. Unlike a struct, however, there is no readonly modifier, so immutability has to be enforced by the developer. This is an updated version of the *Blade Runner* code:

```
public record Movie
{
    public string Title { get; init; }
    public string Director { get; init;  }
    public IEnumerable<string> Cast { get; init; }
}

var bladeRunner = new Movie
    {
        Title = "Blade Runner",
        Director = "Ridley Scott",
        Cast = new []
        {
            "Harrison Ford",
            "Sean Young"
        }
    };
```

The code doesn't look all that different, does it? Records come into their own, though, when we want to create a modified version. Let's imagine for a moment that in our C# 10 application, we want to create a new movie record for the director's cut of *Blade Runner*.[3]

This version is exactly the same for our purposes, except that it has a different title. To save defining data, we'll literally copy over data from the original record but with one modification. With a read-only struct, we'd have to do something like this:

```
public readonly struct Movie
{
    public string Title { get; init; }
    public string Director { get; init;  }
    public IEnumerable<string> Cast { get; init; }
}

var bladeRunner = new Movie
    {
        Title = "Blade Runner",
        Director = "Ridley Scott",
        Cast = new []
        {
            "Harrison Ford",
            "Sean Young"
        }
    };

var bladeRunnerDirectors = new Movie
{
    Title = $"{bladeRunner.Title} - The Director's Cut",
    Director = bladeRunner.Director,
    Cast = bladeRunner.Cast
};
```

The code is following the functional paradigm, and it's not too bad, but it contains another heap of boilerplate we have to include in our applications if we want to enforce immutability.

This becomes important if we have something like a state object that needs to be updated regularly following interactions with the user, or external dependencies of some sort. That's a lot of copying of properties we'd have to do using the read-only struct approach.

Record types give us an absolutely amazing new keyword: with. This is a quick, convenient way of creating a replica of an existing record but with a modification. The updated version of the director's cut code with record types looks like this:

---

3 Vastly superior to the theatrical cut, in my opinion.

```
public record Movie
{
    public string Title { get; init; }
    public string Director { get; init;  }
    public IEnumerable<string> Cast { get; init; }
}

var bladeRunner = new Movie
    {
        Title = "Blade Runner",
        Director = "Ridley Scott",
        Cast = new []
        {
            "Harrison Ford",
            "Sean Young"
        }
    };

var bladeRunnerDirectors = bladeRunner with
{
    Title = $"{bladeRunner.Title} - The Director's Cut"
};
```

Isn't that cool? The sheer amount of boilerplate we can save with record types is staggering.

I recently wrote a text adventure game in functional C#. I made a central GameState record type, containing all the progress the player has made so far. I used a massive pattern-matching statement to work out what the player was doing this turn, and a simple with statement to update state by returning a modified duplicate record. It's an elegant way to code state machines and clarifies intent massively by cutting away so much of the uninteresting boilerplate.

One more neat feature of records is that we can even define them simply in a single line like this:

```
public record Movie(string Title, string Director, IEnumerable<string> Cast);
```

Creating instances of Movie using this style of definition can't be done with curly braces; it has to be done with a function:

```
var bladeRunner = new Movie(
"Blade Runner",
"Ridley Scott",
new[]
{
    "Harrison Ford",
    "Sean Young"
});
```

Note that all properties have to be supplied and in order, unless we use constructor tags like this:

```
var bladeRunner = new Movie(
    Cast: new[]
    {
        "Harrison Ford",
        "Sean Young"
    },
    Director: "Ridley Scott",
    Title: "Blade Runner");
```

We *still* have to provide all the properties, but we can put them in any order we like (for all the good that does…).

Which syntax you use is a matter of preference. In most circumstances, they're equivalent.

Nullable Reference Types

Despite what it sounds like, a nullable reference type isn't actually a new type, as with record types. This is effectively a compiler option, which was introduced in C# 8. This option is set in the CSPROJ file, as in this extract:

```
<PropertyGroup>
  <TargetFramework>net6.0</TargetFramework>
  <Nullable>enable</Nullable>
  <IsPackable>false</IsPackable>
</PropertyGroup>
```

If you prefer using a UI, the option can also be set in the Build section of the project's properties.

Strictly speaking, activating the null reference types feature doesn't change the behavior of the code generated by the compiler, but does add an extra set of warnings to the IDE and the compiler to help avoid a situation where null might end up assigned. Figure 3-1 shows a warning added to our Movie record type, indicating that it's possible for properties to end up null.

Another warning occurs if we try to set the title of the *Blade Runner* director's cut to null, as shown in Figure 3-2.

```
public record Movie
{
    0 references
    public string Title { get; init; }
    0 references
    public string Dire          string Movie.Title { get;
    0 references                 init; }
    public IEnumerable                                    nit; }
}                            CS8618: Non-nullable
                             property 'Title' must
                             contain a non-null value
                             when exiting constructor.
                             Consider declaring the
                             property as nullable.

                             Show potential fixes (Ctrl+.)
```

Figure 3-1. Warning for nullable properties on a record

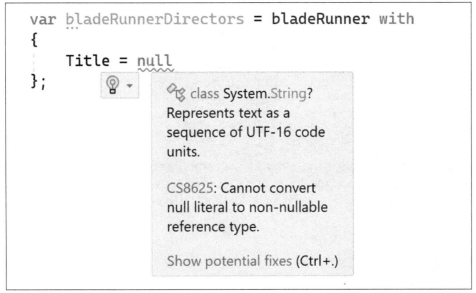

```
var bladeRunnerDirectors = bladeRunner with
{
    Title = null
};              💡 ▾      class System.String?
                          Represents text as a
                          sequence of UTF-16 code
                          units.

                          CS8625: Cannot convert
                          null literal to non-nullable
                          reference type.

                          Show potential fixes (Ctrl+.)
```

Figure 3-2. Warning for setting a property to null

Do bear in mind that these are only compiler warnings. The code will still execute without any errors at all. It's just guiding us to writing code that's less likely to contain null reference exceptions, which can only be a good thing.

Avoiding the use of a null value is generally a good practice, whether you're using FP or not. A null value is the so-called "billion-dollar mistake." Invented by British computer scientist Tony Hoare in the mid '60s, null has been one of the leading causes of bugs in production ever since: an object being passed into something that turns out unexpectedly to be null. This gives rise to a null-reference exception, and you don't need to have been in this business long before you encounter your first one of those!

Having null as a value adds unneeded complexity to your codebase and introduces another source of potential errors. This is why it's worth paying attention to the compiler warning and keeping null out of your codebase wherever possible.

If there's a perfectly good reason for setting a value to be null, we can do so by adding *?* characters to properties, like this:

```
public record Movie
{
    public string? Title { get; init; }
    public string? Director { get; init;  }
    public IEnumerable<string>? Cast { get; init; }
}
```

I'd consider deliberately adding a nullable property to my codebase only if a third-party library requires it. Even then, I wouldn't allow the nullable to be persisted through the rest of my code. I'd probably tuck it away somewhere that the code that parses the external data can see it, and then convert it into a safer, more controlled structure for passing to other areas of the system.

The Future

As of the time of writing, C# 11 is out and well established as part of .NET 7. The full spec for C# 12 is out, and for the first time in many years, it doesn't seem to contain anything especially functional—even if it does contain many generally neat features!

C# 12 Specifications

You can find a description of all the new features of C# 12 on the Microsoft website (*https://oreil.ly/ByZl4*).

Primary constructors are now available to all classes, and not just record types. That's nice, and a way to reduce code noise, but not specifically functional.

Default values can also now be included on lambda expressions. That does make it slightly easier to write composable functions in places, but once again, not *specifically* functional.

Although it's a little disappointing to have to skip a year of having new functional features added to C#, there is still really quite a lot available already that we can play with for now. Especially as Microsoft have said that there are some very exciting things coming on the horizon…

Discriminated Unions

I'm not sure that it's by any means certain that we'll get discriminated unions in C#, but it is a feature that's being actively considered and worked on within Microsoft.

C# 12 Specifications

There's a discussion available on YouTube where you can see Microsoft C# team members discussing this very idea: "Languages and Runtime Community Standup: Considering Discriminated Unions" (*https://oreil.ly/psirr*).

I'm not going to discuss discriminated unions in too much detail here, when you can turn to Chapter 6 for full details of what they are and how we can use them now in an awful lot more detail.

I'm also aware of at least two attempts to implement this concept that are available currently in NuGet:

- Harry McIntyre's OneOf (*https://oreil.ly/bhjGX*)
- Kim Hugener-Olsen's Sundew.DiscriminatedUnions (*https://oreil.ly/Ws3G6*)

In brief, they're a way of having a type that might actually be one of several types. Discriminated unions are available natively in F#, but C# doesn't have them to date, and it's not necessarily a given that we'll ever get them.

As of the time of writing, they're under active consideration for C# 13, and discussions are happening over on GitHub (*https://oreil.ly/E4_OS*), and proposals (*https://oreil.ly/bOX3T*) exist as well. For now, however, we'll just have to keep watching the skies!

Active Patterns

Active patterns is an F# feature I can see being added to C# sooner or later. It's an enhancement to pattern matching that allows functions to be executed in the lefthand "pattern" side of the expression. This is an F# example:

```
let (|IsDateTime|_|) (input:string) =
    let success, value = DateTime.TryParse input
    if success then Some value else None

let tryParseDateTime input =
    match input with
    | IsDateTime dt -> Some dt
    | _ -> None
```

As you can see in this example, F# developers are able to provide their own custom functions for the lefthand "pattern" side of the expression. IsDateTime is the custom function here, defined on the first line. It takes a string and returns a value if the parse worked, and what is effectively a null result if it doesn't.

The pattern-match expression tryParseDateTime() uses IsDateTime as the pattern. If a value is returned from IsDateTime, that case on the pattern-match expression is selected and the resulting DateTime is returned.

Don't worry too much about the intricacies of F# syntax; I'm not expecting you to learn about that here. Other books cover F#, and you could probably do worse than one or more of these resources:

- *F# in Action* or *Get Programming with F#* by Isaac Abraham (Manning)
- *Essential F#* by Ian Russell (LeanPub) (*https://oreil.ly/Npcdt*)
- F# for Fun and Profit website by Scott Wlaschin (*https://oreil.ly/NP8XZ*)

Whether either of these F# features becomes available in a later version of C# remains to be seen, but C# and F# share a common language runtime, so it's not beyond imagining that they might be ported over.

Summary

In this chapter, we looked at all the features of C# that have been released since FP began to be integrated in C# 3 and 4. We looked at what they are, how they can be used, and why they're worth considering.

Broadly, these FP features fall into two categories:

Pattern matching
> Implemented in C# as an advanced form of `switch` statement that allows for incredibly powerful, code-saving logic to be written briefly and simply. We saw how every version of C# has contributed more pattern-matching features to the developer.

Immutability
> The ability to prevent variables from being altered once instantiated. It's highly unlikely that true immutability will ever be made available in C# for reasons of backward compatibility, but new features are being added to C#, such as read-only structs and record types that make it easier for a developer to pretend that immutability exists without having to add a lot of tedious boilerplate code to the application.

The next chapter takes things a step further and demonstrates novel ways to use some existing features of C#, for new additions to your FP tool belt.

CHAPTER 4

Work Smart, Not Hard with Functional Code

Everything I've covered so far has been FP as intended by Microsoft's C# team. You'll find these features, along with examples, on the Microsoft website. In this chapter, however, I want to start being a bit more creative with C#.

I don't know about you, but I like being lazy, or at least I don't like wasting my time with tedious boilerplate code. One of the many wonderful things about FP is its concision, compared to imperative code.

In this chapter, I'm going to show you ways to push the functional envelope further than out-of-the-box C# will allow. You'll also learn to implement some of the more recent functional features introduced in C# in legacy versions of the language, which will hopefully allow you to get on with your day job an awfully lot quicker.

This chapter explores a few categories of functional concepts:

Funcs *in enumerables*
> Func delegates don't seem to get used all that much, but they're incredibly powerful features of C#. I'll show a few ways of using them that help extend C#'s capabilities. In this case, we'll add them to enumerables and operate on them with LINQ expressions.

Funcs *as filters*
> You can also use Func delegates as filters—something that sits between you and the real value you're trying to reach. You can write a few neat bits of code by using these principles.

Custom enumerables

I've discussed the `IEnumerable` interface and how cool it is before, but did you know you can break it open and implement your own customized behavior? I'll show you how.

All these and a host of other concepts too!

It's Time to Get Func-y

The `Func` delegate types are functions stored as variables. You define what parameters they take and what they return, and call them like any other function. Here's a quick example:

```
private readonly Func<Person, DateTime, string> SayHello =
    (Person p, DateTime today) => today + " : " + "Hello " + p.Name;
```

The last generic type in the list between the two angle brackets is the return value; all the previous types are the parameters. This example takes two string parameters and returns a string.

You're going to be seeing an awful lot of `Func` delegates from now on, so please do make sure you're comfortable with them before reading on.

Funcs in Enumerables

I've seen plenty of examples of `Funcs` as parameters to functions, but I'm not sure many developers realize that we can put them in an enumerable and create some interesting behaviors.

First is the obvious one—put them in an array to act on the same data multiple times:

```
private IEnumerable<Func<Employee, string>> descriptors = new []
{
    x => "First Name = " + x.firstName,
    x => "Last Name = " + x.lastName,
    x => "MiddleNames = string.Join(" ", x.MiddleNames)
}

public string DescribeEmployee(Employee emp) =>
    string.Join(Environment.NewLine, descriptors.Select(x => x(emp)));
```

Using this technique, we can have a single original source of data (here, an `Employee` object) and have multiple records of the same type generated from it. In this case, we aggregate using the built-in .NET method `string.Join` to present a single, unified string to the end user.

This approach has a few advantages over a simple `StringBuilder`. First, the array can be assembled dynamically. We could have multiple rules for each property and how it's rendered, which could be selected from a set of local variables depending on custom logic.

Second, this is an enumerable, so by defining it this way, we're taking advantage of a feature of enumerables called *lazy evaluation* (introduced in Chapter 2). The thing about enumerables is that they aren't arrays; they aren't even data. They're just pointers to something that will tell us how to extract the data. It might well be—and, in fact, usually is the case—that the source behind the enumerable is a simple array, but not necessarily. An enumerable requires a function to be executed each time the next item is accessed via a `foreach` loop. Enumerables were developed to transform into actual data only at the very last possible moment—typically, when starting a `foreach` loop iteration. Most of the time, this doesn't matter if an array held in-memory somewhere is feeding the enumerable, but if an expensive function or lookup to an external system is powering it, lazy loading can be incredibly useful to prevent unnecessary work.

The elements of an enumerable are evaluated one at a time and only when their turn has come to be used by whatever process is performing the enumeration. For example, if we use the LINQ `Any` function to evaluate each element in an enumerable, `Any` will stop enumerating the first time an element is found that matches the specified criteria, meaning the remaining elements will be left unevaluated.

Lastly, from a maintenance perspective, this technique is easier to live with. Adding a new line to the final result is as easy as adding a new element to the array. This approach also acts as a restraint to future programmers, making it harder for them to try to put too much complex logic where it doesn't belong.

A Super-Simple Validator

Let's imagine a quick validation function, which typically looks like this:

```
public bool IsPasswordValid(string password)
{
    if(password.Length <= 6)
        return false;

    if(password.Length > 20)
        return false;

    if(!password.Any(x => Char.IsLower(x)))
        return false;

    if(!password.Any(x => Char.IsUpper(x)))
        return false;

    if(!password.Any(x => Char.IsSymbol(x)))
        return false;
```

```
if(password.Contains("Justin", StringComparison.OrdinalIgnoreCase)
    && password.Contains("Bieber", StringComparison.OrdinalIgnoreCase))

    return false;

return true;
}
```

Well, for a start, that's a *lot* of code for what is, in fact, a fairly simple set of rules. The imperative approach forces you to write a whole heap of repetitive boilerplate code. On top of that, if we want to add in another rule, that's potentially around four new lines of code to add when really only one is especially interesting to us.

If only there were a way to compact this code into just a few simple lines. Well, since you asked so nicely, here you go:

```
public bool IsPasswordValid(string password) =>
    new Func<string, bool>[]
    {
        x => x.Length > 6,
        x => x.Length <= 20,
        x => x.Any(y => Char.IsLower(y)),
        x => x.Any(y => Char.IsUpper(y)),
        x => x.Any(y => Char.IsSymbol(y)),
        x => !x.Contains("Justin", StringComparison.OrdinalIgnoreCase)
            && !x.Contains("Bieber", StringComparison.OrdinalIgnoreCase)
    }.All(f => f(password));
```

Not so long now, is it? What have we done here? We've put all the rules into an array of Funcs that turn a `string` into a `bool`—i.e., check a single validation rule. We use a LINQ statement: `.All()`. The purpose of this function is to evaluate whatever lambda expression we give it against all elements of the array it's attached to. If a single one of these returns `false`, the process is terminated early, and `false` is returned from `All()` (as mentioned earlier, the subsequent values aren't accessed, so lazy evaluation saves us time by not evaluating them). If every single one of the items returns `true`, `All()` also returns `true`.

We've effectively re-created the first code sample, but the boilerplate code we were forced to write—`if` statements and early returns—is now implicit in the structure.

This also has the advantage of once again being easy to maintain as a code structure. If we wanted, we could even generalize it into an extension method. I do this often:

```
public static bool IsValid<T>(this T @this, params Func<T,bool>[] rules) =>
    rules.All(x => x(@this));
```

This reduces the size of the password validator yet further and gives us a handy, generic structure to use elsewhere:

```
public bool IsPasswordValid(string password) =>
    password.IsValid(
```

```
        x => x.Length > 6,
        x => x.Length <= 20,
        x => x.Any(y => Char.IsLower(y)),
        x => x.Any(y => Char.IsUpper(y)),
        x => x.Any(y => Char.IsSymbol(y)),
        x => !x.Contains("Justin", StringComparison.OrdinalIgnoreCase)
            && !x.Contains("Bieber", StringComparison.OrdinalIgnoreCase)
    )
```

At this point, I hope you're reconsidering ever writing something as long and ungainly as that first validation code sample ever again.

I think an `IsValid` check is easier to read and maintain, but if we want a piece of code that is much more in line with the original code sample, we can create a new extension method by using `Any()` instead of `All()`:

```
public static bool IsInvalid<T>(
    this T @this,
    params Func<string,bool>[] rules) =>
```

This means that the Boolean logic of each array element can be reversed, as it was originally:

```
public bool IsPasswordValid(string password) =>
    !password.IsInvalid(
        x => x.Length <= 6,
        x => x.Length > 20,
        x => !x.Any(y => Char.IsLower(y)),
        x => !x.Any(y => Char.IsUpper(y)),
        x => !x.Any(y => Char.IsSymbol(y)),
        x => x.Contains("Justin", StringComparison.OrdinalIgnoreCase)
            && x.Contains("Bieber", StringComparison.OrdinalIgnoreCase)
    )
```

If we want to maintain both functions, `IsValid()` and `IsInvalid()`, because each has its place in our codebase, it's probably worth saving some coding effort and preventing a potential maintenance task in the future by simply referencing one in the other:

```
public static bool IsValid<T>(this T @this, params Func<T,bool>[] rules) =>
    rules.All(x => x(@this));

public static bool IsInvalid<T>(this T @this, params Func<T,bool>[] rules) =>
    !@this.IsValid(rules);
```

Use it wisely, my young functional Padawan learner.

Pattern Matching for Old Versions of C#

Pattern matching is one of the best features of C# in recent years, along with record types, but it isn't available in anything except the most recent .NET versions. (See Chapter 3 for more details on native pattern matching in C# 7 and up.)

Is there a way to allow pattern matching to happen, but without needing up upgrade to a newer version of C#? There most certainly is. It is nowhere near as elegant as the native syntax in C# 8, but it provides a few of the same benefits.

In this example, we'll calculate the amount of tax someone should pay based on a grossly simplified version of the UK income tax rules. Note that these really are much simpler than the real thing. I don't want us to get too bogged down in the complexities of taxes.

The rules to apply look like this:

- If yearly income is less than or equal to £12,570, no tax is taken.
- If yearly income is between £12,571 and £50,270, take 20% tax.
- If yearly income is between £50,271 and £150,000, take 40% tax.
- If yearly income is over £150,000, take 45% tax.

If we wanted to write this longhand (nonfunctionally), it would look like this:

```
decimal ApplyTax(decimal income)
{
    if (income <= 12570)
        return income;
    else if (income <=50270)
        return income * 0.8M;
    else if (income <= 150000)
        return income * 0.6M;
    else
        return income * 0.55M;
}
```

Now, in C# 8 and onward, switch expressions would compress this to a few lines. So long as we're running at least C# 7 (.NET Framework 4.7), this is the style of pattern matching we can create:

```
var inputValue = 25000M;
var updatedValue = inputValue.Match(
    (x => x <= 12570, x => x),
    (x => x <= 50270, x => x * 0.8M),
    (x => x <= 150000, x => x * 0.6M)
).DefaultMatch(x => x * 0.55M);
```

We're passing in an array of tuples containing two lambda expressions. The first determines whether the input matches against the current pattern; the second is the transformation in value that occurs if the pattern is a match. There's a final check to see whether the default pattern should be applied—i.e., because none of the other patterns were a match.

Despite being a fraction of the length of the original code sample, this contains all the same functionality. The matching patterns on the lefthand side of the tuple are simple, but they can contain expressions as complicated as we'd like and could even be calls to whole functions containing detailed criteria to match on.

So, how do we make this work? This is an extremely simple version that provides most of the functionality required:

```
public static class ExtensionMethods
{
    public static TOutput Match<TInput, TOutput>(
        this TInput @this,
        params (Func<TInput, bool> IsMatch,
        Func<TInput, TOutput> Transform)[] matches)
    {

        var match = matches.FirstOrDefault(x => x.IsMatch(@this));
        var returnValue = match?.Transform(@this) ?? default;
        return returnValue;
    }
}
```

We use the LINQ method `FirstOrDefault()` to first iterate through the lefthand functions to find one that returns `true` (i.e., one with the right criteria), and then call the righthand conversion `Func` to get the modified value.

This is fine, except that if *none* of the patterns match, we'll be in a bit of a fix. Most likely, we'll have a null reference exception.

To cover this, we must force the need to provide a default match (the equivalent of a simple `else` statement, or the _ pattern match in `switch` expressions). The answer is to have the `Match` function return a placeholder object that either holds a transformed value from the `Match` expressions or executes the `Default` pattern lambda expression. The improved version looks like this:

```
public static MatchValueOrDefault<TInput, TOutput> Match<TInput, TOutput>(
    this TInput @this,
    params (Func<TInput, bool>,
    Func<TInput, TOutput>)[] predicates)
{
    var match = predicates.FirstOrDefault(x => x.Item1(@this));
    var returnValue = match?.Item2(@this);
    return new MatchValueOrDefault<TInput, TOutput>(returnValue, @this);
}

public class MatchValueOrDefault<TInput, TOutput>
{
    private readonly TOutput value;
    private readonly TInput originalValue;

    public MatchValueOrDefault(TOutput value, TInput originalValue)
    {
```

```
        this.value = value;
        this.originalValue = originalValue;
    }
}

public TOutput DefaultMatch(Func<TInput, TOutput> defaultMatch)
{
    if (EqualityComparer<TOutput>.Default.Equals(default, this.value))
    {
        return defaultMatch(this.originalValue);
    }
    else
    {
        return this.value;
    }
}
```

This approach is severely limited compared to what can be accomplished in the latest versions of C#. No object type matching occurs, and the syntax isn't as elegant, but it's still usable and could save an awful lot of boilerplate as well as encourage good code standards.

In versions of C# that are older still and that don't include tuples, we can consider the use of KeyValuePair<T,T>, though the syntax is far from attractive. What, you don't want to take my word? OK, here we go. Don't say I didn't warn you...

The Extension() method itself is about the same and just needs a small alteration to use KeyValuePair instead of tuples:

```
public static MatchValueOrDefault<TInput, TOutput> Match<TInput, TOutput>(
    this TInput @this,
    params KeyValuePair<Func<TInput, bool>, Func<TInput, TOutput>>[] predicates)
{
    var match = predicates.FirstOrDefault(x => x.Key(@this));
    var returnValue = match.Value(@this);
    return new MatchValueOrDefault<TInput, TOutput>(returnValue, @this);
}
```

And here's the ugly bit. The syntax for creating KeyValuePair objects is pretty awful:

```
var inputValue = 25000M;
var updatedValue = inputValue.Match(
    new KeyValuePair<Func<decimal, bool>, Func<decimal, decimal>>(
        x => x <= 12570, x => x),
    new KeyValuePair<Func<decimal, bool>, Func<decimal, decimal>>(
        x => x <= 50270, x => x * 0.8M),
    new KeyValuePair<Func<decimal, bool>, Func<decimal, decimal>>(
        x => x <= 150000, x => x * 0.6M)
).DefaultMatch(x => x * 0.55M);
```

So we *can* still have a form of pattern matching in C# 4, but I'm not sure how much we're gaining by doing it. That's perhaps up to you to decide. At least I've shown you the way.

Make Dictionaries More Useful

Functions don't have to be used only for turning one form of data into another. We can also use them as filters, extra layers that sit between the developer and an original source of information or functionality. This section looks at a way of using functional filtering to improve the use of dictionaries.

One of my absolute favorite things in C# by far is dictionaries. Used appropriately, they can reduce a heap of ugly, boilerplate-riddled code with a few simple, elegant, array-like lookups. They're also efficient to find data in, once created.

Dictionaries have a problem, however, that often makes it necessary to add in a heap of boilerplate that invalidates the whole reason they're so lovely to use. Consider the following code sample:

```
var doctorLookup = new []
{
    ( 1, "William Hartnell" ),
    ( 2, "Patrick Troughton" ),
    ( 3, "Jon Pertwee" ),
    ( 4, "Tom Baker" )
}.ToDictionary(x => x.Item1, x => x.Item2);

var fifthDoctorInfo = $"The 5th Doctor was played by {doctorLookup[5]}";
```

What's up with this code? It falls foul of a code feature of dictionaries that I find inexplicable: if you try looking up an entry that doesn't exist,[1] it will trigger an exception that has to be handled!

The only safe way to handle this is to use one of several techniques available in C# to check against the available keys before compiling the string, like this:

```
var doctorLookup = new []
{
    ( 1, "William Hartnell" ),
    ( 2, "Patrick Troughton" ),
    ( 3, "Jon Pertwee" ),
    ( 4, "Tom Baker" )
}.ToDictionary(x => x.Item1, x => x.Item2);
```

---

[1] Incidentally, it was Peter Davison.

```
var fifthDoctorActor = doctorLookup.ContainsKey(5)
    ? doctorLookup[5]
    : "An Unknown Actor";

var fifthDoctorInfo = $"The 5th Doctor was played by {fifthDoctorActor}";
```

Alternatively, slightly newer versions of C# provide a TryGetValue() function to simplify this code a little:

```
var fifthDoctorActor = doctorLookup.TryGetValue(5, out string value)
    ? value
    : "An Unknown Actor";
```

So, can we use FP techniques to reduce our boilerplate code and give us all the useful features of dictionaries, but without the awful tendency to explode? You betcha!

First we need a quick extension method:

```
public static class ExtensionMethods
{
    public static Func<TKey, TValue> ToLookup<TKey,TValue>(
      this IDictionary<TKey,TValue> @this)
    {
        return x => @this.TryGetValue(x, out TValue? value) ? value : default;
    }

    public static Func<TKey, TValue> ToLookup<TKey,TValue>(
      this IDictionary<TKey,TValue> @this,
      TValue defaultVal)
    {
        return x => @this.ContainsKey(x) ? @this[x] : defaultVal;
    }
}
```

I'll explain further in a minute, but first, here's how we'd use the extension methods:

```
var doctorLookup = new []
{
    ( 1, "William Hartnell" ),
    ( 2, "Patrick Troughton" ),
    ( 3, "Jon Pertwee" ),
    ( 4, "Tom Baker" )
}.ToDictionary(x => x.Item1, x => x.Item2)
    .ToLookup("An Unknown Actor");

var fifthDoctorInfo = $"The 5th Doctor was played by {doctorLookup(5)}";
// output = "The 5th Doctor was played by An Unknown Actor"
```

Notice the difference? If you look carefully, the code is now using parentheses, rather than square array/dictionary brackets to access values from the dictionary. That's because it's technically not a dictionary anymore! It's a function.

If you look at the extension methods, they return functions, but they're functions that keep the original Dictionary object in scope for as long as they exist. Basically, they're like a filter layer sitting between the Dictionary and the rest of the codebase. The functions make a decision on whether use of the Dictionary is safe.

It means we can use a Dictionary, but the exception that occurs when a key isn't found will no longer be thrown, and we can either have the default for the type (usually null) returned, or supply our own default value. Simple.

The only downside to this method is that it's no longer a Dictionary, in effect. We can't modify it any further or perform any LINQ operations on it. If we are in a situation, though, where we're sure we won't need to, this is something we can use.

Parsing Values

Another common cause of noisy, boilerplate code is parsing values from string to other forms. We might use something like this for parsing in a hypothetical settings object, in the event we were working in .NET Framework and the *appsettings.json* and IOption<T> features aren't available:

```
public Settings GetSettings()
{
    var settings = new Settings();

    var retriesString = ConfigurationManager.AppSettings["NumberOfRetries"];
    var retriesHasValue = int.TryParse(retriesString, out var retriesInt);
    if(retriesHasValue)
        settings.NumberOfRetries = retriesInt;
    else
        settings.NumberOfRetries = 5;

    var pollingHrStr = ConfigurationManager.AppSettings["HourToStartPollingAt"];
    var pollingHourHasValue = int.TryParse(pollingHrStr, out var pollingHourInt);
    if(pollingHourHasValue)
        settings.HourToStartPollingAt = pollingHourInt;
    else
        settings.HourToStartPollingAt = 0;

    var alertEmailStr = ConfigurationManager.AppSettings["AlertEmailAddress"];
    if(string.IsNullOrWhiteSpace(alertEmailStr))
        settings.AlertEmailAddress = "test@thecompany.net";
    else
        settings.AlertEmailAddress = aea.ToString();

    var serverNameString = ConfigurationManager.AppSettings["ServerName"];
    if(string.IsNullOrWhiteSpace(serverNameString))
        settings.ServerName = "TestServer";
    else
        settings.ServerName = sn.ToString();
```

```
        return settings;
    }
```

That's a lot of code to do something simple, isn't it? A lot of boilerplate code noise obscures the intention of the code to all but those familiar with these sorts of operations. Also, if a new setting were to be added, it would take five or six lines of new code for each and every one. That's quite a waste.

Instead, we can do things a little more functionally and hide the structure away somewhere, leaving just the intent of the code visible for us to see.

As usual, here's an extension method to take care of business:

```
public static class ExtensionMethods
{
    public static int ToIntOrDefault(this object @this, int defaultVal = 0) =>
        int.TryParse(@this?.ToString() ?? string.Empty, out var parsedValue)
            ? parsedValue
            : defaultVal;

    public static string ToStringOrDefault(
        this object @this,
        string defaultVal = "") =>
        string.IsNullOrWhiteSpace(@this?.ToString() ?? string.Empty)
            ? defaultVal
            : @this.ToString();
}
```

This takes away all the repetitive code from the first example and allows you to move to a more readable, result-driven code sample, like this:

```
public Settings GetSettings() =>
    new Settings
    {
        NumberOfRetries = ConfigurationManager.AppSettings["NumberOfRetries"]
            .ToIntOrDefault(5),
        HourToStartPollingAt =
            ConfigurationManager.AppSettings["HourToStartPollingAt"]
            .ToIntOrDefault(0),
        AlertEmailAddress = ConfigurationManager.AppSettings["AlertEmailAddress"]
            .ToStringOrDefault("test@thecompany.net"),
        ServerName = ConfigurationManager.AppSettings["ServerName"]
            .ToStringOrDefault("TestServer"),

    };
```

It's easy now to see at a glance what the code does, what the default values are, and how we'd add more settings with a single line of code. Any other settings value types besides `int` and `string` would require the creation of an additional extension method, but that's no great hardship.

Custom Enumerations

Most of us have likely used enumerables when coding, but did you know that there's an engine under the surface that we can access and use to create all sorts of interesting custom behaviors? With a custom iterator, we can drastically reduce the number of lines of code needed for more complicated behavior when looping through data.

First, though, it's necessary to understand just how an enumerable works beneath the surface. A class sits beneath the surface of the enumerable, the engine that drives the enumeration, and this class allows us to use `foreach` to loop through values. It's called the enumerator class.

The enumerator has two functions:

Current
> This gets the current item out of the enumerable. This may be called as many times as we want, provided we don't try moving to the next item. If we try getting the `Current` value before first calling `MoveNext()`, an exception is thrown.

MoveNext()
> Moves from the current item and tries to see whether there is another to be selected. Returns `true` if another value is found, `false` if we've reached the end of the enumerable or there were no elements in the first place. The first time `MoveNext()` is called, it points the enumerator at the first element in the enumerable.

Query Adjacent Elements

Let's start with a relatively simple example. Imagine that we want to run through an enumerable of integers, to see whether it contains any numbers that are consecutive. An imperative solution would likely look like this:

```
public IEnumerable<int> GenerateRandomNumbers()
{
    var rnd = new Random();
    var returnValue = new List<int>();
    for (var i = 0; i < 100; i++)
    {
        returnValue.Add(rnd.Next(1, 100));
    }
    return returnValue;
}

public bool ContainsConsecutiveNumbers(IEnumerable<int> data)
{
    // OK, you caught me out: OrderBy isn't strictly imperative, but
    // there's no way I'm going to write out a sorting algorithm out
    // here just to prove a point!
```

```
var sortedData = data.OrderBy(x => x).ToArray();

for (var i = 0; i < sortedData.Length - 1; i++)
{
    if ((sortedData[i] + 1) == sortedData[i + 1])
        return true;
}

return false;
}

var result = ContainsConsecutiveNumbers(GenerateRandomNumbers());
Console.WriteLine(result);
```

To make this code functional, as is often the case, we need an extension method. This would take the enumerable, extract its enumerator, and control the customized behavior.

To avoid use of an imperative-style loop, we'll use recursion here. Recursion (introduced in Chapters 1 and 2) is a way of implementing an indefinite loop by having a function call itself repeatedly.[2]

I'll revisit the concept of recursion in Chapter 9. For now, let's use the standard, simple version of recursion:

```
public static bool Any<T>(this IEnumerable<T> @this, Func<T, T, bool> evaluator)
{
    using var enumerator = @this.GetEnumerator();
    var hasElements = enumerator.MoveNext();
    return hasElements && Any(enumerator, evaluator, enumerator.Current);
}

private static bool Any<T>(IEnumerator<T> enumerator,
        Func<T, T, bool> evaluator,
        T previousElement)
{
    var moreItems = enumerator.MoveNext();
    return moreItems && (evaluator(previousElement, enumerator.Current)
        ? true
        : Any(enumerator, evaluator, enumerator.Current));

}
```

So, what's happening here? This approach is kind of like juggling, in a way. We start by extracting the enumerator and moving to the first item.

Inside the private function, we accept the enumerator (now pointing to the first item), the "are we done" evaluator function, and a copy of that same first item.

---

2 An indefinite loop, but hopefully not infinite!

Then we immediately move to the next item and run the evaluator function, passing in the first item and the new Current, so they can be compared.

At this point, either we find out we've run out of items or the evaluator returns true, in which case we can terminate the iteration. If MoveNext() returns true, we check if the previousValue and Current match our requirement (as specified by evaluator). If they do, we finish and return true; otherwise, we make a recursive call to check the rest of the values.

This is the updated version of the code to find consecutive numbers:

```
public IEnumerable<int> GenerateRandomNumbers()
{
    var rnd = new Random();

    var returnValue = Enumerable.Repeat(0, 100)
        .Select(x => rnd.Next(1, 100));
    return returnValue;
}

public bool ContainsConsecutiveNumbers(IEnumerable<int> data)
{
    var sortedData = data.OrderBy(x => x).ToArray();
    var result = sortedData.Any((prev, curr) => cur == prev + 1);
    return result;
}
```

It would also be easy enough to create an All() method based on the same logic, like so:

```
public static bool All<T>(
    this IEnumerator<T> enumerator,
    Func<T,T,bool> evaluator,
    T previousElement)
{
    var moreItems = enumerator.MoveNext();
    return moreItems
        ? evaluator(previousElement, enumerator.Current)
            ? All(enumerator, evaluator, enumerator.Current)
            : false
        : true;
}

public static bool All<T>(this IEnumerable<T> @this, Func<T,T,bool> evaluator)
{
    using var enumerator = @this.GetEnumerator();
    var hasElements = enumerator.MoveNext();
    return hasElements
        ? All(enumerator, evaluator, enumerator.Current)
        : true;
}
```

The only differences between All() and Any() are the conditions for deciding whether to continue and whether you need to return early. With All(), the point is to check every pair of values and return out of the loop early only if one is found not to meet the criteria.

Iterate Until a Condition Is Met

The technique described in this section is basically a replacement for a while loop, so there's another statement we don't necessarily need.

For this example, let's imagine what the turn system might be like for a text-based adventure game. For younger readers, this is what we had in the old days, before graphics. You used to have to write what you wanted to do, and the game would write what happened—kind of like a book, except you wrote what happened yourself.

 Go and check out the epic adventure game *Zork* if you'd like to see this for yourself. Try not to get eaten by a grue!

The basic structure of one of those games was something like this:

1. Write a description of the current location.
2. Receive user input.
3. Execute the requested command.

Here's how imperative code might handle that situation:

```
var gameState = new State
{
    IsAlive = true,
    HitPoints = 100
};

while(gameState.IsAlive)
{
    var message = this.ComposeMessageToUser(gameState);
    var userInput = this.InteractWithUser(message);
    this.UpdateState(gameState, userInput);

    if(gameState.HitPoints <= 0)
        gameState.IsAlive = false;
}
```

In principle, what we want is a LINQ-style `Aggregate()` function, but one that doesn't loop through all the elements of an array and then finish. Instead, we want the function to loop continuously until our end condition is met (the player is dead). I'm simplifying a little here (obviously, our player in a proper game could *win* as well). But my example game is like life, and life's not fair!

The extension method for this is another place that would benefit from tail-recursion optimized calls, and I'll be presenting options for that in Chapter 9. For now, though, we'll just use simple recursion (which may become an issue if the game has a lot of turns) to avoid introducing too many ideas too soon:

```
public static class ExtensionMethods
{
    public static T AggregateUntil<T>(
      this T @this,
      Func<T,bool> endCondition,
      Func<T,T> update) =>
        endCondition(@this)
            ? @this
            : AggregateUntil(update(@this), endCondition, update);
}
```

Using this, we can do away with the `while` loop entirely and transform the entire turn sequence into a single function, like so:

```
var gameState = new State
{
    IsAlive = true,
    HitPoints = 100
};

var endState = gameState.AggregateUntil(
    x => x.HitPoints <= 0,
    x => {
        var message = this.ComposeMessageToUser(x);
        var userInput = this.InteractWithUser(message);
        return this.UpdateState(x, userInput);
    });
```

This isn't perfect but it's functional now. There are far better ways of handling the multiple steps to update the game's state, and the issue of how to handle user interaction in a functional manner remains too. Chapter 13 covers those topics.

Summary

In this chapter, we looked at ways to use Func delegates, enumerables, and extension methods to extend C# to make it easier to write functional-style code and to get around a few existing limitations of the language. I'm certain that I'm barely scratching the surface with these techniques, and that plenty more are out there to be discovered and used.

The next chapter explores higher-order functions as well as some structures that can be used to take advantage of them to create yet more useful functionality.

PART II

Into the Belly of the Functional

Hail, bold adventurer!

I see you've survived the first part of your journey. Now you can consider yourself promoted from functional apprentice to journeyman.[1] This next road is longer, twistier, and far stranger.

Be not afraid, though, because if you are open to it, wonders await you ahead. This is where we stop thinking entirely in terms of out-of-the-box C# and start looking a little more into functional theory.

I hope you aren't expecting formal definitions, or talk on list theory, because you won't find that here. I'm going to take you up the gentle slope, a step at a time—always with an eye to what's actually useful to you in your daily coding.

Come along. The horses are getting restless. It's time to saddle up!

---

1 *Journeyman* is a historical job title from a less enlightened age, which I felt was too perfect here *not* to use. Please feel free to remove "man" and insert the correct term for yourself.

CHAPTER 5

Higher-Order Functions

Welcome back, my friends, to the show that never ends. In this chapter, we'll look at uses for higher-order functions. I'm going to show you novel ways to use them in C# to save yourself effort and to make code that is less likely to fail.

But, what *are* higher-order functions? This slightly odd name represents something very simple. In fact, you've likely been using higher-order functions for some time if you've spent much time working with LINQ. They come in two flavors; here's the first:

```
var liberatorCrew = new []
{
    "Roj Blake",
    "Kerr Avon",
    "Vila Restal",
    "Jenna Stannis",
    "Cally",
    "Olag Gan",
    "Zen"
};
var filteredList = liberatorCrew.Where(x => x.First() > 'M');
```

Passed into the `Where()` function is an arrow expression, which is just shorthand for writing out an unnamed function. The longhand version would look like this:

```
function bool IsGreaterThanM(char c)
{
    return c > 'm';
}
```

So here, the function has been passed around as the parameter to another function, to be executed elsewhere inside it.

This is another example of the use of higher-order functions:

```
public Func<int, int> MakeAddFunc(int x) => y => x + y;
```

Notice here that there are two arrows, not one. We're taking an integer x and from that returning a new function. In that new function, references to x will be filled in with whatever was provided when MakeAddFunc() was called originally.

For example:

```
var addTenFunction = MakeAddFunc(10);
var answer = addTenFunction(5);
// answer is 15
```

By passing 10 into MakeAddFunc() in this example, we create a new function whose purpose is simply to add 10 to whatever additional integer we pass into it.

In short, a *higher-order function* has one or more of the following properties:

- Accepts a function as a parameter
- Returns a function as its return type

In C#, this is all typically done with either a Func (for functions with a return type) or Action (for functions that return void) delegate type. Higher-order functions are a fairly simple idea that's even easier to implement, but the effect they can have on your codebase is incredible.

In this chapter, I'm going to walk you through ways of using higher-order functions to improve your daily coding. I'll also introduce a next-level usage of higher-order functions called *combinators*. These enable passing around functions to create a more complex and useful behavior.

 Combinators are called that, incidentally, because they originate from a mathematical technique called *combinatory logic*. You won't need to worry about ever hearing that term again or about any references to advanced math—I'm not going there. It's just in case you were curious…

A Problem Report

To get started, let's look at a bit of problem code. Imagine that your company asks you for a function to take a data store (such as an XML file or a JSON file), summarize the number of each possible value, and then transmit that data on to somewhere else. On top of that, the company wants a separate message to be sent in the event that no data is found at all. I run a really loose ship, so let's keep things fun and imagine you work for the Evil Galactic Empire and are cataloguing Rebel Alliance ships on your radar.

The code might look something like this:

```
public void SendEnemyShipWeaponrySummary()
{
    try
    {
        var enemyShips = this.DataStore.GetEnemyShips();
        var summaryNumbers = enemyShips.GroupBy(x => x.Type)
            .Select(x => (Type: x.Key, Count: x.Count()));
        var report = new Report
        {
            Title = "Enemy Ship Type",
            Rows = summaryNumbers.Select(X => new ReportItem
            {
                ColumnOne = X.Type,
                ColumnTwo = X.Count.ToString()
            })
        };

        if (!report.Rows.Any())
            this.CommunicationSystem.SendNoDataWarning();
        else
            this.CommunicationSystem.SendReport(report);
    }
    catch (Exception e)
    {
        this.Logger.LogError(e,
        "An error occurred in " +
            nameof(SendEnemyShipWeaponrySummary) +
            ": " + e.Message);
    }
}
```

This is fine, isn't it? Isn't it? Well, think about this scenario. You're sitting at your desk, eating your daily pot noodle,[1] when you notice that—Jurassic Park style—a rhythmic ripple appears in your coffee. This signals the arrival of your worst nightmare: your boss! Let's imagine that your boss is—thinking totally at random here—a tall, deep-voiced gentleman in a black cape and with appalling asthma. He also hates it when people displease him. *Really* hates it.

He's happy with the first function you create. For this, you can breathe a sigh of relief. But now he wants a second function. This one is going to create another summary, but this time of the level of weaponry in each ship—whether they are unarmed, lightly armed, heavily armed, or capable of destroying planets. That sort of thing.

---

1 Ideally the hottest, spiciest flavor you can find. Flames should be shooting from your mouth as you eat!

Easy, you think. The boss will be so impressed with how quickly you do this. So you do what seems easiest: Ctrl-C, then Ctrl-V to copy and paste the original, change the name, change the property you're summarizing, and you end up with this:

```
public void GenerateEnemyShipWeaponrySummary()
{
    try
    {
        var enemyShips = this.DataStore.GetEnemyShips();
        var summaryNumbers = enemyShips.GroupBy(x => x.WeaponryLevel)
            .Select(x => (Type: x.Key, Count: x.Count()));
        var report = new Report
        {
            Title = "Enemy Ship Weaponry Level",
            Rows = summaryNumbers.Select(X => new ReportItem
            {
                ColumnOne = X.Type,
                ColumnTwo = X.Count.ToString()
            })
        };

        if (!report.Rows.Any())
            this.CommunicationSystem.SendNoDataWarning();
        else
            this.CommunicationSystem.SendReport(report);
    }
    catch (Exception e)
    {
        this.Logger.LogError(e,
        "An error occurred in " +
            nameof(SendEnemyShipWeaponrySummary) +
            ": " + e.Message);
    }
}
```

Five seconds of work, and a day or two of leaning on your figurative shovel with the odd complaint out loud of how hard the work is here, all while you secretly work on today's Wordle. Job done, and slaps on the back all round, right? Right?

Well…there are a couple of problems with this approach.

First, let's think about unit testing. As good, upstanding code citizens, we unit-test all our code. Imagine that you unit-tested the snot out of that first function. When you copied and pasted the second, what was the level of unit-test coverage at that point?

I'll give you a clue: it was between zero and zero. You could copy and paste the tests too, and that would be fine, but that's now an awful lot more code that you're copying and pasting every time.

This isn't an approach that scales up well. What if your boss wanted another function after this one, and another, and another. What if you ended up being asked for 50 functions? Or 100? That's a lot of code. You'd end up with code thousands of lines long, not something I'd be keen to support.

It gets worse when you consider something that happened to me near the beginning of my career. I was working for an organization that had a desktop application that carried out a series of complex calculations for each customer, based on a few input parameters. Each year the rules changed, but the old rule bases had to be replicated because it might be necessary to see what would have been calculated in a previous year.

So, the folks who had been developing the app before I joined the team had copied a whole chunk of code every year. They made a few little changes, added a link somewhere to the new version, and voilà. Job done.

I was tasked with making these annual changes one year, so off I went, young, innocent, and raring to make a difference in the world. When I was making my changes, I noticed something odd. There was a weird error with a field that had nothing to do with my changes. I fixed the bug, but then a thought occurred to me that made my heart sink.

I checked every previous version of the codebase for each previous year and found that nearly all had the same bug. It had been introduced about 10 years before, and every developer since then had replicated the bug precisely. I had to fix it 10 times over, increasing the testing effort by an order of magnitude.

With this in mind, ask yourself: did copying and pasting really save you any time? I routinely work on apps that stay in existence for decades and that show no sign of being put out to pasture anytime soon.

When I decide where to make time-saving measures for coding work, I try to look over the whole life of the application, and try to keep in mind any potential consequences for a decision a decade on.

To return to the subject at hand, how would I have used higher-order functions to solve this problem? Well, are you sitting comfortably? Then I'll begin…

Thunks

A bundle of code that carries a stored calculation, which can be executed later on request, is properly known as a *thunk*. It's the same as the sound a plank of wood makes when it smacks you in the side of the head. There's an argument to be had as to whether that hurts your head more or less than reading this book!

Here in C#, Func delegates are again the way to implement this. We can write functions that take Func delegates as parameter values to allow for certain calculations in our function to be left effectively blank, and which can be filled in from the outside world, via an arrow function.

Although this technique has a serious, proper, mathematical term, I like calling them *doughnut functions*, because it's more descriptive. They're like normal functions but with a hole in the middle! A hole I'd ask someone else to fill with the necessary functionality.

This is one potential way to refactor the problem report function:

```
public void SendEnemyShipWeaponrySummary() =>
    GenerateSummary(x => x.Type, "Enemy Ship Type Summary");

public void GenerateEnemyShipWeaponryLevelSummary() =>
    GenerateSummary(x => x.WeaponryLevel, "Enemy Ship WeaponryLevel");

private void GenerateSummary(
    Func<EnemyShip, string> summarySelector,
    string reportName)
{
    try
    {
        var enemyShips = this.DataStore.GetEnemyShips();
        var summaryNumbers = enemyShips.GroupBy(summarySelector)
            .Select(x => (Type: x.Key, Count: x.Count()));
        var report = new Report
        {
            Title = reportName,
            Rows = summaryNumbers.Select(X => new ReportItem
            {
                ColumnOne = X.Type,
                ColumnTwo = X.Count.ToString()
            })
        };

        if (!report.Rows.Any())
            this.CommunicationSystem.SendNoDataWarning();
        else
            this.CommunicationSystem.SendReport(report);
    }
    catch (Exception e)
    {
        this.Logger.LogError(e,
        $"An error occurred in " + nameof(GenerateSummary) +
            ", report: " + reportName +
            ", message: " + e.Message;
    }
}
```

In this revised version, we've gained a few advantages.

First, the number of additional lines per new report is just one! That's a much tidier codebase and easier to read. The code is kept close to the intent of the new function—i.e., be the same as the first but with a few changes.

Second, after unit-testing function 1, when we create function 2, the unit-test level is still close to 100%. The only difference functionally is the report name and the field to be summarized.

Lastly, any enhancements or bug fixes to the base function will be shared among all report functions simultaneously. That's a lot of benefit for relatively little effort. There's also a very high degree of confidence that if one report function tests well, all the others will do the same.

We could walk away from this version happy. But if it were me, I'd consider going a step further and exposing the private version with its `Func` parameters on the interface for whatever wants to use it:

```
public interface IGenerateReports
{
    void GenerateSummary(Func<EnemyShip, string> summarySelector,
        string reportName)
}
```

The implementation would be the private function from the previous code sample made public instead. This way, there's no need to ever modify the interface or implementing class again, at least not if all that's wanted is an additional report for a different field.

This makes the business of creating reports something that can be done entirely arbitrarily by whatever code module consumes this class. It takes a lot of the burden of maintaining the report set from developers like ourselves and puts it more in the hands of the teams that care about the reports. Imagine the sheer number of requests for change that will now never need to come to a development team.

If we wanted to be really wild, we could expose further `Func` parameters as `Func<ReportLine,string>` to allow users of the report class to define custom formatting. We could also use `Action` parameters to allow for bespoke logging or event handling. This is just in my silly, made-up reporting class. The possibilities for the use of higher-order functions in this way are endless.

Despite being an FP feature, this is keeping us squarely in line with the *O* of the SOLID principles of object-oriented design, the open/closed principle, which states a module should be open to extension but closed to modification.[2]

---

2 Read more about SOLID on Wikipedia (*https://oreil.ly/aY9lU*) or see my YouTube video "SOLID Principles in 5 Nightmares" (*https://oreil.ly/CCvVD*).

It's surprising how well OOP and FP can complement each other in C#. I often think it's important for developers to make sure they are adept at both paradigms so they know how to use them together effectively.

Chaining Functions

Allow me to introduce you to the best friend you never knew you needed: the Map() function. This function is also commonly referred to as *chain and pipe*, but for the sake of consistency, we'll call it Map() throughout this book. I'm afraid that a lot of functional structures tend to have many names in use, depending on the programming language and implementation. I'll try to point out whenever this is the case.

Now, I'm British, and one cliché about British people is that we like talking about the weather. It's entirely true. Our country has been known to go through four seasons in a single day, so the weather is a constant source of fascination to us.

When I used to work for an American company once upon a time, the topic of conversation with my colleagues over video calls would often turn inevitably to the subject of the weather. They'd tell me that the temperature outside was around 100 degrees. I work in Celsius, so to me this sounds rather suspiciously like the boiling point of water. Given that my colleagues were not screaming as their blood boiled away into steam, I suspected something else was at work. It was, of course, that they were working in Fahrenheit, so I had to convert this to something I understood with the following formula:

1. Subtract 32.
2. Multiply by 5.
3. Divide by 9.

This gives a temperature in Celsius of around 38 degrees, which is warm and toasty, but for the most part safe for human life.

How could we code this process in exactly that multistep operation and then finish by returning a formatted string? We *could* stick it all together into a single line like this:

```
public string FahrenheitToCelsius(decimal tempInF) =>
    Math.Round(((tempInF-32) *5 / 9), 2) + "°C";
```

That's not very readable though, is it? Honestly, I probably wouldn't make too much fuss about that in production code, but I'm demonstrating a technique, so bear with me.

The multistep way to write this out is like this:

```
string FahrenheitToCelsius(decimal tempInF)
{
    var a = tempInF - 32;
    var b = a * 5;
    var c = b / 9;
    var d = Math.Round(c, 2);
    var returnValue = d + "°C";
    return returnValue;
}
```

This is much more readable and easier to maintain, but it still has an issue. We're creating variables that are intended to be used a single time and then thrown away. In this little function, this approach is not terribly relevant, but what if this were a gigantic thousand-line function? What if instead of a little decimal variable like these, we had a large, complex object? All the way down at line 1,000, that variable—which is never intended to be used again—is still in scope, and holding up memory. It's also a little messy to create a variable you aren't planning to use beyond the next line. This is where Map() comes in.

Map() is somewhat like the LINQ Select() function, except instead of operating on each element of an enumerable, it operates on an object—any object. You pass it a lambda arrow function just the same as with Select() except that your x parameter refers to the base object. If you applied it to an enumerable, the x parameter would refer to the entire enumerable, not individual elements thereof.

Here's how our modified Fahrenheit conversion would look:

```
public string FahrenheitToCelsius(decimal tempInF)   =>
    tempInF.Map(x => x - 32)
        .Map(x => x * 5)
        .Map(x => x / 9)
        .Map(x => Math.Round(x, 2))
        .Map(x => x + "°C");
```

This code has the same exact functionality, same friendly, multistage operation, but no throwaway variables. Each arrow function is executed; then after it's completed, its contents are subject to garbage collection. The decimal x that is multiplied by 5 is subject for disposal when the next arrow function takes a copy of its result and divides that by 9.

Here's how we implement Map():

```
public static class MapExtensionMethods
{
    public static TOut Map<TIn, TOut>(this TIn @this, Func<TIn, TOut> f) =>
        f(@this);
}
```

It's tiny, isn't it? Despite that, I use this particular method quite a lot—whenever I want to do a multistep transformation of data. It makes it easier to convert whole function bodies into simple arrow functions, like the `Map()`-based `FahrenheitTo Celsius()` function.

This method has far more advanced versions, which include things like error handling, and which I'll be getting into in Chapter 7. For now, though, this is a fantastic little toy that you can start playing with right away. Uncle Simon's early Christmas gift to you. Ho, ho, ho.

A simpler implementation of `Map()` is possible, if you don't want to change types with each transformation. This is cleaner and more concise, if it suits your needs. It could be implemented like this:

```
public static T Map<T>(this T @this, params Func<T,T>[] transformations) =>
    transformations.Aggregate(@this, (agg, x) => x(agg));
```

Using that, the basic Fahrenheit-to-Celsius transformation would look like this:

```
public decimal FahrenheitToCelsius(decimal tempInF)  =>
    tempInF.Map(
        x => x - 32,
        x => x * 5,
        x => x / 9
        x => Math.Round(x, 2);
```

This might be worth using to save a little bit of boilerplate in simpler cases, like the temperature conversion. See Chapter 8 for some ideas on how to make this look even better.

Fork Combinator

A *fork combinator* is used to take a single value, process it in multiple ways simultaneously, and then join up all those separate strands into a single, final value. This process can be used to simplify some fairly complex multistep calculations into a single line of code. I've also heard this process called a *converge*, but I like *fork* because it's more descriptive of exactly how it works.

The process runs roughly like this:

1. Start with a single value.
2. Feed that value into a set of *prong* functions, each of which acts on the original input in isolation to produce some sort of output.
3. A *join* function takes the result of the prongs and merges it into a final result.

Here are a few examples of how we might use it.

If we want to specify the number of arguments in our function definition rather than having an unspecified number of prongs from an array, we could use `Fork()` to calculate an average value:

```
var numbers = new [] { 4, 8, 15, 16, 23, 42 }
var average = numbers.Fork(
    x => x.Sum(),
    x => x.Count(),
    (s, c) => s / c
);
// average = 18
```

Or here's a blast from the past—we can use `Fork` to calculate the hypotenuse of a triangle:

```
var triangle = new Triangle(100, 200);
var hypotenuse = triangle.Fork(
    x => Math.Pow(x.A, 2),
    x => Math.Pow(x.B, 2),
    (a2, b2) => Math.Sqrt(a2 + b2)
);
```

The implementation looks like this:

```
public static class ext
{
    public static TOut Fork<TIn, T1, T2, TOut>(
      this TIn @this,
      Func<TIn, T1> f1,
      Func<TIn, T2> f2,
      Func<T1,T2,TOut> fout)
    {
        var p1 = f1(@this);
        var p2 = f2(@this);
        var result = fout(p1, p2);
        return result;
    }
}
```

Note that having two generic types, one for each prong, means that any combination of types can be returned by those functions.

We could easily go out and write versions for any number of parameters beyond two as well, but each additional parameter we want to consider would require an additional extension method.

If we want to go further and have an unlimited number of prongs, that's easily done, provided we are OK with having the same intermediate type generated by each:

```
public static class ForkExtensionMethods
{
    public static TEnd Fork<TStart, TMiddle, TEnd>(
        this TStart @this,
        Func<TMiddle, TEnd> joinFunction,
        params Func<TStart, TMiddle>[] prongs
    )
    {
```

```
    var intermediateValues = prongs.Select(x => x(@this));
    var returnValue = joinFunction(intermediateValues);
    return returnValue;
}
```

We could use this, for instance, to create a text description based on an object:

```
var personData = this.personRepository.GetPerson(24601);
var description = personData.Fork(
    prongs => string.Join(Environment.NewLine, prongs),
    x => "My name is " + x.FirstName + " " + x.LastName,
    x => "I am " + x.Age + " years old.",
    x => "I live in " + x.Address.Town
)

// This might, for example, produce:
//
// My name is Jean Valjean
// I am 30 years old
// I live in Montreuil-sur-mer
```

In this example, we're acting multiple times on a complex object (Person); there is no enumerable of properties that we can operate on with a Select() statement to get the list of descriptive strings we want. Using a fork combinator, we can effectively convert a single item *into* an array of items that we can then apply list operations to, in order to convert it into a more usable final result.

Also when using Fork like this, it's easy enough to add as many more lines of description as we want but still maintain the same level of complexity and readability.

Alt Combinator

An *alt combinator* is used to bind together a set of functions to achieve the same end, but which should be tried one after the other until one of them returns a value. I've also seen this referred to as *or*, *alternate*, or *alternation*.

Think of it as working like this: "Try method A; if that doesn't work, try method B; if that doesn't work, try method C; if that doesn't work, I suppose we're out of luck."

Let's imagine a scenario where we might want to find something by trying multiple methods:

```
var jamesBond = "007"
    .Alt(x => this.hotelService.ScanGuestsForSpies(x),
        x => this.airportService.CheckPassengersForSpies(x),
        x => this.barService.CheckGutterForDrunkSpies(x));

if(jamesBond != null)
    this.deathTrapService.CauseHorribleDeath(jamesBond);
```

So long as one of those three methods returns a value corresponding to a hard-drinking, borderline-misogynist, thuggish employee of the British government, then the jamesBond variable won't be null. Whichever function returns a value first is the last function to be run.

So how do we implement this function before we find our enemy has fled? Like this:

```
public static TOut Alt<TIn, TOut>(
    this TIn @this,
    params Func<TIn, TOut>[] args) =>
    args.Select(x => x(@this))
    .First(x => x != null);
```

Remember here that the LINQ Select() function operates on a lazy-loading principle, so even though we appear to be converting the whole of the Func array into concrete types, we're not, because the First() function will prevent any elements from being executed after one of them has returned a non-null value. Isn't LINQ great?

A slightly more real-world usage for this concept might occur with multiple stores for the same data, where each in turn needs to be checked. Maybe we have several sources for employee data, which either don't all contain the same lists of people or might be unavailable periodically, requiring a fallback to an alternative means:

```
public Person GetEmployee(int empId) =>
    empId.Alt(
        x => this.employeeDbRepo.GetById(x),
        x => this.ActiveDirectoryClient.GetById(x),
        x => this.EmergencyBackupCsvClient.GetById(x)
    );
```

In this scenario, three levels of data are checked to find our employee's information. First preference is given to our system's database. This probably assumes the employee has been seen by the system before and it has stored something about them previously. Perhaps our employee is a new starter, and there are no database records? In that case, the only source of data available is Active Directory, from which we can get a few bits of essential information that can perhaps be padded out later. Finally, in the event that some sort of network outage occurs, the system can finally consider checking a local CSV file for cached information. I'm not saying that I'd necessarily do that last step, as security implications probably exist, but I'm demonstrating how flexible this approach allows you to be.

Compose

A common feature of functional languages is the ability to build up a complex function from a collection of smaller, simpler functions. Any process that involves combining functions is called *composing*.

JavaScript libraries like Ramda (*https://ramdajs.com*) have terrific composing features available, but C#'s strong typing works against them in this instance.

C# has a few methods for composing functions. The first is the simplest, just using basic `Map()` functions, as described earlier in this chapter:

```
var input = 100M;
var f = (decimal x) => x.Map(x => x - 32)
    .Map(x => x * 5)
    .Map(x => x / 9)
    .Map(x => Math.Round(x, 2))
    .Map(x => $"{x} degrees");
var output = f(input);
// output = "37.78 degrees"
```

The `f` here is a composed higher-order function. The five functions (e.g., `x => x - 32`, those steps of the calculation) used to create `f` are described as anonymous lambda expressions. They combine like LEGO bricks to form a larger, more complex behavior.

A valid question here is what's the point of composing functions? The answer is that we don't necessarily have to do the whole thing all at once. We could build the logic we want in pieces and then ultimately create many functions by using those same base pieces.

Imagine now that we want to also hold a `Func` delegate that represents the opposite conversion—we'd end up with two functions like this:

```
var input = 100M;
var fahrenheitToCelsius = (decimal x) =>
    x.Map(x => x - 32)
        .Map(x => x * 5)
        .Map(x => x / 9)
        .Map(x => Math.Round(x, 2))
        .Map(x => $"{x} degrees");
var output = fahrenheitToCelsius(input);
Console.WriteLine(output);.
// 37.78 degrees

var input2 = 37.78M;
var celsiusToFahrenheit =    (decimal x) =>
    x.Map(x => x * 9)
        .Map(x => x / 5)
        .Map(x => x + 32)
        .Map(x => Math.Round(x, 2))
        .Map(x => $"{x} degrees");
var output2 = celsiusToFahrenheit(input2);
Console.WriteLine(output2);
// 100.00 degrees
```

The last two lines of each function are identical. Isn't it a bit wasteful to repeat them each time? We can eliminate the repetition by using a Compose() function:

```
var formatDecimal = (decimal x) => x
    .Map(x => Math.Round(x, 2))
    .Map(x => $"{x} degrees");

var input = 100M;
var celsiusToFahrenheit = (decimal x) => x.Map(x => x - 32)
    .Map(x => x * 5)
    .Map(x => x / 9);
var fToCFormatted = celsiusToFahrenheit.Compose(formatDecimal);
var output = fToCFormatted(input);
Console.WriteLine(output);

var input2 = 37.78M;
var celsiusToFahrenheit =    (decimal x) =>
    x.Map(x => x * 9)
    .Map(x => x / 5)
    .Map(x => x + 32);
var cToFFormatted = celsiusToFahrenheit.Compose(formatDecimal);
var output2 = cToFFormatted(input2);
Console.WriteLine(output2);
```

Functionally, these new versions using Compose() are identical to the previous versions exclusively using Map().

The Compose() function performs nearly the same task as Map(), with the subtle difference that we're ultimately producing a Func delegate at the end, not a final value. This is the code that performs the Compose() process:

```
public static class ComposeExtensionMethods
{
    public static Func<TIn, NewTOut> Compose<TIn, OldTOut, NewTOut>(
        this Func<TIn, OldTOut> @this,
        Func<OldTOut, NewTOut> f) =>
            x => f(@this(x));
}
```

By using Compose(), we've eliminated some unnecessary replication. Any improvements to the format process will be shared by both Func delegate objects simultaneously.

A limitation, exists, however. In C#, extension methods can't be attached to lambda expressions or to functions directly. We can attach an extension to a lambda expression if it's referenced as a Func or Action delegate, but for that to happen, it first needs to be assigned to a variable, where it will be automatically set as a delegate type for us. This is why it's necessary in the preceding examples to assign the chains of Map() functions to a variable before calling Compose()—otherwise, it would be possible to simply call Compose() at the end of the Map() chain and save ourselves a variable assignment.

This process is not unlike reusing code via inheritance in OOP, except it's done at the individual line level and requires significantly less boilerplate. It also keeps these similar, related pieces of code together, rather than having them be spread out over separate classes and files.

Transduce

A *transducer* is a way of combining list-based operations, like Select() and Where(), with some form of aggregation to perform multiple transformations to a list of values, before finally collapsing it down into a single, final value.

While Compose() is a useful feature, it has limitations. It effectively always takes the place of a Map() function—i.e., it acts on the object as a whole and can't perform LINQ operations on enumerables. We *could* Compose() an array and put Select() and Where() operations inside each, but honestly that looks pretty messy:

```
var numbers = new [] { 4, 8, 15, 16, 23, 42 };
var add5 = (IEnumerable<int> x) => x.Select(y => y + 5);
var Add5MultiplyBy10 = add5.Compose(x => x.Select(y => y * 10));

var numbersGreaterThan100 = Add5MultiplyBy10.Compose(x => x.Where(y => y > 100));

var composeMessage = numbersGreaterThan100.Compose(x => string.Join(",", x));
Console.WriteLine("Output = " + composeMessage(numbers));
// Output = 130,200,210,280,470
```

If you're happy with that, by all means use it. Nothing is wrong with it per se, aside from being rather inelegant.

We can use another structure, though: Transduce. A Transduce operation acts on an array and represents all the stages of a functional flow:

Filter()—*i.e.,* .Where()
  Reduce the number of elements.

Transform()—*i.e.,* .Select()
  Convert them to a new form.

Aggregate()—*i.e., erm...actually it is* Aggregate
  Whittle down the collection of many items to a single item by using these rules.

This could be implemented in C# in many ways, but here's one possibility:

```
public static TFinalOut Transduce<TIn, TFilterOut, TFinalOut>(
    this IEnumerable<TIn> @this,
    Func<IEnumerable<TIn>, IEnumerable<TFilterOut>> transformer,
```

```
Func<IEnumerable<TFilterOut>, TFinalOut> aggregator) =>
    aggregator(transformer(@this));
```

This extension method takes a transformer method, which can be any combination of Select() and Where() the user defines to transform the enumerable ultimately from one form and size to another. The method also takes an aggregator, which converts the output of the transformer into a single value.

This is how the Compose() function we defined previously could be implemented with this version of the Transduce() method:

```
var numbers = new [] { 4, 8, 15, 16, 23, 42 };

// N.B - I could make this a single line with brackets, but
// I find this more readable, and it's functionally identical due
// to lazy evaluation of enumerables
var transformer = (IEnumerable<int> x) => x
    .Select(y => y + 5)
    .Select(y => y * 10)
    .Where(y => y > 100);

var aggregator = (IEnumerable<int> x) => string.Join(", ", x);

var output = numbers.Transduce(transformer, aggregator);
Console.WriteLine("Output = " + output);
// Output = 130, 200, 210, 280, 470
```

Alternatively, if you'd prefer to handle everything as Func delegates, so that you can reuse the Transduce() method, it could be written in this way:

```
var numbers = new [] { 4, 8, 15, 16, 23, 42 };
var transformer = (IEnumerable<int> x) => x
    .Select(y => y + 5)
    .Select(y => y * 10)
    .Where(y => y > 100);

var aggregator = (IEnumerable<int> x) => string.Join(", ", x);

var transducer = transformer.ToTransducer(aggregator);
var output2 = transducer(numbers);
Console.WriteLine("Output = " + output2);
```

This is the updated extension method:

```
public static class TransducerExtensionMethod
{
    public static Func<IEnumerable<TIn>, TO2> ToTransducer<TIn, TO1, TO2>(
        this Func<IEnumerable<TIn>,
        IEnumerable<TO1>> @this,
        Func<IEnumerable<TO1>, TO2> aggregator) =>
            x => aggregator(@this(x));
}
```

We've now generated a Func delegate variable that can be used as a function on as many arrays of integers as we want, and that single Func will perform any number of transformations and filters required, and then aggregate the array down to a single, final value.

Tap

A common concern I hear raised about chains of functions is that it's impossible to perform logging within them—unless we make one of the links in the chain a reference to a separate function that does have logging calls within it.

An FP technique can be used to inspect the contents of a function chain at any point: a Tap() function. A Tap() function is a bit like a wiretap in old detective films.[3] It allows a stream of information to be monitored and acted on, but without disrupting or altering it.

The way to implement Tap() is like this:

```
public static class Extensions
{
    public static T Tap<T>(this T @this, Action<T> action)
    {
        action(@this);
        return @this;
    }
}
```

An Action delegate is effectively like a void returning function. In this instance, it accepts a single parameter: a generic type, T. The Tap() function passes the current value of the object in the chain into the Action, where logging can take place, then returns an unmodified copy of that same object.

We could use it like this:

```
var input = 100M;
var fahrenheitToCelsius = (decimal x) => x.Map(x => x - 32)
    .Map(x => x * 5)
    .Map(x => x / 9)
    .Tap(x => this.logger.LogInformation("the un-rounded value is " + x))
    .Map(x => Math.Round(x, 2))
    .Map(x => $"{x} degrees");
var output = fahrenheitToCelsius(input);
Console.WriteLine(output);
// 37.78 degrees
```

---

3 I'd guess that's where they get their name.

In this new version of the Fahrenheit-to-Celsius functional chain, we're now tapping into it after the basic calculation is completed, but before we start rounding and formatting it to a string. Here we've added a call to a logger in `Tap()`, but we could switch that for a `Console.WriteLine` or whatever else we'd like.

Try/Catch

We can use several more advanced structures in FP for handling errors. If you just want something quick and easy that you can quickly implement in a few lines of code, but that has its limitations, keep reading. Otherwise, try having a look ahead at Chapters 6 and 7. You'll find plenty there on handling errors without side effects.

For now, though, let's see what we can do with a few simple lines of code…

In theory, in the middle of functional-style code, no errors should be possible. If everything is done in line with the functional principles of side-effect-free code, immutable variables, and so on, then we should be safe. On the fringes, though, some interactions might be considered unsafe.

Let's imagine we want to run a lookup in an external system with an integer ID. This external system could be a database, a web API, a flat file on a network share, anything at all. The thing all these possibilities have in common is that any can fail for many reasons, few, if any, of which are the fault of the developer.

There could be network issues, hardware issues on the local or remote computers, inadvertent human intervention. The list goes on.

This is one method by which we deal with that situation in object-oriented code:

```
pubic IEnumerable<Snack> GetSnackByType(int typeId)
{
  try
    {
        var returnValue = this.DataStore.GetSnackByType(typeId);
        return returnValue;
    }
    catch(Exception e)
    {
        this.logger.LogError(e, $"There aren't any pork scratchings left!");
        return Enumerable.Empty<Snack>()
    }
}
```

I dislike two aspects of this code block. The first is the amount of boilerplate bulking out the code. We have to add a lot of industrial-strength coding to protect ourselves from problems that we didn't cause.

The other method often deployed to handle these scenarios is to have something that rethrows an exception up to a higher level to `catch` again. I really dislike this approach. It depends on defensive code having been written higher up and can cause unexpected behavior to occur, because we've disrupted the standard order of operations. We can't say when and by what the error will be caught, or even *if* it'll be caught. It could result in an unhandled Exception, which could terminate the application altogether.

The other issue is with try/catch blocks themselves. They break the order of operations, moving execution of the program from where we were to a potentially hard-to-find location. In this case, we have a nice, simple, compact little function, and the location of the catch is easy to determine. I've worked in codebases where the catch was several layers of functions higher than the place the fault occurred. Bugs were common in that codebase because assumptions were made about certain lines of code being reached when they weren't because of the strange positioning of the try/catch block.

I probably wouldn't have too many issues with this code block in production, but left unchecked, bad coding practices can leak in. Nothing in the code prevents future coders from introducing multilevel nested functions in here.

I think the best solution is to use an approach that removes all the boilerplate and makes it hard, or even impossible, to introduce bad code structure later. Consider something like this:

```
pubic IEnumerable<Snack> GetSnackByType(int typeId)
{
    var result = typeId.MapWithTryCatch(this.DataStore.GetSnackByType)
        ?? Enumerable.Empty<Snack>();
    return result;
}
```

We're running a Map() function with an embedded try/catch. The new Map() function returns either a value if everything works or null if a failure occurs.

The extension method looks like this:

```
public static class Extensions
{
    public static TO MapWithTryCatch<TIn,TO>(this TIn @this, Func<TIn,TO> f)
    {
        try
        {
            return f(@this);
        }
        catch()
        {
            return default;
        }
    }
}
```

This isn't quite a perfect solution, though. What about error logging? This is committing the cardinal sin of swallowing error messages unlogged.

We could think about solving this in a few ways. Any of these are equally fine, so proceed as your fancy takes you.

One option is to instead have an extension method that takes an ILogger instance to return a Func delegate containing the try/catch functionality:

```
public static class TryCatchExtensionMethods
{
    public static TOut CreateTryCatch<TIn,TOut>(this TIn @this, ILogger logger)
    {
        Func<TIn,TOut> f =>
        {
            try
            {
                return f(@this);
            }
            catch(Exception e)
            {
                logger.LogError(e, "An error occurred");
                return default;
            }

        }
    }
}
```

The usage is pretty similar:

```
public IEnumerable<Snack> GetSnackByType(int typeId)
{
    var tryCatch = typeId.CreateTryCatch(this.logger);
    var result = tryCatch(this.DataStore.GetSnackByType)
        ?? Enumerable.Empty<Snack>();
    return result;
}
```

Only a single additional line of boilerplate is added, and now logging is being done. Sadly, we can't add anything specific in the message besides the error itself. The extension method doesn't know where it's called from, or the context of the error, which is perfect for reusing the method all over the codebase.

If we don't want the try/catch being aware of the ILogger interface, or we want to provide a custom error message every time, we need to look at something a little more complicated to handle error messaging.

One option is to return a metadata object that contains the return value of the function that's being executed, and a bit of data about whether the code worked, whether errors occurred, and what they were. We could use something like this:

```
public class ExecutionResult<T>
{
    public T Result { get; init; }
    public Exception Error { get; init; }
}

public static class Extensions
{
    public static ExtensionResult<TOut> MapWithTryCatch<TIn,TOut>(
        this TIn @this,
        Func<TIn,TOut> f)
    {
        try
        {
         var result = f(@this);
         return new ExecutionResult<TOut>
         {
             Result = result
         };
        }
        catch(Exception e)
        {
            return new ExecutionResult<TOut>
            {
                Error = e
            };
        }
    }
}
```

I don't really like this approach. It's breaking one of the SOLID principles of object-oriented design, the interface segregation principle. Well, sort of. Technically, that applies to interfaces, but I try to apply it everywhere, even if I do write functional code. The idea is that we shouldn't be forced to include something in a class or interface that we don't need. Here, we're forcing a successful run to include an Exception property that it'll never need, and likewise, a failure run will have to include the Result property it'll never need.

We could do this in other ways, but I'm making it simple, and returning either a version of the ExecutionResult class with the result or a default value of Result with the Exception.

This means we can use the extension method like this:

```
pubic IEnumerable<Snack> GetSnackByType(int typeId)
{
    var result = typeId.MapWithTryCatch(this.DataStore.GetSnackByType);
    if(result.Value == null)
    {
        this.Logger.LogException(result.Error, "We ran out of jammy dodgers!");
        return Enumerable.Empty<Snack>();
```

```
    }

        return result.Result;
    }
```

The unnecessary fields aside, this approach has another issue: the onus is now on the developer using the try/catch function to add additional boilerplate to check for errors.

Skip ahead to Chapter 6 for an alternative way of handling this sort of return value in a more purely functional manner. For now, here's a slightly cleaner way of handling it.

First, we add in another extension method, one that attaches to the ExecutionResult object this time:

```
public static T OnError<T>(
    this ExecutionResult<T> @this,
    Action<Exception> errorHandler)
    {
    if (@this.Error != null)
        errorHandler(@this.Error);
        return @this.Result;
    }
```

Here, we're first checking for an error. If an error exists, we execute the user-defined Action, which will presumably be a logging operation. It finishes by unwrapping the ExecutionResult into just its actual returned data object.

All of that means we can now handle the try/catch like this:

```
public IEnumerable<Snack> GetSnackByTypeId(int typeId) =>
    typeId.MapWithTryCatch(DataStore.GetSnackByType)
        .OnError(e => this.Logger.LogError(e, "We ran out of custard creams!"));
```

This solution is far from perfect, but without moving on to another level in functional theory, it's workable and elegant enough that it's not setting off my internal perfectionist. It also forces the user to consider error handling when using this, which can only be a good thing!

Handling Nulls

Aren't null reference exceptions annoying? If you want someone to blame, it's a guy called Tony Hoare who invented the concept of null back in the '60s. Actually, let's not blame anyone. I'm sure he's a lovely person, beloved by everyone who knows him. In any case, we can hopefully all agree that null reference exceptions are an absolute pain.

So, is there a functional way to deal with them? If you've read this far, you probably know that the answer is a resounding yes![4]

The Unless() function takes in a Boolean condition and an Action delegate, and executes the Action only if the Boolean is false—i.e., the Action is always executed *unless* the condition is true.

The most common usage for something like this is—you guessed it—checking for null. Here's an example of exactly the sort of code we'd want to replace. This is a rarely seen bit of source code for a Dalek:[5]

```
public void BusinessAsUsual()
{
    var enemies = this.scanner.FindLifeforms('all');
    foreach(var e in enemies)
    {
        this.Gun.Blast(e.Coordinates.Longitude, e.Coordinates.Latitude);
        this.Speech.ScreamAt(e, "EXTERMINATE");
    }
}
```

This is all well and good, and probably leaves a lot of people killed by a psychotic mutant in a mobile pepper-pot-shaped tank. But what if the Coordinates object was null for some reason? That's right—null reference exception.

This is where we make this functional and introduce an Unless() function to prevent the exception from occurring. This is what Unless() looks like:

```
public static class UnlessExtensionMethods
{
    public void Unless<T>(this T @this, Func<bool> condition, Action<T> f)
    {
        if(!condition(@this)
        {
            f(@this);
        }
    }
}
```

The Unless() function has to be a void, unfortunately. If we swapped the Action for a Func, then it's fine to return the result of the Func from the extension method. What about when the condition is true, though, and we don't execute? What do we return then? There isn't really an answer to that question.

---

4 Also, congratulations for making it this far—although it probably didn't take you anywhere so much time as it did me!

5 For the uninitiated, these are the main baddies in the British SF TV series *Doctor Who*. You can see them in action on YouTube (*https://oreil.ly/tNf6D*).

This is how we could use the Unless() function to make a new, super-duper, even more deadly functional Dalek:

```
public void BusinessAsUsual()
{
    var enemies = this.scanner.FindLifeforms('all');

    foreach(var e in enemies)
    {
        e.unless(
            x => x.Coordinates == null,
            x => this.Gun.Blast(e.Coordinates.Longitude, e.Coordinates.Latitude)
        )

        // May as well do this anyway, since we're here.
            this.Speech.ScreamAt(e, "EXTERMINATE");
    }
}
```

Using this, a null Coordinates object won't result in an exception; the gun simply won't be fired.

The next few chapters provide more ways to prevent null exceptions—ways that require more advanced coding and a little theory, but that are much more thorough in the way they work. Stay tuned.

Update an Enumerable

I'm going to finish off this section with a useful example. It involves updating an element in an enumerable without changing any data at all!

The thing to remember about enumerables is that they are designed to use lazy evaluation—i.e., they don't convert from a set of functions pointing at a data source to actual data until the last possible moment. Quite often, the use of Select() functions doesn't trigger an evaluation, so we can use them to effectively create filters sitting between the data source and the place in the code where enumeration of the data will take place.

Here's an example of altering an enumerable so that the item at position x is replaced:

```
var sourceData = new []
{
    "Hello", "Doctor", "Yesterday", "Today", "Tomorrow", "Continue"
}

var updatedData = sourceData.ReplaceAt(1, "Darkness, my old friend");
var finalString = string.Join(" ", updatedData);
// Hello Darkness, my old friend Yesterday Today Tomorrow Continue
```

This calls a function to replace the element at position 1 ("Doctor") with a new value. Despite having two variables, nothing is done to the source data at all. The variable SourceData remains the same after this code snippet has come to the end. Furthermore, no replacement is made until calling string.Join, because that's the very moment at which concrete values are required.

This is how it's done:

```
public static class Extensions
{
    public static IEnumerable<T> ReplaceAt(this IEnumerable<T> @this,
        int loc,
        T replacement) =>
        @this.Select((x, i) => i == loc ? replacement : x);
}
```

This enumerable, returned here, points at the original enumerable and gets its values from there, but with one crucial difference. If the index of the element ever equals the user-defined value (1, the second element, in this example), all other values are passed through, unaltered.

If we were so inclined, we could provide a function to perform the update—giving the user the ability to base the new version of the data item on the old version that is being replaced. This is how we'd achieve that:

```
public static class Extensions
{
    public static IEnumerable<T> ReplaceAt(this IEnumerable<T> @this,
        int loc,
        Func<T, T> replacement) =>
        @this.Select((x, i) => i == loc ? replacement(x) : x);
}
```

The code is easy enough to use too:

```
var sourceData = new []
{
    "Hello", "Doctor", "Yesterday", "Today", "Tomorrow", "Continue"
}

var updatedData = sourceData.ReplaceAt(1, x => x + " Who");
var finalString = string.Join(" ", updatedData);
// Hello Doctor Who Yesterday Today Tomorrow Continue
```

It's also possible that we don't know the ID of the element we want to update—in fact, we could have multiple items to update. The next example is an alternative enumerable update function based on providing a Func that takes T as a parameter and returns a bool (i.e., Func<T,bool>) to identify the records that should be updated.

This example is based on board games—one of my favorite hobbies, much to the annoyance of my ever-patient wife! In this scenario, there is a Tag property on the `BoardGame` object, which contains metadata tags that describe the game ("family", "co-op", "complex", stuff like that) and that will be used by a search engine app. It's been decided that another tag should be added to games suitable for one player—"solo":

```
var sourceData = this.DataStore.GetBoardGames();

var updatedData = sourceData.ReplaceWhen(
    x => x.NumberOfPlayersAllowed.Contains(1),
    x => x with { Tags = x.Tags.Append("solo") });
this.DataStore.Save(updatedData);
```

The implementation is a variation on code we've already covered:

```
public static class ReplaceWhenExtensions
{
    public static IEnumerable<T> ReplaceWhen<T>(this IEnumerable<T> @this,
        Func<T, bool> shouldReplace,
        Func<T, T> replacement) =>
        @this.Select(x => shouldReplace(x) ? replacement(x) : x);
}
```

This function can be used to replace the need for many instances of `if` statements, and reduce them to simpler, more predictable operations.

Summary

In this chapter, we looked at various ways to use higher-order functions to provide rich functionality to our codebase, avoiding the need for OOP-style statements.

Do get in touch if you have any ideas of your own for higher-order function uses. You never know, it might end up in a future edition of this book!

The next chapter delves into discriminated unions and how this functional technique can help better model business logic concepts in your codebase, and remove the need for a lot of defensive code typically needed with nonfunctional projects. Enjoy!

CHAPTER 6

Discriminated Unions

Discriminated unions (DUs) are a way of defining a type (or class in the OOP world) that is actually one of a set of different types. Which type an instance of a DU actually is at any given moment has to be checked before use.

F# has DUs available natively, and it's a feature used extensively by F# developers. Despite sharing a common runtime with C#, and the feature being there for us *in theory*, there are only plans in place to introduce them into C# at some point, but it's not certain how or when. In the meantime, we can roughly simulate them with abstract classes, and that's the technique I'm going to talk about in this chapter.

This chapter is our first dabble into some of the more advanced areas of FP. Earlier chapters were more focused on how you, the developer, can work smart, not hard. We've also looked at ways to reduce boilerplate and to make code more robust and maintainable.

DUs are a programming structure that will do all of this too,[1] but are more than a simple extension method, or a single-line fix to remove a little bit of boilerplate. DUs are closer in concept to a design pattern—in that they have a structure and some logic that needs to be implemented around it.

Holiday Time

Let's imagine an old-school object-oriented problem of creating a system for package holidays (or *vacations* in the US). You know, the sort where the travel agency arranges a customer's travel and accommodations, all in one. I'll leave you to imagine which

---

1 Let me please reassure everyone that despite being called *discriminated unions*, they bear no connection to anyone's view of love and/or marriage or to worker's organizations.

lovely destination our customer is off to. Personally, I'm quite fond of the Greek islands.

Here's a set of C# data classes that represent two different kinds of holiday—one with and one without complimentary meals provided:

```csharp
public class Holiday
{
    public int Id { get; set; }
    public Location Destination { get; set; }
    public Location DepartureAirport { get; set; }
    public DateTime StartDate { get; set; }
    public int DurationOfStay { get; set; }
}

public class HolidayWithMeals : Holiday
{
    public int NumberOfMeals { get; set; }
}
```

Now imagine we are creating, say, an account page for our customer and want to list everything they've bought so far.[2] That's not all that difficult, really. We can use a relatively new is statement to build the necessary string. Here's one way to do it:

```csharp
public string formatHoliday(Holiday h) =>
    "From: " + h.DepartureAirport.Name + Environment.NewLine +
    "To: " + h.Destination.Name + Environment.NewLine +
    "Duration: " + h.DurationOfStay + " Day(s)" +
    (
        h is HolidayWithMeals hm
            ? Environment.NewLine + "Number of Meals: " + hm.NumberOfMeals
            : string.Empty
    );
```

If we want to quickly improve this with a few functional ideas, we could consider introducing a Fork combinator (see Chapter 5), The basic type would be Holiday, and the subtype would be HolidayWithMeals. We'd have essentially the same thing, but with an extra field or two.

Now, what if there was a project started up in the company to offer other types of services, separate from holidays. The company is going to also start providing day trips that don't involve hotels, flights, or anything else of that sort. Entrance into Tower Bridge in London, perhaps.[3] Or a quick jaunt up the Eiffel Tower in Paris. Whatever you fancy. The world is your oyster.

---

2 Didn't I tell you? We're in the travel business now, you and I! Together, we'll flog cheap holidays to unsuspecting punters until we retire rich and contented. That, or carry on doing what we're doing now. Either way.

3 It's not London Bridge, that famous one you're thinking of. London Bridge is elsewhere. In Arizona, in fact. No, really. Look it up.

The object would look something like this:

```
public class DayTrip
{
    public int Id { get; set; }
    public DateTime DateOfTrip { get; set; }
    public Location Attraction { get; set; }
    public bool CoachTripRequired { get; set; }
}
```

The point is, though, that if we want to represent this new scenario with inheritance from a `Holiday` object, it doesn't work. An approach I've seen some people follow is to merge all the fields together, along with a Boolean to indicate which fields are the ones we should be looking at:

```
public class CustomerOffering
{
    public int Id { get; set; }
    public Location Destination { get; set; }
    public Location DepartureAirport { get; set; }
    public DateTime StartDate { get; set; }
    public int DurationOfStay { get; set; }
    public bool CoachTripRequired { get; set; }
    public bool IsDayTrip { get; set; }
}
```

This is a poor idea for several reasons. For one, we're breaking the interface segregation principle. Whichever sort of holiday an instance of `CustomerOffering` represents, we're forcing it to hold fields that are irrelevant to it. We've also doubled up the concepts of `Destination` and `Attraction`, as well as `DateOfTrip` and `StartDate` here, to avoid duplication, but it means that we've lost some of the terminology that makes code dealing with day trips meaningful.

The other option is to maintain the objects as entirely separate types with no relationship between them at all. Doing that, we'd lose the ability to have a nice, concise, simple loop through every object. We wouldn't be able to list everything in a single table in date order. We would need multiple tables.

None of the possibilities seem all that good. But this is where DUs come charging to the rescue. In the next section, I'll show you how to use them to provide an optimum solution to this problem.

Holidays with Discriminated Unions

In F#, we can create a union type for our customer-offering example, like this:

```
type CustomerOffering =
    | Holiday
    | HolidayWithMeals
    | DayTrip
```

This means we can instantiate a new instance of `CustomerOffering`, but there are three separate types it could be, each potentially with its own entirely different properties.

This is the nearest we can get to this approach in C#:

```
public abstract class CustomerOffering
{
    public int Id { Get; set; }
}

public class Holiday : CustomerOffering
{
    public Location Destination { get; set; }
    public Location DepartureAirport { get; set; }
    public DateTime StartDate { get; set; }
    public int DurationOfStay { get; set; }
}

public class HolidayWithMeals : Holiday
{
    public int NumberOfMeals { get; set; }
}

public class DayTrip : CustomerOffering
{
    public DateTime DateOfTrip { get; set; }
    public Location Attraction { get; set; }
    public bool CoachTripRequired { get; set; }
}
```

On the face of it, the code doesn't seem entirely different from the first version of this set of classes, but there's an important difference. The base is abstract—we can't actually create a `CustomerOffering` class. Instead of being a family tree of classes with one parent at the top that all others conform to, all the subclasses are different, but equal in the hierarchy.

The class hierarchy diagram in Figure 6-1 should clarify the difference between the two approaches.

The `DayTrip` class is in no way forced to conform to any concept that makes sense to the `Holiday` class. `DayTrip` is completely its own thing: it can use property names that correspond exactly to its own business logic, rather than having to retrofit a few of the properties from `Holiday`. In other words, `DayTrip` isn't an *extension* of `Holiday`; it's an *alternative* to it.

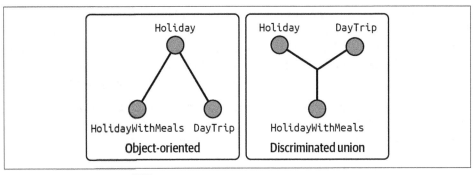

Figure 6-1. OOP versus DU

This also means we can have a single array of all CustomerOfferings, even though they're wildly different. We don't need separate data sources.

We'd handle an array of CustomerOffering objects in code by using a pattern-matching statement:

```
public string formatCustomerOffering(CustomerOffering c) =>
    c switch
    {
        HolidayWithMeals hm => this.formatHolidayWithMeal(hm),
        Holiday h => this.formatHoliday(h),
        DayTrip dt => this.formatDayTrip(tp)
    };
```

This simplifies the code everywhere the DU is received, and gives rise to more descriptive code that more accurately indicates all the possible outcomes of a function.

Schrödinger's Union

If you want an analogy of how these DU things work, think of poor old Schrödinger's cat. This was a thought experiment proposed by Austrian physicist Erwin Schrödinger to highlight a paradox in quantum mechanics. He imagined a box containing a cat and a radioactive isotope that had a 50-50 chance of decaying and killing the cat.[4] The point was that, according to quantum physics, until someone opens the box to check on the cat, both states—alive and dead—exist at the same time (meaning that the cat is both alive and dead at the same time).[5]

---

4 No one has ever done this. I'm not aware of a single cat ever being sacrificed in the name of quantum mechanics.

5 Somehow. I've never really understood this part of it.

This also means that if Herr Schrödinger were to send his cat/isotope box in the mail to a friend, they'd have a box that could contain one of two states inside, and until they open it, they don't know which.[6] Of course, the postal service being what it is, chances are the cat would be dead upon arrival *either way*. This is why you really shouldn't try this one at home. Trust me (I'm not a doctor, nor do I play one on TV).

That's kind of how a DU works. It has a single returned value, but that value may exist in two or more states. We don't know which until we examine it. If a class doesn't care which state, we can even pass it along to its next destination unopened.

Schrödinger's cat as code might look like this:

```
public abstract class SchrödingersCat { }

public class AliveCat : SchrödingersCat { }

public class DeadCat : SchrödingersCat { }
```

I'm hoping you're now clear on what exactly DUs *are*. I'm going to spend the rest of this chapter demonstrating a few examples of what they are *for*.

Naming Conventions

Let's imagine a code module for writing out people's names from the individual components. If you have a traditional British name, like my own, this is fairly straightforward. A class to write a name like mine would look something like this:

```
public class BritishName
{
    public string FirstName { get; set; }
    public IEnumerable<string> MiddleNames { get; set; }
    public string LastName { get; set; }
    public string Honorific { get; set; }
}

var simonsName = new BritishName
{
    Honorific = "Mr.",
    FirstName = "Simon",
    MiddleNames = new [] { "John" },
    LastName = "Painter
};
```

---

6 Wow. What a horrible birthday present that would be. Thanks, Schrödinger!

The code to render that name to string would be as simple as this:

```
public string formatName(BritishName bn) =>
    bn.Honorific + " " bn.FirstName + " " + string.Join(" ", bn.MiddleNames) +
    " " + bn.LastName;
// Results in "Mr Simon John Painter"
```

All done, right? Well, this works for traditional British names, but what about Chinese names? They aren't written in the same order as British names. Chinese names are written as *<family name> <given name>*, and many Chinese people take a *courtesy name*, a Western-style name that is used professionally.

Let's take the example of the legendary actor, director, writer, stuntman, singer, and all-round awesome human being Jackie Chan. His real name is Fang Shilong. In that set of names, his family name (surname) is Fang. His personal name (often in English called the first name, or Christian name) is Shilong. Jackie is a courtesy name he's used since he was very young. This style of name doesn't work whatsoever with the formatName() function we've created.

We *could* mangle the data a bit to make it work:

```
var jackie = new BritishName
{
    Honorific = "Xiānsheng", // equivalent of "Mr."
    FirstName = "Fang",
    LastName = "Shilong"
}
// results in "xiānsheng Fang Shilong"
```

So fine, this correctly writes his two official names in the required order. What about his courtesy name, though? The code provides nothing to write that out. Also, the Chinese equivalent of "Mr."—Xiānsheng[7]—goes *after* the name, so this is really pretty shoddy, even if we try repurposing the existing fields.

We could add an awful lot of if statements into the code to check for the nationality of the person being described, but that approach would rapidly turn into a nightmare if we tried to scale it up to include more than two nationalities.

Once again, a better approach would be to use a DU to represent the radically different data structures in a form that mirrors the reality of the thing they're trying to represent:

```
public abstract class Name { }

public class BritishName : Name
{
```

---

7 "先生." It literally means "one who was born earlier." Interestingly, if you were to write the same letters in Japanese, it would be pronounced "Sensei." I'm a nerd—I love stuff like this!

```
    public string FirstName { get; set; }
    public IEnumerable<string> MiddleNames { get; set; }
    public string LastName { get; set; }
    public string Honorific { get; set; }
}

public class ChineseName : Name
{
    public string FamilyName { get; set; }
    public string GivenName { get; set; }
    public string Honorific { get; set; }
    public string CourtesyName { get; set; }
}
```

In this imaginary scenario, there are probably separate data sources for each name type, each with its own schema. Maybe a web API for each country?

Using this union, we can create an array of names containing both me and Jackie Chan:[8]

```
var names = new Name[]
{
    new BritishName
    {
        Honorific = "Mr.",
        FirstName = "Simon",
        MiddleNames = new [] { "John" },
        LastName = "Painter"
    },
    new ChineseName
    {
        Honorific = "Xiānsheng",
        FamilyName = "Fang",
        GivenName = "Shilong",
        CourtestyName = "Jackie"
    }
}
```

We could then extend the formatting function with a pattern-matching expression:

```
public string formatName(Name n) =>
    n switch
    {
    BritishName bn => bn.Honorific + " " bn.FirstName + " "
        + string.Join(" ", bn.MiddleNames) + " " + bn.LastName,
    ChineseName cn => cn.FamilyName + " " + cn.GivenName + " " +
        cn.Honorific + " \"" + cn.CourtesyName + "\""
    };
```

---

8 Sadly, this is the closest I'll ever get to him for real. Do watch some of his Hong-Kong films if you haven't already! I'd start with the *Police Story* series.

```
var output = string.Join(Environment.NewLine, names);
// output =
// Mr. Simon John Painter
// Fang Shilong Xiānsheng "Jackie"
```

This same principle can be applied to any style of naming for anywhere in the world, and the names given to fields will always be meaningful to that country, as well as always being correctly styled without repurposing existing fields.

Database Lookup

In my C# code, I often consider using DUs as the return type of functions. I'm especially likely to use this technique in lookup functions to data sources. Let's imagine for a moment we want to find someone's details in a system of some kind somewhere. The function is going to take an integer ID value and return a Person record.

At least, that's what you'd often find people doing. You might see something like this:

```
public Person  GetPerson(int id)
{
    // Fill in some code here.  Whatever data
    // store you want to use.  Except mini-disc.
}
```

But if you think about it, returning a Person object is only *one* of the possible return states of the function.

What if an ID is entered for a person who doesn't exist? We *could* return null, I suppose, but that doesn't describe what actually happened. What if there were a handled exception that resulted in nothing being returned? The null doesn't tell us *why* it was returned.

The other possibility is an Exception being raised. It might well not be the fault of our code, but nevertheless it could happen if network or other issues arise. What would we return in this case?

Rather than returning an unexplained null and forcing other parts of the codebase to handle it, or an alternative return type object with metadata fields containing exceptions, we could create a DU:

```
public abstract class PersonLookupResult
{
    public int Id { get; set; }
}

public class PersonFound : PersonLookupResult
{
    public Person Person { get; set; }
}
```

```
public class PersonNotFound : PersonLookupResult
{

}

public class ErrorWhileSearchingPerson : PersonLookupResult
{
    public Exception Error { get; set; }
}
```

We can now return a single class from our `GetPersonById()` function, which tells the code utilizing the class that one of these three states has been returned, and that state has already been determined. The returned object doesn't need to have logic applied to it to determine whether it worked, and the states are completely descriptive of each case that needs to be handled.

The function would look something like this:

```
public PersonLookupResult  GetPerson(int id)
{
    try
    {
        var personFromDb = this.Db.Person.Lookup(id);
        return personFromDb == null
            ? new PersonNotFound { Id = id }
            : new PersonFound
                {
                    Person = personFromDb,
                    Id = id
                };
    }
    catch(Exception e)
    {
        return new ErrorWhileSearchingPerson
        {
            Id = id,
            Error = e
        }
    }
}
```

And consuming it is once again a matter of using a pattern-matching expression to determine what to do:

```
public string DescribePerson(int id)
{
    var p = this.PersonRepository.GetPerson(id);
    return p switch
    {
        PersonFound pf => "Their name is " + pf.Name,
        PersonNotFound _ => "Person not found",
```

```
        ErrorWhileSearchingPerson e => "An error occurred" + e.Error.Message
    };
}
```

Sending Email

The preceding example is fine when we're expecting a value back, but what about when there's no return value? Let's imagine I've written some code to send an email to a customer or to a family member I can't be bothered to write a message to myself.[9]

I don't expect anything back, but I might like to know if an error has occurred, so this time I'm especially concerned with only two states. This is how I'd define my three possible outcomes from sending an email:

```
public abstract class EmailSendResult
{

}

public class EmailSuccess : EmailSendResult
{

}

public class EmailFailure : EmailSendResult
{
    pubic Exception Error { get; set; }
}
```

Use of this class in code might look like this:

```
public EmailSendResult SendEmail(string recipient, string message)
{
  try
    {
        this.AzureEmailUtility.SendEmail(recipient, message);
        return new EmailSuccess();
    }
    catch(Exception e)
    {
        return new EmailFailure
        {
            Error = e
        };
    }
}
```

---

9 Just kidding, folks, honest! Please don't take me off your Christmas card lists!

Using the function elsewhere in the codebase would look like this:

```
var result = this.EmailTool.SendEmail(
    "Season's Greetings",
    "Hi, Uncle John. How's it going?");

var messageToWriteToConsole = result switch
{
    EmailFailure ef => "Error occurred sending the email: " + ef.Error.Message,
    EmailSuccess _ => "Email send successful",
    _ => "Unknow Response"
};

this.Console.WriteLine(messageToWriteToConsole);
```

This, once again, means we can return an error message and failure state from the function, but without anything anywhere depending on properties it doesn't need.

Console Input

Some time ago I came up with the mad idea to try out my FP skills by converting an old text-based game written in HP Time-Shared BASIC to functional-style C#.

The game, called *Oregon Trail*, dated all the way back to 1975. Hard as it is to believe, the game is even older than I am! Older even than *Star Wars*. In fact, it even predates monitors and had to effectively be played on something that looked like a typewriter. In those days, when the code said print, it meant it!

One of the most crucial things the game code had to do was to periodically take input from the user. Most of the time, an integer was required—either to select a command from a list or to enter an amount of goods to purchase. Other times, it was important to receive text and to confirm what the user typed—such as in the hunting mini-game, where the user was required to type BANG as quickly as possible to simulate attempting to accurately hit a target.

I *could* have simply had a module in the codebase that returned raw user input from the console. This would mean that every place in the entire codebase that required an integer value would have to carry out an empty string check, followed by parsing the string to an int, before getting on with whatever logic was actually required.

A smarter idea is to use a DU to represent the different states the logic of the game recognizes from user input, and keep the necessary int check code in a single place:

```
public abstract class UserInput
{

}

public class TextInput : UserInput
```

```
{
    public string Input { get; set; }
}

public class IntegerInput : UserInput
{
    public int Input { get; set; }
}

public class NoInput : UserInput
{
}

public class ErrorFromConsole : UserInput
{
  public Exception Error { get; set; }
}
```

I'm not honestly sure what errors are possible from the console, but I don't think it's wise to rule them out, especially as they're beyond the control of the application code.

The idea here is that we're gradually shifting from the impure area beyond the code-base and into the pure, controlled area within it (see Figure 6-2)—like a multistage airlock.

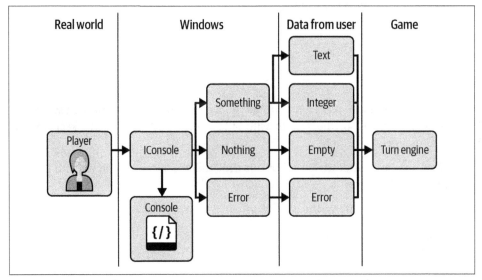

Figure 6-2. Stages of text input

Speaking of the console being beyond our control: if we want to keep our codebase as functional as possible, it's best to hide it behind an interface. Then we can inject mocks during testing and push back the nonpure area of our code a little further:

```
public interface IConsole
{
    UserInput ReadInput(string userPromptMessage);
}

public class ConsoleShim : IConsole
{
    public UserInput ReadInput(string userPromptMessage)
    {
        try
        {
            Console.WriteLine(userPromptMessage);
            var input = Console.ReadLine();
            return new TextInput
            {
                Input = input
            };
        }
        catch(Exception e)
        {
            return new ErrorFromConsole
            {
                Error = e
            };
        }
    }
}
```

That was the most basic representation possible of an interaction with the user. That's because that's an area of the system with side effects, and we want to keep that as small as possible.

After that, we create another layer, but this time there is some logic applied to the text received from the player:

```
public class UserInteraction
{
    private readonly IConsole _console;
    public UserInteraction(IConsole console)
    {
        this._console = console;
    }

    public UserInput GetInputFromUser(string message)
    {
        var input = this._console.ReadInput(message);
        var returnValue = input switch
        {
```

```
                TextInput x when string.IsNullOrWhiteSpace(x.Input) =>
                new NoInput(),
                TextInput x when int.TryParse(x.Input, out var _)=>
                new IntegerInput
                {
                    Input = int.Parse(x.Input)
                },
                TextInput x => new TextInput
                {
                    Input = x.Input
                }
            };

            return returnValue;
        }
    }
```

If we want to prompt the user for input and guarantee that they give us an integer, it's now easy to code:

```
public int GetPlayerSpendOnOxen()
{
    var input =
        this.UserInteraction.GetInputFromUser(
            "How much do you want to spend on Oxen?")
    var returnValue = input switch
    {
        IntegerInput ii => ii.Input,
        _ => {
            this.UserInteraction.WriteMessage("Try again");
            return GetPlayerSpendOnOxen();
        }
    };

    return returnValue;
}
```

In this code block, we're prompting the player for input. Then, we check whether it's the integer we expected—based on the check already done on it via a DU. If it's an integer, great. Job's a good 'un; return that integer.

If not, the player needs to be prompted to try again, and we call this function again, recursively. We could add more detail about capturing and logging any errors received, but I think this demonstrates the principle soundly enough.

Note also that there isn't a need for a try/catch in this function. That is already handled by the lower-level function.

There are many, many places this code checking for integer are needed in this *Oregon Trail* conversion. Imagine how much code we've saved ourselves by wrapping the integer check into the structure of the return object!

Generic Unions

All the DUs so far are entirely situation specific. Before wrapping up this chapter, I want to discuss a few options for creating entirely generic, reusable versions of the same idea.

First, let me reiterate: we can't have DUs that we can simply declare easily, on the fly, as the folks in F# can. It's just not a thing we can do. Sorry. The best we can do is emulate it as closely as possible, with some sort of boilerplate trade-off.

Here are a couple of functional structures we can use. There are, incidentally, more advanced ways to use these coming up in Chapter 7. Stay tuned for that.

Maybe

If our intention with using a DU is to represent that data might not have been found by a function, then the Maybe structure might be the one for us. Implementations look like this:

```
public abstract class Maybe<T>
{
}

public class Something<T> : Maybe<T>
{
    public Something(T value)
    {
        this.Value = value;
    }

    public T Value { get; init; }
}

public class Nothing<T> : Maybe<T>
{

}
```

We're basically using the Maybe abstract as a wrapper around another class, the actual class our function returns; but by wrapping it in this manner, we are signaling to the outside world that there may not necessarily be anything returned.

Here's how we might use it for a function that returns a single object:

```
public Maybe<DoctorWho> GetDoctor(int doctorNumber)
{
    try
    {
        using var conn = this._connectionFactory.Make();
        // Dapper query to the db
        var data = conn.QuerySingleOrDefault<Doctor>(
```

```
            "SELECT * FROM [dbo].[Doctors] WHERE DocNum = @docNum",
            new { docNum = doctorNumber });
        return data == null
            ? new Nothing<DoctorWho>();
            : new Something<DoctorWho>(data);
    }
    catch(Exception e)
    {
        this.logger.LogError(e, "Error getting doctor " + doctorNumber);
        return new Nothing<DoctorWho>();
    }

}
```

We'd use that something like this:

```
// William Hartnell.  He's the best!
var doc = this.DoctorRepository.GetDoctor(1);
var message = doc switch
{
    Something<DoctorWho> s => "Played by " + s.Value.ActorName,
    Nothing<DoctorWho> _ => "Unknown Doctor"
};
```

This doesn't handle error situations especially well. A Nothing state at least prevents unhandled exceptions from occurring, and we are logging, but nothing useful has been passed back to the end user.

Result

An alternative to Maybe is Result, which represents the possibility that a function might throw an error instead of returning anything. It might look like this:

```
public abstract class Result<T>
{
}

public class Success : Result<T>
{
    public Success<T>(T value)
    {
     this.Value = value;
    }

    public T Value { get; init; }
}

public class Failure<T> : Result<T>
{
    public Failure(Exception e)
    {
        this.Error = e;
```

```
    }

    public Exception Error { get; init; }
}
```

Now, the `Result` version of the `GetDoctor()` function looks like this:

```
public Result<DoctorWho> GetDoctor(int doctorNumber)
{
    try
    {
        using var conn = this._connectionFactory.Make();
        // Dapper query to the db
        var data = conn.QuerySingleOrDefault<Doctor>(
            "SELECT * FROM [dbo].[Doctors] WHERE DocNum = @docNum",
            new { docNum = doctorNumber });
            return new Success<DoctorWho>(data);
    }
    catch(Exception e)
    {
        this.logger.LogError(e, "Error getting doctor " + doctorNumber);
        return new Failure<DoctorWho>(e);
    }

}
```

And we might consider using it like this:

```
// Sylvester McCoy.  He's the best too!
var doc = this.DoctorRepository.GetDoctor(7);
var message = doc switch
{
    Success<DoctorWho> s when s.Value == null => "Unknown Doctor!",
    Success<DoctorWho> s2 => "Played by " + s2.Value.ActorName,
    Failure<DoctorWho> e => "An error occurred: " e.Error.Message
};
```

Now this covers the error scenario in one of the possible states of the DU, but the
burden of null checking falls to the receiving function.

Maybe Versus Result

Here's a perfectly valid question at this point: which is better to use, `Maybe` or `Result`?
`Maybe` gives a state that informs the user that no data has been found, removing
the need for null checks, but effectively silently swallows errors. It's better than an
unhandled exception but could result in unreported bugs. `Result` handles errors
elegantly but puts the burden on the receiving function to check for null.

My personal preference? This might not be strictly within the standard definition of these structures, but I combine them into one. I usually have a three-state Maybe: Something, Nothing, Error. That handles just about anything the codebase can throw at me.

This would be my solution to the problem:

```
public abstract class Maybe<T>
{
}

public class Something<T> : Maybe<T>
{
    public Something(T value)
    {
        this.Value = value;
    }

    public T Value { get; init; }
}

public class Nothing<T> : Maybe<T>
{

}

public class Error<T> : Maybe<T>
{
    public Error(Exception e)
    {
        this.CapturedError = e;
    }

    public Exception CapturedError { get; init; }
}
```

And I'd use it like this:

```
public Maybe<DoctorWho> GetDoctor(int doctorNumber)
{
    try
    {
        using var conn = this._connectionFactory.Make();
        // Dapper query to the db
        var data = conn.QuerySingleOrDefault<Doctor>(
            "SELECT * FROM [dbo].[Doctors] WHERE DocNum = @docNum",
            new { docNum = doctorNumber });
        return data == null
            ? new Nothing<DoctorWho>();
            : new Something<DoctorWho>(data);
    }
    catch(Exception e)
```

```
    {
        this.logger.LogError(e, "Error getting doctor " + doctorNumber);
        return new Error<DoctorWho>(e);
    }

}
```

The receiving function can now handle all three states elegantly with a pattern-matching expression:

```
// Peter Capaldi.  The other, other best Doctor!
var doc = this.DoctorRepository.GetDoctor(12);
var message = doc switch
{
    Nothing<DoctorWho> _ => "Unknown Doctor!",
    Something<DoctorWho> s => "Played by " + s.Value.ActorName,
    Error<DoctorWho> e => "An error occurred: " e.Error.Message
};
```

I find this allows me to provide a full set of responses to any given scenario when returning from a function that requires a connection to the cold, dark, hungry-wolf-filled world beyond my program, and easily allows a more informative response to the end user.

Before we finish on this topic, here's how I'd use that same structure to handle a return type of IEnumerable:

```
public Maybe<IEnumerable<DoctorWho>> GetAllDoctors()
{
    try
    {
        using var conn = this._connectionFactory.Make();
        // Dapper query to the db
        var data = conn.Query<Doctor>(
            "SELECT * FROM [dbo].[Doctors]");
            return data == null || !data.Any()
                ? new Nothing<IEnumerable<DoctorWho>>();
                : new Something<IEnumerable<DoctorWho>>(data);
    }
    catch(Exception e)
    {
        this.logger.LogError(e, "Error getting doctor " + doctorNumber);
        return new Error<IEnumerable<DoctorWho>>(e);
    }

}
```

This allows me to handle the response from the function like this:

```
// Great chaps.  All of them!
var doc = this.DoctorRepository.GetAllDoctors();
var message = doc switch
{
```

```
            Nothing<IEnumerable<DoctorWho>> _ => "No Doctors found!",
            Something<IEnumerable<DoctorWho>> s => "The Doctors were played by: " +
                string.Join(Environment.NewLine, s.Value.Select(x => x.ActorName),
            Error<IEnumerable<DoctorWho>> e => "An error occurred: " e.Error.Message
    };
```

Once again, the code is nice and elegant, and everything has been considered. This is an approach I use all the time in my everyday coding, and I hope after reading this chapter that you will too!

Either

Something and Result—in one form or another—now generically handle returning from a function when there's some uncertainty as to how it might behave. What if we want to return two or more entirely different types?

This is where the Either type comes in. The syntax isn't the nicest, but it does work:

```
public abstract class Either<T1, T2>
{

}

public class Left<T1, T2> : Either<T1, T2>
{
    public Left(T1 value)
    {
        Value = value;
    }

    public T1 Value { get; init; }
}

public class Right<T1, T2> : Either<T1, T2>
{
    public Right(T2 value)
    {
        Value = value;
    }

    public T2 Value { get; init; }
}
```

We could use it to create a type that might be left or right, like this:

```
public Either<string, int> QuestionOrAnswer() =>
    new Random().Next(1, 6) >= 4
        ? new Left<string, int>("What do you get if you multiply 6 by 9?")
        : new Right<string, int>(42);

var data = QuestionOrAnswer();
var output = data switch
```

```
{
    Left<string, int> l => "The ultimate question was: " + l.Value,
    Right<string, int> r => "The ultimate answer was: " + r.Value.ToString()
};
```

We could, of course, expand this to have three or more possible types. I'm not entirely sure what we'd call each of them, but it's certainly possible. A lot of awkward boilerplate is needed, in that we have to include all the references to the generic types in a lot of places. At least it works, though.

Summary

This chapter covered discriminated unions: what exactly they are, how they are used, and just how incredibly powerful they are as a code feature. DUs can be used to massively cut down on boilerplate code, and make use of a data type that descriptively represents all possible states of the system in a way that strongly encourages the receiving function to handle them appropriately.

DUs can't be implemented quite as easily as in F# or other functional languages, but C# at least offers possibilities.

In the next chapter, I'll present more advanced functional concepts that will take DUs up to the next level!

CHAPTER 7

Functional Flow

Calls to external systems such as databases and web APIs are an absolute pain, aren't they? Before using your data—the most important part of the function you're writing—you have to do the following:

1. Catch and handle any exceptions. Maybe the network was glitching, or the database server was offline?

2. Check that what has come back from the database is not `null`.

3. Check that there's an actual, reasonable set of data, even if it isn't `null`.

This entails a lot of tedious boilerplate, which gets in the way of your business logic.

Use of the `Maybe` DU from the previous chapter will help somewhat with returning something other than `null` for records not found or errors encountered, but boilerplate is still required even then.

What if I were to tell you there is a way to never have to see another unhandled exception again? Not only that, but you'd never even need to use a `try/catch` block again. As for `null` checks? Forget 'em. You won't ever have to do that again either.

Don't believe me? Well, strap in; I'm going to introduce you to one of my favorite FP features. I use it all the time in my day job, and I'm hoping that after reading this chapter, you might too.

Maybe, Revisited

I'd like to revisit that `Maybe` DU from Chapter 6 now, but this time I'm going to show you how it can be even more useful than you could ever have imagined.

What I'm going to do is walk you through adding in a version of the Map() extension method from a couple of chapters ago. As you may remember, the Map() combinator in "Chaining Functions" on page 104 works similarly to the LINQ Select() method, except it acts on the entire source object, not individual elements from it.

This time, though, we're going to add a bit of logic inside Map(), something that will determine which type is going to come out. We'll give it a different name this time—Bind():[1]

```
public static Maybe<TOut> Bind<TIn, TOut>(
    this Maybe<TIn> @this,
    Func<TIn, TOut> f)
{
    try
    {
        Maybe<TOut> updatedValue = @this switch
        {
            Something<TIn> s when !EqualityComparer<TIn>.Default.Equals(
                s.Value, default) =>
                    new Something<TOut>(f(s.Value)),
            Something<TIn> _ => new Nothing<TOut>(),
            Nothing<TIn> _ => new Nothing<TOut>(),
            Error<TIn> e => new Error<TOut>(e.ErrorMessage),
            _ => new Error<TOut>(new Exception(
                "New Maybe state that isn't coded for!: " +
                @this.GetType())))
        };
        return updatedValue;
    }
    catch (Exception e)
    {
        return new Error<TOut>(e);
    }
}
```

So what's happening here? One of a few possible things:

- The current value of This (the current object held by Maybe) is a Something—i.e., an actual nondefault valued object or primitive,[2] in which case the supplied function is executed and whatever comes from it is returned in a new Something.

- The current value of This is a Something, but the value inside it is the default (null, in most cases), in which case instead of Something, we now return a Nothing.

---

1 The first few examples of a Bind() function presented in this chapter are modeled after those used by Enrico Buonanno in his book *Functional Programming in C#* (Manning). The rest are my own derivatives of his work.

2 I would say non-null, but integers default to 0 and Booleans to false.

- The current value of This is a Nothing, in which case we return another Nothing. No point doing anything else.

- The current value of This is an error. Again, there's no point doing anything except passing it on.

What's the point of all this? Well, imagine the following procedural code:

```
public string MakeGreeting(int employeeId)
{
    try
    {
        var e = this.empRepo.GetById(employeeId);
        if(e != null)
        {
            return "Hello " + e.Salutation + " " + e.Name
        }

        return "Employee not found";
    }

    catch(Exception e)
    {
        return "An error occurred: " + e.Message;
    }
}
```

When you look at it, the purpose of this code is incredibly simple: fetch an employee; and if there are no issues, say hello to them. But, since null and unhandled exceptions are a thing, we have to write so much defensive code—null checks and try/catch blocks—not just here, but all over our codebase.

What's worse is that we make it the problem of the code calling this function to know what to do with it. How do we signal that an error occurred or that the employee wasn't found? In this example, we just return a string for whatever application we've written to display blindly. The other option would be to return some sort of return object with metadata attached (e.g., bool DataFound, bool ExceptionOccurred, exception CapturedException).

By using a Maybe and Bind() function, none of that is necessary. We could rewrite the code like this:

```
public Maybe<string> MakeGreeting(int employeeId) =>
    new Something(employeeId)
        .Bind(x => this.empRepo.GetById(x))
        .Bind(x => "Hello " + x.Salutation + " " + x.Name);
```

Think about the possible results for each bind listed here.

If the employee repository returns a null value, the next Bind() call will identify a Something with a default (null) value, and not execute the function that constructs a greeting string; instead it will return Nothing.

If an error occurs in the repository (maybe a network connection issue, something impossible to predict or prevent), the error will simply be passed on instead of the function executing.

The ultimate point I'm making is that the arrow function that assembles a greeting will execute only if the previous step (a) returns an actual value and (b) doesn't throw an unhandled exception. This means that the small function written with use of the Bind() method is functionally identical to the previous version, covered with defensive code.

It gets better...

We're not returning a string anymore; we're returning a Maybe<string>. This is a DU that can be used to inform whatever is calling our function of the result of the execution, whether it worked, and so on. That can be used in the outside world to decide how to handle the resulting value, or it can be used in subsequent chains of Bind() calls.

We can use the DU like this:

```
public Interface IUserInterface
{
    void WriteMessage(string s);
}

// Bit of magic here because it doesn't matter
this.UserInterface = Factory.MakeUserInterface();

var message = makeGreetingResult switch
{
    Something s => s.Value,
    Nothing _ => "Hi, but I've never heard of you.",
    Error _ => "An error occurred, try again"
};

this.UserInterface.WriteMessage(message);
```

Alternatively, we could adapt the UserInterface module so that it takes Maybe as a parameter:

```
public Interface IUserInterface
{
    void WriteMessage(Maybe<string> s);
}

// Bit of magic here because it doesn't matter
this.UserInterface = Factory.MakeUserInterface();
```

```
var logonMessage = MakeGreeting(employeeId)
    .Bind(x => x + Environment.NewLine + MakeUserInfo(employeeId));
this.UserInterface.WriteMessage(logonMessage);
```

Swapping out a concrete value in an Interface for a Maybe<T> is a sign to the class that consumes it that there is no certainty that the operation will work, and forces the consuming class to consider each of the possibilities and how to handle them. It also puts the onus on deciding how to respond entirely in the hands of the consuming class. There's no need for the class returning the Maybe to have any interest in what happens next.

The best description I've ever encountered for this style of programming was in a talk and related articles by Scott Wlaschin called "Railway Oriented Programming" (*https://oreil.ly/aMDgh*). Wlaschin describes the process as being like a railway line with a series of points. Each set of points is a Bind() call. The train starts on the Something line, and every time a function passed to a Bind() is executed, the train either carries on to the next set of points or switches to the Nothing path, and simply glides along to the station at the end of the line without doing any more work.

It's a beautiful, elegant way of writing code that cuts out so much boilerplate it isn't even funny. If only there were a handy technical term for this structure. Oh wait, there is! It's called a *monad*!

I said way back at the beginning of the book that they might pop up somewhere. If anyone ever says to you that monads are complicated, I hope you can see now that they're wrong.

Monads are like a wrapper around a value of some kind—like an envelope or a burrito. They hold the value but make no comment about what it's actually set to. What they do is give us the ability to hang functions off them that provide a safe environment to perform operations without having to worry about negative consequences—such as null reference exceptions.

The Bind() function is like a relay race; each call does some sort of operation and then passes its value to the next runner. Bind() also handles errors and nulls for us, so we don't need to worry about writing so much defensive code.

If you like, imagine a monad being like an explosion-proof box. You have a package you want to open but don't know whether it's something safe like a letter[3] or something explosive just waiting to take you down when you lift the lid. If you pop the package inside the monad container, the package can open safely or explode, but the monad will keep you safe from the consequences.

---

3 Or the living Schrödinger's cat. Actually, *is* that the safe option? I've owned cats; I know what they're like!

That's really all there is too it. Well, mostly.

In the rest of this chapter, I'll show you what else we can do with monads, and what other sorts of monads there are. Don't worry, though. The "hard" part is over now; if you've reached this point and you're still with me, the rest of this book is going to be a piece of cake.[4]

Maybe and Debugging

A comment I hear sometimes regarding strings of `Bind()` statements is that they make it harder to use debug tools in Visual Studio to step through the changes—especially when you have scenarios like this:

```
var returnValue = idValue.ToMaybe()
    .Bind(transformationOne)
    .Bind(transformationTwo)
    .Bind(transformationThree);
```

Stepping through the changes is actually possible in most versions of Visual Studio, but you'd need make sure you keep mashing the F11 "Step-in" key on the keyboard to enter the nested arrow functions inside the `Bind()` call. This approach is still hardly the best for working out what's happening if a value isn't being calculated correctly. It's even worse when you consider Step-in will enter the `Maybe`'s `Bind()` function and need a few more steps to be taken before seeing the result of the arrow function.

I tend to write my `Bind()` functions one to a line, each storing a variable containing its individual output:

```
var idMaybe = idValue.ToMaybe();
var transOne = idMaybe.Bind(x => transformationOne(x));
var transTwo = transOne.Bind(x => transformationTwo(x));
var returnValue = transTwo.Bind(x => transformationThree(x));
```

Functionally, these two samples are identical. It's just that we're capturing each output separately rather than immediately feeding it into another function and discarding them.

The second sample is easier to diagnose issues with, though, as we can inspect each intermediate value. Debugging is made easier because of the FP technique of never modifying a variable after it's set. This means that every intermediate step in the process is set in stone to work through what exactly happened, as well as how and where things went wrong in the event of a bug.

These intermediate values will remain in scope for the entirety of the life of whatever larger function they're part of, though. If it's an especially large function, and one of

---

4 Cheesecake, preferably. Paul Hollywood would be very disappointed to learn I don't like many cakes, but New York–style cheesecake is most certainly one that I like!

the intermediate values is hefty, merging them might be worthwhile so that the large intermediate value is descoped as early as possible.

This decision is mostly a matter of personal style and one or two codebase constraints. Whichever you choose is fine.

Map() Versus Bind()

Strictly speaking, the preceding code is not implementing the Bind() function in accordance with the functional paradigm. Two functions *should be* attached to the Maybe: Map() and Bind(). They're nearly the same, but with a small and subtle difference.

The Map() function is like the one I described in the previous section—it attaches to a Maybe<T1> and needs a function that gives you the value of type T1 from inside the Maybe and requires you to turn it into a type T2.

An actual Bind() needs you to pass in a function that returns a Maybe of the new type—i.e., Maybe<T2>. It still returns the same result as the Map() function:

```
public static Maybe<TOut> Map<TIn, TOut>(
    this Maybe<TIn> @this,
    Func<TIn, TOut> f) => // Some implementation

public static Maybe<TOut> Bind<TIn, TOut>(
    this Maybe<TIn> @this,
    Func<TIn, Maybe<TOut>> f) => // Some Implementation
```

If, for example, we have a function that calls a database and returns a type of Maybe<IEnumerable<Customer>> to represent a list of customers that may or may not have been found—then we call that with a Bind() function.

Any subsequent chained functions to change the IEnumerable of customers into another form would be done with a Map() call, since those changes are data-to-data, not data-to-maybe.

Here's how we might go about implementing a proper Bind():

```
public static Maybe<TOut> Bind<TIn, TOut>(
    this Maybe<TIn> @this,
    Func<TIn, Maybe<TOut>> f)
{
    try
    {
        var returnValue = @this switch
        {
            Something<TIn> s => f(s.Value),
            _ => new Nothing<TOut>()
        };
        return returnValue;
```

```
        }
        catch (Exception _)
        {
            return new Nothing<TOut>();
        }
    }
```

And here's an example of how to use the function:

```
public Interface CustomerDataRepo
{
    Maybe<Customer> GetCustomerById(int customerId);
}

public string DescribeCustomer(int customerId) =>
    new Something<int>(customerId)
        .Bind(x => this.customerDataRepo.GetCustomerById(x))
        .Map(x => "Hello " + x.Name);
```

Use this new `Bind()` function and rename the previous one `Map()`, and you're conforming to the functional paradigm a little closer.

In production code, however, I don't personally do this. I just use a function called `Bind()` for both purposes. Why, you might ask? It's mostly to prevent confusion, in all honesty. JavaScript has a native `Map()` function, but it operates like a C# `Select()` on individual elements of arrays. C# also has a `Map()` function in Jimmy Bogard's AutoMapper library (*https://automapper.org*), which is used to convert an array of objects from one type to another.[5]

With both of these instances of a `Map()` function already in use in many C# codebases, I thought adding another `Map()` into the mix might confuse other folks looking at my code. For this reason, I use `Bind()` for all purposes, as C# and JavaScript don't have a `Bind()` function—except in libraries implementing the functional paradigm.

You can choose whether to use the more strictly accurate version with both `Map()` and `Bind()`, or the route that—in my opinion—is less confusing and more pragmatic, which is to simply use multiple instances of the `Bind()` function to serve every purpose. I'm going to carry on assuming that second option for the rest of this book.

Maybe and the Primitives

Maybe and the Primitives sounds like the title of an amazing pulp adventure novel that was never written. It would probably involve our heroine, Captain Maybe, swinging to the rescue somewhere in a lost civilization populated by aggressive cave-dwelling nasties.

---

5 This library can be used for quickly and easily converting between types, if that's something you do a lot in your code.

In fact, a *primitive type* in C# is one of a set of built-in types that *don't* default to null:

- bool
- byte
- sbyte
- char
- decimal
- double
- float
- int

- uint
- nint
- nuint
- long
- ulong[6]
- short
- ushort

The point here is that if we were to use any of these on a Bind() function from the previous sections and set their value to 0, it would fall foul of the check against default, because most of these default to 0.[7]

Here's an example of a unit test that would fail (I'm using xUnit with Fluent Assertions for a friendlier, human-readable assert style):

```
[Fact]
public Task primitive_types_should_not_default_to_nothing()
{
    var input = new Something<int>(0);
    var output = input.Bind(x => x + 10);
    (output as Something<int>).Value.Should().Be(10);
}
```

This test stores an integer with the value of 0 in a Maybe and then attempts to Bind() it into a value 10 higher—i.e., it should equal 10. In the existing code, the switch operation inside Bind() would consider the value 0 to be default and would switch the return type from Something<int> to Nothing<int>. The function to add 10 wouldn't be carried out, meaning that output in the unit test would be switched into a null, and the test would fail with a null reference exception.

Arguably, though, this isn't correct behavior, as 0 is a valid value of int. The code is easily fixed with an additional line in the Bind() function, however:

```
public static Maybe<TOut> Bind<TIn, TOut>(
    this Maybe<TIn> @this,
    Func<TIn, TOut> f)
{
```

---

6 Not a kind of tea! Nor is it a porcine character from Dragonball.

7 Except bool, which defaults to false, and char, which defaults to '\0'.

```
try
{
    Maybe<TOut> updatedValue = @this switch
    {
        Something<TIn> s when
            !EqualityComparer<TIn>.Default.Equals(s.Value, default) =>
                new Something<TOut>(f(s.Value)),
            // This is the new line
        Something<TIn> s when
        s.GetType().GetGenericArguments()[0].IsPrimitive =>
            new Something<TOut>(f(s.Value)),
        Something<TIn> _ => new Nothing<TOut>(),
        Nothing<TIn> _ => new Nothing<TOut>(),
        Error<TIn> e => new Error<TOut>(e.ErrorMessage),
        _ => new Error<TOut>(
            new Exception("New Maybe state that isn't coded for!: " +
                @this.GetType()))
    };
    return updatedValue;
}
catch (Exception e)
{
    return new Error<TOut>(e);
}
}
```

The new line checks the first generic argument of the Maybe<T>—i.e., the "real" type of T. All the types I listed at the beginning of this section would have a value of IsPrimitive set to true.

If we were to rerun the unit test with this modified Bind() function, the 0-valued int still wouldn't match on the check against not being default, but the next line would match, because int is a primitive.

This does now mean that all primitives are *incapable* of being a Nothing<T>. Whether that's right or wrong is a matter for you to assess. You might want to consider it a Nothing<T> if T is a bool, for example. If that's the case, another case would need to be added to the switch between the first two lines to handle the specific case of T being bool.

It might also be important to a calculation that it be possible for a Boolean false to be passed into a function to perform a calculation. As I said, it's a question you can best answer yourself.

One way to avoid this situation altogether is to always pass a nullable class around as T so you can be sure that you're getting the correct behavior when trying to decide whether what you're looking at is Something or Nothing.

Maybe and Logging

Another thing worth considering for the use of monads in a professional environment is the all-important developer's tool: logging. Logging information—not just errors, but also all sorts of important information—about the status of a function's progress is often crucial. Not just errors, but also all sorts of important information.

It's possible to do something like this, of course:

```
var idMaybe = idValue.ToMaybe();
var transOne = idMaybe.Bind(x => transformationOne(x));
if(transOne is Something<MyClass> s)
{
    this.Logger.LogInformation("Processing item " + s.Value.Id);
}
else if (transOne is Nothing<MyClass>)
{
    this.Logger.LogWarning("No record found for " + idValue");
}
else if (transOne is Error<MyClass> e)
{
    this.Logger.LogError(e, "An error occurred for " + idValue);
}
```

But this approach is likely to balloon out of hand if we do much of it—especially if there are many binds in the process that all require logging.

We might be able to leave out the error log until the very end, or even all the way out in the controller or whatever else ultimately originated this request. The error message would be passed from hand to hand untouched. But that still leaves occasional log messages for information or warning purposes.

I prefer to add extension methods to the `Maybe` to provide a set of event handler functions:

```
public static class MaybeLoggingExtensions
{
    public static Maybe<T> OnSomething(this Maybe<T> @this, Action<T> a)
    {
        if(@this is Something<T>)
        {
            a(@this);
        }

      return @this;
    }

    public static Maybe<T> OnNothing(this Maybe<T> @this, Action a)
    {
        if(@this is Nothing<T> _)
        {
            a();
```

```
    }

    return @this;

    public static Maybe<T> OnError(this Maybe<T> @this, Action<Exception> a)
    {
        if(@this is Error<T> e)
        {
            a(e.CapturedError);
        }

        return @this;
    }
}
```

The way I'd use this then, is more like this:

```
var idMaybe  idValue.ToMaybe();
var transOne = idMaybe.Bind(x => transformationOne(x))
    .OnSomething(x => this.Logger.LogInformation("Processing item " + x.Id))
    .OnNothing(() => this.Logger.LogWarning("No record found for " + idValue))
    .OnError(e => this.Logger.LogError(e, "An error occurred for " + idValue));
```

This is fairly usable, although it does have a drawback. The OnNothing() and OnError() states will proliferate from Bind() to Bind() unmodified, so if we have a long list of Bind() calls with OnNothing() or OnError() handler functions, they'll all fire every time, like this:

```
var idMaybe  idValue.ToMaybe();
var transOne = idMaybe.Bind(x => transformationOne(x))
    .OnNothing(() => this.Logger.LogWarning("Nothing happened one"));
var transTwo = transOne.Bind(x => transformationTwo(x))
    .OnNothing(() => this.Logger.LogWarning("Nothing happened two"));
var returnValue = transTwo.Bind(x => transformationThree(x))
    .OnNothing(() => this.Logger.LogWarning("Nothing happened three"));
```

In this code sample, all three OnNothing() functions will fire, and three warning logs will be written. You may want that or you may not. It might not be all that interesting after the first Nothing.

I *do* have a solution for this issue, but it means quite a lot more coding. Create a new instance of Nothing and Error that descend from the originals:

```
public class UnhandledNothing<T> : Nothing<T>
{
}

public class UnhandledError<T> : Error<T>
{
}
```

We'd also need to modify the Bind() function so that these are the types that are returned when switching from the Something path to one of these:

```
public static Maybe<TOut> Bind<TIn, TOut>(
    this Maybe<TIn> @this,
    Func<TIn, TOut> f)
{
    try
    {
        Maybe<TOut> updatedValue = @this switch
        {
            Something<TIn> s when
                !EqualityComparer<TIn>.Default.Equals(s.Value, default) =>
                    new Something<TOut>(f(s.Value)),
            Something<TIn> s when
                s.GetType().GetGenericArguments()[0].IsPrimitive =>
                    new Something<TOut>(f(s.Value)),
            Something<TIn> _ => new UnhandledNothing<TOut>(),
            Nothing<TIn> _ => new Nothing<TOut>(),
            UnhandledNothing<TIn> _ => new UnhandledNothing<TOut>(),
            Error<TIn> e => new Error<TOut>(e.ErrorMessage),
            UnhandledError<TIn> e => new UnhandledError<TOut>(e.CapturedError),
            _ => new Error<TOut>(
                new Exception("New Maybe state that isn't coded for!: " +
                    @this.GetType()))
        };
        return updatedValue;
    }
    catch (Exception e)
    {
        return new UnhandledError<TOut>(e);
    }
}
```

Then, finally, we need to update the handler functions:

```
public static class MaybeLoggingExtensions
{

  public static Maybe<T> OnNothing(this Maybe<T> @this, Action a)
    {
        if(@this is UnhandledNothing<T> _)
        {
            a();
            return new Nothing<T>();
        }

        return @this;
    }

    public static Maybe<T> OnError(this Maybe<T> @this, Action<Exception> a)
    {
        if(@this is UnhandledError<T> e)
```

```
        {
            a(e.CapturedError);
            return new Error<T>(e.CapturedError);
        }

        return @this;
    }
}
```

When a switch happens from Something to one of the other states, the Maybe switches to a state that not only signals that either Nothing or an Exception occurred, but also that nothing has yet handled that state.

Once one of the handler functions is called, and an unhandled state is found, then the callback is triggered to log (or whatever) and a new object is returned that maintains the same state type, but this time indicating that is no longer unhandled.

In the previous example with multiple Bind() calls with OnNothing() functions attached, only the first OnNothing() will actually be triggered; the rest will be ignored.

Nothing is stopping you from still using a pattern-matching statement to examine the type of the Maybe to perform an action after the Maybe reaches its final destination, elsewhere in the codebase.

Maybe and Async

I know what you're going to ask me next. Look, I'm going to have to let you down gently. I'm already married. Oh? My mistake. Async and monads. Yeah, OK. Moving on…

How do you handle calls inside a monad to processes that are asynchronous? Honestly, it's not all that hard. Leave the Maybe Bind() functions we've already written and add these to the codebase as well:

```
public static async Task<Maybe<TOut>> BindAsync<TIn, TOut>(
    this Maybe<TIn> @this,
    Func<TIn, Task<TOut>> f)
{
    try
    {
        Maybe<TOut> updatedValue = @this switch
        {
            Something<TIn> s when
                EqualityComparer<TIn>.Default.Equals(s.Value, default) =>
                    new Something<TOut>(await f(s.Value)),
            Something<TIn> _ => new Nothing<TOut>(),
            Nothing<TIn> _ => new Nothing<TOut>(),
            Error<TIn> e => new Error<TOut>(e.ErrorMessage),
            _ => new Error<TOut>(
                new Exception("New Maybe state that isn't coded for!: " +
```

```
                    @this.GetType()))
        };
        return updatedValue;
    }
    catch (Exception e)
    {
        return new Error<TOut>(e);
    }
}
```

All we've done here is wrap another layer around the value we're passing around. The first layer is the Maybe—representing that the operation we're trying may not have worked. The second layer is the Task—representing that an async operation needs to be carried out first, before we can get to the Maybe.

Using this out in your wider codebase is probably best done a line at a time so you can avoid mixing up the async and non-async versions in the same chain of Bind() calls. Otherwise, you could end up with a Task<T> being passed around as a type, rather than the actual type, T. Also, it means you can separate out each async call and use an await statement to get the real value to pass along to the next Bind() operation.

Nested Maybes

A problem scenario can occur with the Maybes I've shown so far. I came to realize this scenario existed only after I'd changed an awful lot my interfaces to have Maybe<T> as the return type for anything involving an external interaction.

Imagine that we've created a couple of data loaders of some description. They could be databases, web APIs, or something else; it doesn't matter:

```
public interface DataLoaderOne
{
    Maybe<string> GetStringOne();
}

public interface DataLoaderTwo
{
    Maybe<string> GetStringTwo(string stringOne);
}

public interface DataLoaderThree
{
    Maybe<string> GetStringThree(string stringTwo);
}
```

In some other part of the code, we want to orchestrate calls to each of these interfaces in turn by using a Bind() call.

Note that the point of the Maybe<string> return type is that we can reference them through Bind() functions, and if any of the dataLoader calls fail, the subsequent steps *won't* be executed and we'll get a Nothing<string or Error<string> at the end to examine:

```
var finalString = dataLoaderOne.GetStringOne()
    .Bind(x => dataLoaderTwo.GetStringTwo(x))
    .Bind(x => dataLoaderThree.GetStringThree(x));
```

What we'll find, though, is that this code won't compile. Why do you suppose that is?

Three function calls are at work here, and all three return the type Maybe<string>. Look at what happens a line at a time:

1. GetStringOne() returns a Maybe<string>. So far, so good.

2. The Bind() call attaches to the Maybe<string> and unpacks it to a string to pass to GetStringTwo(), whose return type is popped into a new Maybe for safekeeping.

3. The next Bind() call unwraps the return type of that last bind so that it's only the return type of GetStringTwo()—but GetStringTwo() didn't return a string; it returned Maybe<string>. So, on this second Bind() call, x is actually equal to Maybe<string>, which can't be passed into GetStringThree()!

We *could* solve this by directly accessing the value out of the Maybe stored in x, but first we'd need to cast it to a Something. What if it weren't a something, though? What if an error had occurred in GetStringOne() talking to the database? What if no string could be found?

We basically need a way to unpack a nested Maybe, but *only* in the event that it returns a Something containing a real value. In all other cases, we need to match its unhappy path (Nothing or Error).

One way to do it is with another Bind() function to sit alongside the other two already created, but this one specifically handles the issue of nested Maybes.

We could do it like this:

```
public static Maybe<TOut> Bind<TIn, TOut>(
    this Maybe<Maybe<TIn>> @this, Func<TIn, TOut> f)
{
    try
    {
        var returnValue = @this switch
        {
            Something<Maybe<TIn>> s => s.Value.Bind(f),
            Error<Maybe<TIn>> e => new Error<TOut>(e.ErrorMessage),
            Nothing<Maybe<TIn>> => new Nothing<TOut>(),
```

```
            _ => new Error<TOut>(
                new Exception(
                    "New Maybe state that isn't coded for!: " + @this.GetType())))
        };
        return returnValue;


    }
    catch (Exception e)
    {
        return new Error<TOut>(e);
    }
}
```

We're taking the nested bind (Maybe<Maybe<string>>) and calling Bind() on it, which unwraps the first layer, leaving simply Maybe<string> inside the Bind() callback function. From there, we can just use the exact same logic on the Maybe as in previous Bind() functions.

We would need do this for the async version as well:

```
public static async Task<Maybe<TOut>> BindAsync<TIn, TOut>(
    this Maybe<Maybe<TIn>> @this,
    Func<TIn, TOut> f)
{
    try
    {
        var returnValue = await @this.Bind(async x =>
        {
            var updatedValue = @this switch
            {
              Something<TIn> s when
                EqualityComparer<TIn>.Default.Equals(s.Value, default(TIn)) =>
                  new Something<TOut>(await f(s.Value)),
              Something<TIn> _ => new Nothing<TOut>(),
              Nothing<TIn> _ => new Nothing<TOut>(),
              Error<TIn> e => new Error<TOut>(e.CapturedError)
            }
            return updatedValue;
        });
        return returnValue;
    }
    catch(Exception e)
    {
        return new Error<TOut>(e);
    }
}
```

If you want another way to think about this process, think of the SelectMany() function in LINQ. If we feed it an array of arrays—a multidimensional array—we get back a single-dimension, flat array. This handling of nested Maybe objects now allows us to do the same thing with monads. This is actually one of the "laws" of monads—the properties that anything that calls itself a monad is expected to follow.

In fact, that leads me neatly onto the next topic. What exactly are laws, what are they for, and how do we make sure our C# monads follow them too?

The Laws

Strictly speaking, a true monad must conform to a set of rules (known as *laws*). I'll briefly talk through each of these laws so you'll know for yourself whether you're looking at a real monad.

Left Identity Law

The *left identity law* states that a monad, given a function as a parameter to its `Bind()` method, will return something that is entirely the equivalent of just running the function directly with no side effects. Here's some C# code to demonstrate:

```
Func<int, int> MultiplyByTwo = x => x * 2;
var input = 100;
var runFunctionOutput = MultiplyByTwo(input);

var monadOutput = new Something<int>(input).Bind(MultiplyByTwo);

// runFunctionOutput and monadOutput.Value should both
// be identical - 200 - to conform to the Left Identity Law.
```

Right Identity Law

Before I explain the right identity law, I need to move back a few steps. First, I need to explain *functors*. These are functions that convert a thing, or list of things, from one form into another. `Map()`, `Bind()`, and `Select()` are all examples of functors.

The simplest functor that exists is the *Identity functor*. This is a function that, given an input, returns it unaltered and with no side effects. The Identity functor can have its uses, when you're composing functions together.

The only reason to be interested in it here and now is that it's the basis of the second monad law: the *right identity law*. This law indicates that a monad, when given an Identity functor in its `Bind()` function, will return the original value with no side effects.

We could test the `Maybe` created in Chapter 6 like this:

```
Func<int,int> identityInt = (int x) => x;
var input = 200;
var result = new Something<int>(input).Bind(identityInt);
// result = 200
```

The `Maybe` takes a function that doesn't result in an error or `null`, executes it, and then returns exactly whatever comes out of it and nothing else.

The basic gist of both of these first two laws is simply that the monad can't interfere in any way with the data coming in or going out, or in the execution of the function provided as a parameter to the `Bind()` method. A monad is simply a pipe down which functions and data flow.

Associativity Law

The first two laws should be fairly trivial, and our `Maybe` implementation fulfills them both. The last law, the *associativity law*, is a bit harder to explain.

It basically means that the way the monads are nested doesn't matter; you always end up with a single monad containing a value at the end. Here's a simple C# example:

```
var input = 100;
var op1 = (int x) => x * 2;
var op2 = (int x) => x + 100;

var versionOne = new Something<int>(input)
    .Bind(op1)
    .Bind(op2);

    // versionOne.Value = 100 * 2 + 100 = 300

    var versionTwo = new Something<int>(input)
        .Bind(x => new Something<int>(x).Bind(op1)).Bind(op2);

    // If we don't implement something to fulfill the
    // associativity law, we'll end up with a type of
    // Something<Something<int>>, where we want this to be
    // the exact same type and value as versionOne
```

Look back to my description of how to deal with nested `Maybe`s in "Nested Maybes" on page 161 and you'll see how this code is implemented.

With any luck, now that you've seen the three monad laws, I've proven that my `Maybe` is a proper, no-holds-barred, honest-to-dog monad.

In the next section, I'll show you another monad you might use to do away with the need for storing variables that need to be shared.

Reader

Let's imagine for a moment that we're putting together a report of some kind. It does a series of pulls of data from an SQL Server database.

First, we need to grab the record for a given user. Next, using that record, we get their most recent order from our entirely imaginary bookshop.[8] Finally, we turn the most recent Order record into a list of items from the order and return a few details from them in a report.

We want to take advantage of a monad-style Bind() operation, so how do we ensure that the data from each step is passed along with the database connection object? That's no problem; we can throw together a tuple and simply pass along both objects:

```
public string MakeOrderReport(string userName) =>
    (
        Conn: this.connFactory.MakeDbConnection(),
        userid
    )
    .Bind(x => (
        x.Conn,
        Customer: this.customerRepo.GetCustomer(x.Conn, x.userName)
    )
    .Bind(x => (
        x.Conn,
        Order: this.orderRepo.GetCustomerOrders(x.Conn, x.Customer.Id)
    ),
    .Bind(x => this.Order.Items.First())
    .Bind(x => string.Join("\r\n", x));
```

This is a workable solution, but it's a bit ugly. A few repeated steps exist only to allow the connection object to be persisted between Bind() operations. It's harming the readability of the function.

The function isn't pure either, if you think about it. It has to create a database connection, which is a form of side effect.

We can use another functional structure to solve all these problems: the Reader monad. It's FP's answer to dependency injection, but on the functional level, rather than into a class.

In the case of the preceding function, it's the IDbConnection that we want to inject so it can be instantiated elsewhere, leaving the MakeOrderReport() pure—i.e., free of any side effects.

Here's an incredibly simple use of Reader:

```
var reader = new Reader<int, string>(e => e.ToString());
var result = reader.Run(100);
```

---

8 I'm the imaginary owner, and you can be the imaginary person who helps customers find what they want. Aren't I generous?

This code defines a `Reader`, which takes a function that it stores but doesn't execute. The function has an "environment" variable type as its parameter—this is the currently unknown value we're going to inject in the future—and returns a value based on that parameter (in this case, an integer).

The "int → string" function is stored in `Reader` on the first line. On the second line, we call the `Run()` function, which provides the missing environment variable value (here, 100). Since the environment has finally been provided, `Reader` can therefore use it to return a real value.

Since this is a monad, that also means we should have `Bind()` functions to provide a flow. This is how they'd be used:

```
var reader = new Reader<int, int>(e => e * 100)
    .Bind(x => x / 50)
    .Bind(x => x.ToString());

var result = reader.Run(100);
```

Note that the type of the `reader` variable is `Reader<int, string>`. That's because every `Bind()` call places a wrapper around the previous function that has the same alternate return type but a different parameter. In the first line with the parameter `e => e * 100`, that function will be executed later, after `Run()`. And so on...

This is a more realistic use of `Reader`:

```
public Customer GetCustomerData(string userName, IDbConnection db) =>
    new Reader(this.customerRepo.GetCustomer(userName, x))
    .Run(db);
```

Alternatively, we can simply return `Reader` and then allow the outside world to continue using `Bind()` calls to modify it further before the `Run()` function turns it into a proper value:

```
public Reader<IdbConnection, User> GetCustomerData(string userName) =>
    new Reader(this.customerRepo.GetCustomer(userName, x));
```

This way, the same function can be called many times, with the `Reader`'s `Bind()` function used to convert it to the actual type we want. For example, say we want to get the customer's order data:

```
var dbConn = this.DbConnectionFactory.GetConnection();

var orders = this._customerRepo.GetCustomerData("simon.painter")
    .Bind(X => x.OrderData.ToArray())
    .Run(dbConn);
```

Think of this approach as creating a box that can be opened only by inserting a variable of the correct type.

The use of `Reader` also means it's easy to inject a mock `IDbConnection` into these functions and write unit tests based on them.

Depending on how we want to structure our code, we could even consider exposing `Readers` on interfaces. We don't have to pass in a dependency like a `DbConnection`; we could pass in an ID value for a database table or anything we like—something like this, perhaps:

```
public interface IDataStore
{
    Reader<int,Customer> GetCustomerData();
    Reader<Guid,Product> GetProductData();
    Reader<int,IEnumerable<Order>> GetCustomerOrders();
}
```

You could use this in all sorts of ways; the choice is all a matter of what suits you and what you're trying to do. In the next section, I'll show a variation on this idea—the `State` monad.

State

In principle, a `State` monad is similar to `Reader`. A container is defined that requires some form of state object to convert itself into a proper final piece of data. `Bind()` functions are used to provide additional data transformations, but nothing will happen until `State` is provided.

`State` differs from `Reader` in two ways:

- Instead of an environment type, it's known as the *state* type.
- Two items, not one, are being passed between `Bind()` operations.

In a `Reader` monad, the original environment type is seen only at the beginning of the chain of `Bind()` functions. With a `State` monad, the type persists all the way through to the end. The `State` type, and whatever the current value is set to, are stored in a tuple that is passed from one step to the next. Both the value and `State` can be replaced with new values each time. The value can change types, but `State` is a single type throughout the whole process that can have its values updated, if required.

You can also arbitrarily fetch or replace the `State` object in the `State` monad at any time by using functions.

My implementation doesn't strictly adhere to the way you'll see it in languages like Haskell, but I'd argue that implementations of that kind are a pain in C#, and I'm not convinced that there's any point to doing it. The version I'm showing you here could well have some use in daily C# coding:

```
public class State<TS, TV>
{
    public TS CurrentState { get; init; }
    public TV CurrentValue { get; init; }
    public State(TS s, TV v)
    {
        CurrentValue = v;
        CurrentState = s;
    }
}
```

The State monad doesn't have multiple states, so there's no need for a base abstract class. It's just a simple class with two properties—a value and a state (i.e., the thing we'll pass along through every instance).

The logic has to be implemented in extension methods:

```
public static class StateMonadExtensions
{

public static State<TS, TV> ToState<TS, TV>(this TS @this, TV value) =>
    new(@this, value);

public static State<TS, TV> Update<TS, TV>(
        this State<TS, TV> @this,
        Func<TS, TS> f
    ) => new(f(@this.CurrentState), @this.CurrentValue);
}
```

As usual, we don't have a lot of code to implement but plenty of interesting effects.

This is the way I'd use it:

```
public IEnumerable<Order> MakeOrderReport(string userName) =>
    this.connFactory.MakeDbConnection().ToState(userName)
        .Bind((s, x) => this.customerRepo.GetCustomer(s, x))
        .Bind((s, x) => this.orderRepo.GetCustomreOrders(s, x.Id))
```

The idea here is that the state object is being passed along the chain as s, and the result of the last Bind() is passed as x. Based on both of those values, we can determine what the next value should be.

This just leaves out the ability to update the current state. We'd do that with this extension method:

```
public static State<TS, TV>Update<TS,TV>(
    this State<TS,TV> @this,
    Func<TS, TS> f
) => new(@this.CurrentState, f(@this.CurrentState));
```

Here's a simple example for the sake of illustration:

```
var result = 10.ToState(10)
    .Bind((s, x) => s * x)
```

```
.Bind((s, x) => x - s) // s=10, x = 90
.Update(s => s - 5) // s=5, x = 90
.Bind((s, x) => x / 5); // s=5, x = 18
```

Using this technique, we can have arrow functions with a few bits of state that will flow from one Bind() operation to the next, and that we can even update when needed. The technique prevents us from either being forced to turn our neat arrow function into a full function with curly braces, or passing a large, ungainly tuple containing the read-only data through each Bind().

This implementation has left off the form you'll find in Haskell, where the initial State value is passed in only when the complete chain of Bind() functions has been defined, but I'd argue that in a C# context, this version is more useful and certainly an awful lot easier to code!

Maybe a State?

You may notice in the previous code sample that there is no way to use the Bind() function like a Maybe, to capture error conditions and null results coming back in any of the several possible states. Is it possible to merge Maybe and Reader into a single monad that both persists a State object *and* handles errors?

Yes, and we could accomplish this in several ways, depending on how exactly we're planning to use the monad. I'll show you my preferred solution. First, we adjust the State class so that instead of a value, it stores a Maybe containing the value:

```
public class State<TS, TV>
{
    public TS CurrentState { get; init; }
    public Maybe<TV> CurrentValue { get; init; }
    public State(TS s, TV v)
    {
        CurrentValue = new Something<TV>(v);
        CurrentState = s;
    }
}
```

Then we adjust the Bind() function to take Maybe into account, but without changing the signature of the function:

```
public static State<TS, TNew> Bind<TS, TOld, TNew>(
    this State<TS, TOld> @this, Func<TS, TOld, TNew> f) =>
    new(@this.CurrentState, @this.CurrentValue.Bind(
        x => f(@this.CurrentState, x))
    );
```

The usage is just about exactly the same, except that Value is now of type Maybe<T> instead of simply T. That affects only the return value from the container function, though:

```
public Maybe<IEnumerable<order>> MakeOrderReport(string userName) =>
    this.connFactory.MakeDbConnection().ToState(userName)
        .Bind((s, x) => this.customerRepo.GetCustomer(s, x))
        .Bind((s, x) => this.orderRepo.GetCustomerOrders(s, x.Id))
```

Whether you want to merge the concepts of the Maybe and the State monads in this way or would rather keep them separate is entirely up to you. If you do follow this approach, you'd just need to make sure to use a switch expression to translate Maybe into a single, concrete value at some point.

Here's a last point to bear in mind too: the CurrentValue object of the State monad doesn't have to be data; it can be a Func delegate, allowing you to have a bit of functionality ported between Bind() calls.

In the next section, I'll show you what *else* might be a monad you've already been using in C#.

Examples You're Already Using

Believe it or not, you've likely already been using monads for a while if you've been working with C# for any amount of time. Let's take a look at a few examples.

Enumerable

If an enumerable isn't a monad, it's as close as it gets, at least after we invoke LINQ, which as you already know is developed based on FP concepts.

The enumerable Select() method operates on individual elements within an enumerable, but it still obeys the left identity law:

```
var op = x => x * 2;
var input = new [] { 100 };

var enumerableResult = input.Select(op);
var directResult = new [] { op(input.First()) };
// both equal the same value - { 200 }
```

The enumerable also obeys the right identity law:

```
var op = x => x;
var input = new [] { 100 };

var enumerableResult = input.Select(op);
var directResult = new [] { op(input.First()) };
// both equal the same value - { 100 }
```

That just leaves the associativity law, which is still a necessity to be considered a true monad. Does the enumerable follow that? It does, of course. By use of SelectMany().

Consider this:

```
var createEnumerable = (int x) => Enumerable.Range(0, x);
var input = new [] { 100, 200 }
var output = input.SelectMany(createEnumerable);
// output = single dimension array with 300 elements
```

There we have it, nested enumerables outputted as a single enumerable. That's the associativity law. Ipso facto, QED, and so on. Yeah. Enumerables are monads.

Task

What about tasks? Are they monads too? I bet you a beer of your choice that they're absolutely monads, and I can prove it.[9] Let's run through the laws once again.

According to the left identity law, a function call with a task should match calling the function call directly. That's slightly tricky to prove, in that an async method always returns a type of Task or Task<T>, which is the same as Maybe<T> in many ways, if you think about it. It's a wrapper around a type that might or might not resolve to actual data. But if we move back a level of abstraction, we can still demonstrate that the law is obeyed:

```
public Func<int> op = x => x * 2;
public async Task<int> asyncOp(int x) => await Task.FromResult(op(x));

var taskResult = await asyncOp(100);
var nonTaskResult = op(100);
// The result is the same - 200
```

I'm not saying that this is C# code I'd necessarily be proud of, but it does at least prove the point that whether we call op through an async wrapper method or not, the result is the same. That's the left identity law confirmed. How about the right identity law? Honestly, that's roughly the same code again:

```
// Notice the function is simply returning x back again unchanged this time.
public Func<int> op = x => x;
public async Task<int> asyncOp(int x) => await Task.FromResult(op(x));

var taskResult = await asyncOp(100);
var nonTaskResult = op(100);
// The result is the same as the initial input - 100
```

That's the identity laws settled. What about the equally important associativity law? Believe it or not, there is a way to demonstrate this with tasks:

---

9 I like dark ales and European-style lagers. That strong stuff they make in Minnesota is terrific too.

```
async Task<int> op1(int x) => await Task.FromResult(10 * x);
async Task<int> pp2() => await Task.FromResult(100);
var result = await op1(await pp2());
// result = 1,000
```

Here we have a `Task<int>` being passed into another `Task<int>` as a parameter, but with nested calls to `await`, it's all possible to flatten out to a simple `int`, which is the actual type of result.

Hopefully, I've earned my beer. Mine's a pint, please.[10] A European-style half-liter is fine as well.

Other Structures

Honestly and truly—if you're OK with my version of the `Maybe` monad and aren't bothered about going further, feel free to skip ahead to Chapter 8. You can easily achieve most of what you likely want with `Maybe` alone. I'm going to describe a few other kinds of monads that exist out there in the wider FP language world, which you *might* want to consider implementing in C#.

These monads might be of interest if squeezing out the last few vestiges of non-functional code from C# is your intention. They might also be of interest from a theoretical perspective. It's entirely up to you, though, whether to take the monad concept further and continue to implement these others.

Now, strictly speaking, the version of the `Maybe` monad I've been building up over this chapter and Chapter 6 is a mix of two monads. A true `Maybe` monad has only two states: `Something` (or `Just`) and `Nothing` (or `Empty`). That's it.

The monad for handling error states is the `Either` (aka `Result`) monad. That has two states: `Left` and `Right`. `Right` is the "happy" path, where every function passed into the `Bind()` command works, and all is right with the world. `Left` is the "unhappy" path, where an error of some kind occurs, and the error is contained in `Left`.

The `Left` and `Right` naming convention presumably comes from the recurring concept in many cultures that the left hand is evil and the right hand is good. This is even captured in bits of our language—the Latin word for "left" is "sinister." In these enlightened days, however, we no longer drive out left-handed folks from our homes or whatever it is they used to do.[11]

---

10 That's 568 milliliters. I'm aware other countries have other definitions of the word.

11 My brother is among the lefties. Hi, Mark—you've been mentioned in a programming book! I wonder whether you'll ever know about it.

I won't spell out that implementation here; you can basically achieve it by taking my version of Maybe and removing the Nothing class.

Similarly, you can make a true Maybe by removing the Error class—although I'd argue that by combining the two into a single entity, you have something that can handle just about any situation you're likely to encounter when interacting with external resources.

Is my approach pure and fully correct classical functional theory? No. Is it useful in production code? 100% yes.

Many more monads exist beyond Maybe and Either, and if you move into a programming language like Haskell, you'll likely make regular use of them. Here are a few examples:

Identity
> A monad that simply returns whatever value you feed in. This monad can be useful when getting into deeper functional theory in a more purely functional language, but doesn't really have an application here in C#.

IO
> Used to allow interactions with external resources without introducing impure functions. In C#, we can follow the inversion-of-control pattern (i.e., dependency injection) to allow us to get around any issues for testing, etc.

Writer
> Used to allow something like a logfile entry to be generated with each Bind() operation that's passed to the monad. I'm not sure there's any special benefit to implementing this in C#, however.

As you can see from this list, many other monads are available in the FP world, but I'd argue that most or all don't provide any real benefit to us. At the end of the day, C# is a hybrid functional/object-oriented language. It has been extended to allow support for FP concepts, but it's never going to be a purely functional language, and there's no benefit to trying to treat it as such.

I strongly recommend experimenting with the Maybe/Either monad, but beyond that, I honestly wouldn't bother, unless you're curious to see just how far you can push the idea of FP in C#.[12] It's not necessarily something for your production environment, though.

---

12 C# rather than .NET in general; F# is .NET as well.

In the final section, I'll provide a complete worked example of how to use monads in an application.

A Worked Example

OK, here we go. Let's put it all together in one great, epic heap of monady-functional goodness. We've already talked holidays in this chapter's examples, so this time I'm going to focus on how we're going to get to the airport. This will need a series of lookups and data transformations, all of which would normally require error handling and branching logic if we were to follow a more conventional, object-oriented approach. I hope you'll agree that by using FP techniques and monads, the code looks quite considerably more elegant.

First off, we need our interfaces. We're not going to code each and every single dependency of the code here, so let's just define the interfaces we'll need:

```
public interface IMappingSystem
{
    Maybe<Address> GetAddress(Location l);
}

public interface IRoutePlanner
{
    Task<Maybe<Route>> DetermineRoute(Address a, Address b);
}

public interface ITrafficMonitor
{
    Maybe<TrafficAdvice> GetAdvice(Route r);
}

public interface IPricingCalculator
{
    decimal PriceRoute(Route r);
}
```

Now we'll write the code to consume them all. In the specific scenario I'm imagining, it's the near future. Driverless cars have become a thing. Most people no longer own personal vehicles and simply use an app on their phones to have a car brought out of the cloud of automated vehicles, direct to their homes.

Here's the process:

1. The initial inputs are the starting location and destination, provided by the user.
2. Each of these locations needs to be looked up in a mapping system and converted to proper addresses.
3. The user's account needs to be fetched from the internal data store.
4. The route needs to be checked with a traffic service.
5. A pricing service has to be called to determine a charge for the journey.
6. The price is returned to the user.

In code, that process might look like this:

```
public Maybe<decimal> DeterminePrice(Location from, Location to)
{
    var addresses = this.mapping.GetAddress(from).Bind(x =>
        (From: x,
         To: this.mapping.GetAddress(to)));

    var route = await addresses.BindAsync (async x =>
        await this.router.DetermineRoute(x.From, x.To));

    var trafficInfo = route.Bind(x => this.trafficAdvisor.GetAdvice(x));
    var hasRoadWorks = trafficInfo is Something<TrafficAdvice> s &&
        s.Value.RoadworksOnRoute;

    var price = route.Bind(x => this.pricing.PriceRoute(x));
    var finalPrice = route.Bind(x => hasRoadWorks ? x *= 1.1 : x);

    return finalPrice;
}
```

This is far easier, isn't it? Before I end this chapter, I want to unpack a few details of what's happening in this code sample.

First, there's no error handling anywhere. Any of those external dependencies could result in an error being thrown, or no details being located in their respective data stores. The monad Bind() function handles all that logic. If, for example, the router is unable to determine a route (maybe a network error occurs), Maybe will be set to an Error<Route> at that point, and none of the subsequent operations will be executed. The final return type will be Error<decimal>, because the Error class is re-created at each step, but the actual Exception is passed between instances. The outside world is responsible for doing something with the final returned value once it receives that value and checks to see whether it's a Something<decimal> or a form of error state. The receiving code can then decide how to communicate this information to the end user.

If we followed the OOP approach to this code, the function would most likely be two to three times longer, in order to include try/catch blocks and checks against each object to confirm that they're valid.

I've used tuples when I want to build up a set of inputs. In the case of the Address objects, this means that if the first address isn't found, the lookup for the second won't be attempted. It also means that both of the inputs required by the second function to be run are available in a single location, which we can then access with another Bind() call (assuming a real value is returned by the address lookup).

The final few steps don't actually involve calls to external dependencies, but by continuing to use the Bind() function, anything inside its parameter lambda expression can be written with the assumption that a real value is available, because if there weren't, the lambda wouldn't be executed.

And there we have it, a pretty much fully functional bit of C# code. I hope it is to your liking.

Summary

In this chapter, we explored the dreaded FP concept that has been known to make grown developers tremble in their inexpensive footwear. All being well, monads shouldn't be a mystery to you any longer.

I've shown you how to do the following:

- Massively reduce the amount of required code
- Introduce an implicit error-handling system

You've accomplished this by using the Maybe monad, along with learning how to make one yourself.

In the next chapter, I'll briefly present the concept of currying. I'll see you on the next page.

CHAPTER 8

Currying and Partial Application

Currying and partial application are two more functional concepts that come straight out of old math papers. The former has absolutely nothing to do with Indian food, delicious though it is;[1] in fact, it's named after the preeminent American mathematician Haskell Brooks Curry, after whom no fewer than three programming languages are named.[2]

As noted in Chapter 1, *currying* came from Curry's work on combinatory logic, which served as a basis for modern FP. Rather than give a dry, formal definition, I'll explain by example. This is a bit of vaguely C#-like pseudocode for an Add() function:

```
public interface ICurriedFunctions
{
    decimal Add(decimal a, decimal b);
}

var curry = // some logic for obtaining an implementation of the interface

var answer = curry.Add(100, 200);
```

In this example, we'd expect the answer to simply be 300 (i.e., 100 + 200), which is indeed what it would be.

What if we were to provide only a single parameter, however? Like this:

```
public interface ICurriedFunctions
{
    decimal Add(decimal a, decimal b);
```

---

1 Food tip: if you're ever in Mumbai, try a Tibb's Frankie from Shivaji Park; you won't regret it!

2 Haskell, obviously, but also Brook and Curry, two lesser-known languages.

```
    }

    var curry = // some logic for obtaining an implementation of the interface

    var answer = curry.Add(100); // What could it be?
```

In this scenario, if this were a hypothetical curried function, what do you think you'd have returned to you in answer?

I've devised a rule of thumb when working in FP, as I mentioned in Chapter 1—if there's a question, the answer is likely to be "functions." And that's the case here.

If this were a curried function, the answer variable would be a function. It would be a modified version of the original Add() function, but with the first parameter now set in stone as the value 100, effectively making it a new function that adds 100 to whatever we provide.

We might use the function like this:

```
    public interface ICurriedFunctions
    {
        decimal Add(decimal a, decimal b);
    }

    var curry = // some logic for obtaining an implementation of the interface

    var add100 = curry.Add(100); // Func<decimal,decimal>, adds 100 to the input

    var answerA = add100(200); // 300 -> 200+100
    var answerB = add100(0);   // 100 -> 0+100
    var answerC = add100(900); // 1000 -> 900+100
```

This code is basically a way to start with a function that has a number of parameters, and from it, create multiple, more specific versions of that function. One single base function can become many different functions. You *could* compare it to the OOP concept of inheritance, if you like. But in reality, it's *nothing* at all like inheritance. Only a single function has any logic behind it—the rest are effectively pointers to that base function holding parameters, ready to feed into it.

What exactly is the point of currying, though? How do we use it? I'll explain in the next section.

Currying and Large Functions

In the preceding Add() example, we have only a single pair of parameters, and so we have only two options for what we could do with them when currying is possible:

- Supply the first parameter and get back a function.

- Supply both parameters and get back a value.

How would currying handle a function with more than two base parameters? For this, I'll use an example of a simple CSV parser—i.e., something that takes a CSV text file, breaks it into records by line, and then uses a delimiter (typically, a comma) to break it up again into individual properties within the record.

Let's imagine we've written a parser function to load in a batch of book data:

```
// Input in the format:
//
//title,author,publicationDate
//The Hitch-Hiker's Guide to the Galaxy,Douglas Adams,1979
//Dimension of Miracles,Robert Sheckley,1968
//The Stainless Steel Rat,Harry Harrison,1957
//The Unorthodox Engineers,Colin Kapp,1979

public IEnumerable<Book> ParseBooks(string fileName) =>
    File.ReadAllText(fileName)
        .Split("\r\n")
        .Skip(1) // Skip the header
        .Select(x => x.split(",").ToArray())
        .Select(x => new Book
        {
            Title = x[0],
            Author = x[1],
            PublicationDate = x[2]
        });

var bookData = parseBooks("books.csv");
```

This is all well and good, except that the next two sets of books have different formats. The *books2.csv* file uses pipes instead of commas to separate fields, and *books3.csv* comes from a Linux environment and has \n line endings instead of the Windows-style \r\n.

We could get around this by creating three functions that are near replicas of one another. I'm not keen on unnecessary replication, though, since it adds too many problems for future developers who want to maintain the codebase.

A more reasonable solution is to add in parameters for everything that could possibly change:

```
public IEnumerable<Book> ParseBooks(
  string lineBreak,
  bool skipHeader,
  string fieldDelimiter,
  string fileName
) =>
```

```
File.ReadAllText(fileName)
    .Split(lineBreak)
    .Skip(skipHeader ? 1 : 0)
    .Select(x => x.split(fieldDelimiter).ToArray())
    .Select(x => new Book
    {
        Title = x[0],
        Author = x[1],
        PublicationDate = x[2]
    });

var bookData = ParseBooks(Environment.NewLine, true, ",", "books.csv");
```

Now, if we wanted to follow the nonfunctional approach to the use of this function, we'd have to fill in every parameter for every possible style of CSV file, like this:

```
var bookData1 = ParseBooks(Environment.NewLine, true,  ",", "books.csv");
var bookData2 = ParseBooks(Environment.NewLine, true, "|", "books2.csv");
var bookData3 = ParseBooks("\n", false, ",", "books3.csv");
```

What currying actually means is to supply the parameters one at a time. Any calls to a curried function result either in a new function with one fewer parameter or a concrete value if all parameters for the base function have been supplied.

The calls with the full set of supplied parameters, from the previous code sample, could be replaced like this:

```
// First some magic that curries the parseBooks function
// I'll look into implementation details later, let's just
// understand the theory for now.

var curriedParseBooks = ParseBooks.Curry();

// these two have 3 parameters - string, string, string
var parseSkipHeader = curriedParseBooks(true);
var parseNoHeader = curriedParseBooks(false);

// 2 parameters
var parseSkipHeaderEnvNl = parseSkipHeader(Environment.NewLine);
var parseNoHeaderLinux = parseNoHeader("\n");

// 1 parameter each
var parseSkipHeaderEnvNlCommarDel = parseSkipHeaderEnvNl(",");
var parseSkipHeaderEnvNlPipeDel = parseSkipHeaderEnvNl("|");
var parseNoHeaderLinuxCommarDel = parseNoHeaderLinux(",");


// Actual data, enumerables of Book data
var bookData1 = parseSkipHeaderEnvNlCommarDel("books.csv");
var bookData2 = parseSkipHeaderEnvNlPipeDel("books2.csv");
var bookData3 = parseNoHeaderLinuxCommarDel("books3.csv");
```

The point is that currying turns a function with x parameters into a sequence of x functions, each of which has a single parameter—the last one returning the final result.

We could even write the preceding function calls like this (if we really, really wanted to):

```
var bookData1 = parseBooks(true)(Environment.NewLine)(",")("books.csv")
var bookData2 = parseBooks(true)(Environment.NewLine)("|")("books2.csv")
var bookData3 = parseBooks(true)("\n")(",")("books3.csv")
```

The point of the first example of currying is that we're gradually building up a hyper-specific version of the function that takes only a filename as a parameter. In addition, we're storing all the intermediate versions for potential reuse in building up other functions.

What we're effectively doing here is building up functions like a wall made of LEGO bricks, where each brick is a function. Or, if you want to think about it another way, we have a family tree of functions, with each choice made at each stage causing a branch in the family, as shown in Figure 8-1.

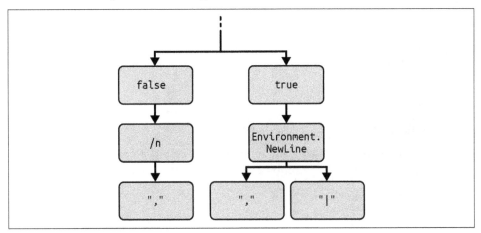

Figure 8-1. A family tree of the parseBooks() functions

Another example that might have uses in production is splitting up a logging function into multiple, more specific functions:

```
// For the sake of this exercise, the parameters are
// an enum (log type - warning, error, info, etc.) and a string
// containing a message to store in the logfile
var logger = getLoggerFunction()
var curriedLogger = logger.Curry();

var logInfo = curriedLogger(LogLevel.Info);
var logWarning = curriedLogger(LogLevel.Warning);
```

```
var logError = curriedLogger(LogLevel.Error);

// You'd use them then, like this:

logInfo("This currying lark works a treat!");
```
This approach has a few useful features:

- We've created only one single function at the end of the day, but from it, managed to create at least three usable variations that can be passed around, requiring only a filename to be usable. That's taking code reuse to an extra level!

- All the intermediate functions are available too. These can either be used directly or as a starting point for creating additional new functions.

C# has another use for currying as well. I'll discuss that in the next section.

Currying and Higher-Order Functions

What if we want to use currying to create a few functions to convert between Celsius and Fahrenheit? We'd start with curried versions of each of the basic arithmetic operations, like this:

```
// once again, the currying process is just magic for now.
// Keep reading for the implementation

var add = ((x,y) => x + y).Curry();
var subtract = ((x,y) => y - x).Curry();
var multiply = ((x,y) => x * y).Curry();
var divide = ((x,y) => y / x).Curry();
```

Using this, along with the map function from a previous chapter, we can create a fairly concise set of function definitions:

```
var celsiusToFahrenheit = x =>
    x.Map(multiply(9))
    .Map(divide(5))
    .Map(add(32));

var fahrenheitToCelsius = x=>
    x.Map(subtract(32))
    .Map(multiply(5))
    .Map(divide(9));
```

Whether you find any of this useful is largely dependent on your use case—what you're trying to achieve and whether currying fits in with it. It's available for you in C# now, as you can see—if, that is, we can find a way to implement it in C#…

Currying in .NET

More functional-based languages can do currying natively with *all* functions in your codebase. So, the big question: can we do anything like this in .NET?

The short answer is "no-ish." The longer answer is "yes, sort of." Currying is not as elegant as in a functional language (e.g., F#), where this is all available out of the box. We either need to hardcode it, create a static class, or hack around with the language a bit and jump through a few hoops.

The hardcoded method assumes that we will always use the function in a curried manner, like this:

```
var Add = (decimal x) => (decimal y) => x + y;
var Subtract = (decimal x) => (decimal y) => y - x;
var Multiply = (decimal x) => (decimal y) => x * y;
var Divide = (decimal x) => (decimal y) => y / x;
```

Note that each function has two sets of arrows, meaning that we've defined one Func delegate that returns another—i.e., the actual type is Func<decimal,Func <decimal,decimal>>. So long as we're using C# 10 or later, we'll be able to take advantage of implicit typing with the var keyword, as in this example. Older versions of C# may need to implicitly state the type of the delegates in the code sample.

The second option is to create a static class that can be referenced from anywhere in the codebase. You can call it what you'd like, but I'm going with F for *functional*:

```
public static class F
{
    public static Func<T1, Func<T2, TOut>> Curry<T1, T2, TOut>(
        Func<T1, T2, TOut> functionToCurry) =>
            (T1 x) => (T2 y) => functionToCurry(x, y);

    public static Func<T1, Func<T2, Func<T3, TOut>>> Curry<T1, T2, T3, TOut>(
        Func<T1, T2, T3, TOut> functionToCurry) =>
            (T1 x) => (T2 y) => (T3 z) => functionToCurry(x, y, z);

    public static Func<T1, Func<T2, Func<T3, Func<T4, TOut>>>>
        Curry<T1, T2, T3, T4, TOut>(
        Func<T1, T2, T3, T4, TOut> functionToCurry) =>
            (T1 x) => (T2 y) => (T3 z) => (T4 a) => functionToCurry(x, y, z, a);
}
```

This effectively places layers of Func delegates between calls to the end function that's being curried, and the areas of code that use it that way.

The downside to this method is that we'll have to create a Curry() method for every possible number of parameters. This example covers functions with two, three, or four parameters. Functions with more than that would need another Curry() method constructed, based on the same formula.

The other issue is that Visual Studio is unable to implicitly determine the type for the function being passed in, so it's necessary to define the function to be curried within the call to F.Curry(), declaring the type of each parameter, like this:

```
var Add = F.Curry((decimal x, decimal y) => x + y);
var Subtract = F.Curry((decimal x, decimal y) => y - x);
var Multiply = F.Curry((decimal x, decimal y) => x * y);
var Divide = F.Curry((decimal y, decimal y) => y / x);
```

The final option—and my preferred option—is to use extension methods to cut down somewhat on the boilerplate code necessary. The definitions would look like this for two, three, and four parameter functions:

```
public static class Ext
{
    public static Func<T1,Func<T2, T3>> Curry<T1,T2,T3>(
    this Func<T1,T2,T3> @this) =>
        (T1 x) => (T2 y) => @this(x, y);

    public static Func<T1,Func<T2,Func<T3,T4>>>Curry<T1,T2,T3,T4>(
    this Func<T1,T2,T3,T4> @this) =>
        (T1 x) => (T2 y) => (T3 z) => @this(x, y, z);

    public static Func<T1,Func<T2,Func<T3,Func<T4,T5>>>>Curry<T1,T2,T3,T4,T5>(
    this Func<T1,T2,T3,T4,T5> @this) =>
        (T1 x) => (T2 y) => (T3 z) => (T4 a) => @this(x, y, z, a);
}
```

That's a fairly ugly block of code, isn't it? The good news is we can just shove that somewhere deep down at the back of our codebase and largely forget it exists.

The usage looks like this:

```
// specifically define the function on one line
// it has to be stored as a `Func` delegate, rather than a
// Lambda expression
var Add = (decimal x, decimal y) => x + y;
var CurriedAdd = Add.Curry();

var add10 = CurriedAdd(10);
var answer = add10(100);
// answer = 110
```

So that's currying. The eagle-eyed among you may have noticed that this chapter is called "Currying *and* Partial Application."

What on earth is partial application? Well, since you asked so very nicely...

Partial Application

Partial application works similarly to currying, but there's a subtle difference. The two terms are often even used (incorrectly) interchangeably.

Currying deals *exclusively* with converting a function with a set of parameters into a series of successive function calls, each with a single parameter (the technical term is a *unary* function). Partial application, on the other hand, allows us to apply as many parameters in one go as we want. Data emerges if all the parameters are filled in.

Returning to our earlier example of the parse function, these are the formats we're working with:

books1
> Windows line endings, header, commas for fields

books2
> Windows line endings, header, pipes for fields

books3
> Linux line endings, no header, commas for fields

With the currying approach, we're creating intermediate steps for setting each parameter of *books3*, even though they're ultimately the only use of each of those parameters. We're also doing the same for the `SkipHeader` and `LineEndings` parameters for *books1* and *books2*, even though they're the same.

We could use code like this to save space:

```
var curriedParseBooks = parseBooks.Curry();

var parseNoHeaderLinuxCommaDel = curriedParseBooks(false)("\n")(",");

var parseWindowsHeader = curriedParseBooks(true)(Environment.NewLine);
var parseWindowsHeaderComma = parseWindowsHeader(",");
var parseWindowsHeaderPipe = parseWindowsHeader("|");

// Actual data, enumerables of Book data
var bookData1 = parseWindowsHeaderComma("books.csv");
var bookData2 = parseWindowsHeaderPipe("books2.csv");
var bookData3 = parseNoHeaderLinuxCommaDel("books3.csv");
```

But the code is much cleaner if we can just use partial application to apply the two parameters neatly:

```
// I'm using an extension method called Partial to apply
// parameters.  Check out the next section for implementation details

var parseNoHeaderLinuxCommarDel = ParseBooks.Partial(false,"\n",",");
```

```
var parseWindowsHeader =
 curriedParseBooks.Partial(true,Environment.NewLine);
var parseWindowsHeaderComma = parseWindowsHeader.Partial(",");
var parseWindowsHeaderPipe = parseWindowsHeader.Partial("|");

// Actual data, enumerables of Book data
var bookData1 = parseWindowsHeaderComma("books.csv");
var bookData2 = parseWindowsHeaderPipe("books2.csv");
var bookData3 = parseNoHeaderLinuxCommarDel("books3.csv");
```

I think that's pretty elegant as a solution, and it still allows us to have reusable intermediate functions where we need them, but still only a single base function. In the next section, I'll show you how to implement this code.

Partial Application in .NET

Here is the bad news: there's absolutely no way whatsoever to elegantly implement partial application in C#. We're going to have to create an extension method for each and every combination of the number of parameters going in and the number of parameters going out.

In the preceding example, we'd need the following:

- Four parameters to one for parseNoHeaderLinuxCommaDel

- Four parameters to two for parseWindowsHeader

- Two parameters to one for parseWindowsHeaderComma and parseWindowsHeader Pipe

Here's what each of those examples looks like:

```
public static class PartialApplicationExtensions
{
    // 4 parameters to 1
    public static Func<T4,TOut> Partial<T1,T2,T3,T4,TOut>(
        this Func<T1,T2,T3,T4,TOut> f,
        T1 one, T2 two, T3 three) => (T4 four) => f(one, two, three, four);

    // 4 parameters to 2
    public static Func<T3,T4,TOut>Partial<T1,T2,T3,T4,TOut>(
        this Func<T1,T2,T3,T4,TOut> f,
        T1 one, T2 two) => (T3 three, T4 four) => f(one, two, three, four);

    // 2 parameters to 1
    public static Func<T2, TOut> Partial<T1,T2,TOut>(
        this Func<T1,T2,TOut> f, T1 one) =>
         (T2 two) => f(one, two);

}
```

If you decide that partial application is a technique you'd like to pursue, you could either add partial methods to your codebase as you feel they're needed, or put aside a block of time to create as many as you think you're ever likely to need.

Summary

Currying and partial application are two powerful, related FP concepts. Sadly, they're not available natively in C# and aren't ever likely to be.

They can be implemented via static classes or extension methods. However, this adds some boilerplate to the codebase, which is ironic, considering that these techniques are intended in part to reduce boilerplate.

Given that C# doesn't support higher-order functions to the same level as F# and other functional languages. C# can't necessarily pass functions around unless they're converted to Func delegates.

Even if functions are converted over to Func, the Roslyn compiler can't always determine parameter types correctly. These techniques will never be as useful in the C# world as they are in other languages. Despite that, though, they have their uses in reducing boilerplate and in enabling a greater level of code reusability than would otherwise be possible.

The decision of whether to use them is a matter of personal preference. I wouldn't regard them as essential for functional C#, but they may be worth exploring nevertheless.

In the next chapter, we'll be exploring the deeper mysteries of indefinite loops in functional C#, and what on earth tail call optimization is.

CHAPTER 9

Indefinite Loops

You've seen in previous chapters how FP replaces `for` and `foreach` loops with LINQ functions like `Select()` or `Aggregate()`. That's absolutely terrific, provided you are working with a fixed-length array, or an enumerable that will determine for itself when it's time to finish iterating.

But what do you do when you aren't at all sure how long you'll want to iterate for? What if you're iterating indefinitely until a condition is met?

I'll start in this chapter by giving you a nonfunctional implementation of the ancient Indian board game Snakes and Ladders.[1] Here are the rules for anyone who had a childhood tragically bereft of this board-game classic:

- The board consists of 100 squares. The players start on square 1 and aim to reach square 100.
- Each player takes a turn to roll a single die and to move their token forward the number of spaces indicated.
- Landing on the bottom of a ladder means the playing piece should "climb" it to the top, advancing closer to square 100.
- Landing on the head of a snake means the playing piece should "slide" down it to the end of the tail, moving farther away from square 100.
- A player who rolls a 6 may take another turn.
- The first player to reach square 100 wins.

---

1 Also known as *Chutes and Ladders* in the US.

This game has all sort of variations, but I'm going with these relatively simple, basic rules. Every edition of the game positions the snakes and ladders in all sorts of ways. The game we'll be making, based on a version published in the early 20th century, looks like Figure 9-1.

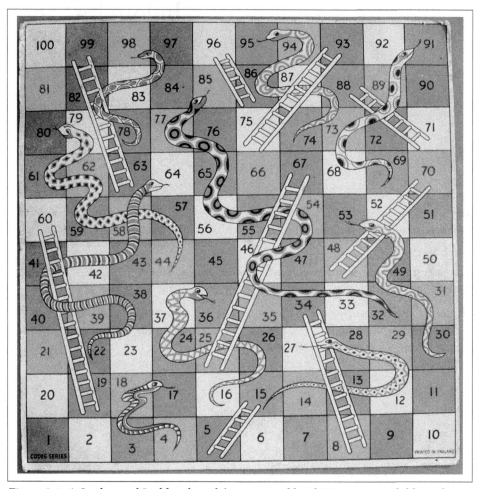

Figure 9-1. A Snakes and Ladders board (source: Auckland Museum; available under CC BY 4.0 license: https://oreil.ly/L_Z0A)

Now, there's no special reason we have to contain the logic for Snakes and Ladders separately— both do the same job. If a player lands on square *x*, move them instantly to square *y*. The only difference between the two is whether the player moves their piece up or down. Logically then, we can treat them as the same thing.

To start off the code, here's a Dictionary of all Snakes and Ladders, which square they start on, and which square they end on:

```
private static readonly Dictionary<int, int> SnakesAndLadders =
    new Dictionary<int, int>
{
    { 5, 15 },
    { 8, 34 },
    { 17, 4 },
    { 19, 60 },
    { 25, 67 },
    { 27, 15 },
    { 36, 16 },
    { 48, 70 },
    { 53, 30 },
    { 63, 99 },
    { 64, 22 },
    { 71, 88 },
    { 75, 93 },
    { 80, 44 },
    { 86, 96 },
    { 91, 69 },
    { 95, 74 },
    { 98. 78 }
};
```

This is what the imperative solution looks like:

```
public int PlaySnakesAndLaddersImperative(int noPlayers, IDieRoll die)
{
    var currentPlayer = 1;
    var playerPositions = new Dictionary<int, int>();
    for (var i = 1; i <= noPlayers; i++)
    {
        playerPositions.Add(i, 1);
    }

    while (!playerPositions.Any(x => x.Value >= 100))
    {
        var dieRoll = die.Roll();
        playerPositions[currentPlayer] += dieRoll;
        if (SnakesAndLadders.ContainsKey(playerPositions[currentPlayer]))
            playerPositions[currentPlayer] =
                SnakesAndLadders[playerPositions[currentPlayer]];
        // another turn for this player if they roll a 6
        if (dieRoll == 6) continue;
            currentPlayer += 1;
        if (currentPlayer > noPlayers)
            currentPlayer = 1;
    }

    return currentPlayer;

}
```

You can't possibly implement this functionality with a `Select()` statement. We can't say when the criteria will be met, and we'll continue to iterate around the `while` loop until one of them is.

So how can we make this functional? A `while` loop is a statement (specifically, a control flow statement), and as such it's not preferred by FP languages.

We have a few options, and I'll describe each, but this is one of those areas requiring some sort of trade-off. Each choice has consequences, and I'll do my best to explain their respective pros and cons.

Buckle up your seat belts, because here we go.

Recursion

The classic FP method for handling indefinite loops is to use recursion. In brief, for those of you unfamiliar with it, *recursion* is the use of a function that calls itself. A condition of some sort determines whether there should be another iteration or whether to actually return data.

If the decision is made at the end of the recursive function, this is known as *tail recursion*.

A functional and recursive implementation of Snakes and Ladders might look like this:

```
public record Player
{
    public int Position { get; set; }
    public int Number { get; set; }
}

public record GameState
{
    public IEnumerable<Player> Players { get; set; }
    public int CurrentPlayer { get; set; }
    public int NumberOfPlayers { get; set; }
}

private static Player UpdatePlayer(Player player, int roll)
{
    var afterDieRoll = player with { Position = player.Position + roll };
    var afterSnakeOrLadder = afterDieRoll with
    {
        Position = SnakesAndLadders.ContainsKey(afterDieRoll.Position)
            ? SnakesAndLadders[afterDieRoll.Position]
            : afterDieRoll.Position
    };
    return afterSnakeOrLadder;
}
```

```
private static GameState PlaySnakesAndLaddersRecursive(
    GameState state,
    IDieRoll die)
{
    var roll = die.Roll();

    var newState = state with
    {
        CurrentPlayer = roll == 6
            ? state.CurrentPlayer
            : state.CurrentPlayer == state.NumberOfPlayers
                ? 1
                : state.CurrentPlayer + 1,
        Players = state.Players.Select(x =>
            x.Number == state.CurrentPlayer
                ? UpdatePlayer(x, roll)
                : x
            ).ToArray()
    };

    return newState.Players.Any(x => x.Position >= 100)
        ? newState
        : PlaySnakesAndLaddersRecursive(newState, die);
}

public int PlaySnakesAndLaddersRecursive(int noPlayers, IDieRoll die)
{
    var state = new GameState
    {
        CurrentPlayer = 1,
        Players = Enumerable.Range(1, noPlayers)
            .Select(x => (x, 1))
            .Select(x => new Player
            {
                Number = x.Item1,
                Position = x.Item2
            }),
        NumberOfPlayers = noPlayers
    };

    var finalState = PlaySnakesAndLaddersRecursive(state, die);
    return finalState.Players.First(x => x.Position >= 100).Number;
}
```

Job done, right? Well, not really, and I would think very carefully before using a function like this one. The issue is that every nested function call adds a new item onto the stack in the .NET runtime, and if the code has a lot of recursive calls, that can either negatively affect performance or kill the application with a stack overflow exception.

If there are guaranteed to be only a handful of iterations, nothing is fundamentally wrong with the recursive approach. You'd also have to be sure that this is revisited if the code's usage is ever significantly changed following an enhancement. This rarely used function with a few iterations one day could turn into something heavily used with hundreds of iterations. If that ever happens, the business might wonder why its wonderful application suddenly becomes near unresponsive almost overnight.

So, as I said, think very carefully before using a recursive algorithm in C#. This has the advantage of being relatively simple and not requiring you to write any boilerplate to make it happen.

F# and many other more strongly functional languages have a feature called *tail call optimization*, which means it's possible to write recursive functions without them exploding the stack. This isn't available in C#, however, and there are no plans to make it available in the future. Depending on the situation, the F# optimization will either create IL code with a while(true) loop, or use an IL command called goto to physically move the execution environment's pointer back to the beginning of the loop.

I did investigate the possibility of referencing a generic tail optimized recursion call from F# and exposing it via a compiled DLL to C#, but that has its own performance issues that makes it a waste of effort.

I've seen another possibility discussed online, and that's to add a post-build event that directly manipulates the .NET IL that C# compiles to so that C# makes retrospective use of the F# tail call optimization feature. That's clever but sounds too much like hard work to me. It would be a potential extra maintenance task too.

In the next section, I'll present a technique to simulate tail call optimization in C#.

Trampolining

I'm not entirely sure where the term *trampolining* came from, but it predates .NET. The earliest references I could find were academic papers from the '90s, looking at implementing some of the features of LISP in C. I'd guess it's even a little older than that, though.

The basic idea of trampolining is that we have a function that takes a *thunk* as a parameter, a thunk being a block of code stored in a variable. In C#, these are implemented as Func or Action. Having got the thunk, we create an indefinite loop with while(true) and some way of assessing a condition that determines whether the loop should terminate. This might be done with an additional Func that returns a bool or some sort of wrapper object that needs to be updated with each iteration by the thunk.

But at the end of the day, what we're looking at is basically hiding a while loop at the back of our codebase. It's true that while isn't purely functional, but this is one of those places where we might need to compromise. Fundamentally, C# is a hybrid language, supporting both OOP and FP paradigms. There are always going to be places where it's not going to be possible for C# to behave in exactly the way F# does. This is one of them.

We could implement trampolining in numerous ways, but this is the one I'd tend to go for:

```
public static class FunctionalExtensions
{
    public static T IterateUntil<T>(
        this T @this,
        Func<T, T> updateFunction,
        Func<T, bool> endCondition)
    {
        var currentThis = @this;

        while (!endCondition(currentThis))
        {
            currentThis = updateFunction(currentThis);
        }

        return currentThis;
    }
}
```

By attaching to type T, which is a generic, this extension method therefore attaches to everything in the C# codebase. The first parameter is a Func delegate that updates the type that T represents to a new form based on whatever rules the outside world defines. The second is another Func that returns the condition that will cause the loop to terminate.

Since this is a simple while loop, there aren't any issues with the size of the stack. The code is not pure FP, though. It's a compromise. At the very least, it's a single instance of a while loop that's hidden somewhere, deep in the codebase. It may also be that one day Microsoft will release a new feature that enables proper tail call optimization to be implemented somehow, in which case this function can be reimplemented and the code should continue to work as it did, but with one instance fewer of imperative code features:

```
public int PlaySnakesAndLaddersTrampolining(int noPlayers, IDieRoll die)
{
    var state = new GameState
    {
```

```
        CurrentPlayer = 1,
        Players = Enumerable.Range(1, noPlayers)
            .Select(x => (x, 1))
            .Select(x => new Player
            {
                Number = x.Item1,
                Position = x.Item2
            }),
        NumberOfPlayers = noPlayers
    };

    var finalState = state.IterateUntil(x =>
    {
        var roll = die.Roll();

        var newState = state with
        {
            CurrentPlayer = roll == 6
                ? state.CurrentPlayer
                : state.CurrentPlayer == state.NumberOfPlayers
                    ? 1
                    : state.CurrentPlayer + 1,
            Players = state.Players.Select(x =>
                x.Number == state.CurrentPlayer
                    ? UpdatePlayer(x, roll)
                    : x
            ).ToArray()
        };

        return newState;
    }, x => x.Players.Any(y => y.Position >= 100));

    return finalState.Players.First(x => x.Position >= 100).Number;
}
```

There is another way you can implement trampolining. Functionally, it behaves the same as a hidden while loop and it is pretty much the same in terms of performance as well.

I'm not necessarily convinced that this approach has any additional benefit, and I *personally* feel it looks a little less friendly than a while loop. But it is probably ever so slightly more in accordance with the functional paradigm in that it dispenses with the while statement. Use this alternative version of trampolining if you prefer, but it's a matter of personal preference, in my view.

This version is implemented using a C# command that under just about any other circumstance I'd *implore* you not to use. It has existed in coding since at least the days of BASIC and is still around in some form today: the goto command.

In BASIC, you could move to any arbitrary line of code you wanted by calling goto and specifying the line number. That's often how loops were implemented in BASIC. In C#, however, you need to create tags, and it's only to these tags that goto will move.

Here's a reimplementation of IterateUntil() using two tags. One is called Loop Beginning, which is the equivalent of the { character at the beginning of a while loop. The second tag is called LoopEnding, which represents the } character at the end of a while loop:

```
public static T IterateUntil<T>(
  this T @this,
  Func<T, T> updateFunction,
  Func<T, bool> endCondition)
{
    var currentThis = @this;

  LoopBeginning:

      currentThis = updateFunction(currentThis);
      if(endCondition(currentThis))
          goto LoopEnding;
      goto LoopBeginning;

  LoopEnding:

      return currentThis;
}
```

I'll leave it to you to decide which version you prefer. They're pretty much equivalent. Whatever you do, don't go using goto anywhere else in your code unless you absolutely, positively, completely, and utterly know what you're doing and why there's *no* better option. Like a certain snake-loving, noseless, evil wizard, the goto command is both great and yet also terrible if used unwisely.

It's powerful in that you can create effects and improve efficiency (in some cases) in ways that are impossible via any other means. It's also dangerous in that you no longer have a predictable order of operations—during execution, the pointer can jump to an arbitrary point in the codebase, regardless of whether it makes any sense at all to do so. Used improperly, you could end up with inexplicable, hard-to-debug issues in your codebase.

Use the goto statement with great caution.

A third option, presented in the next section, requires quite a bit more boilerplate but ultimately looks a little friendlier than the previous versions. Have a look, and see what you think.

Custom Iterator

The third option is to hack around with the IEnumerable and IEnumerator interfaces. The thing about IEnumerable is that it isn't actually an array; it's just a pointer to the current item of data, and an instruction on how to go and fetch the next item. That being the case, we can create our own implementation of the IEnumerable interface but with our own behavior.

For our Snakes and Ladders example, we want an IEnumerable that's going to iterate until a player has reached square 100 and therefore won the game. We start by creating an implementation of IEnumerable itself, which has only a single function that has to be implemented: GetEnumerator(). The IEnumerator class sits behind the scenes and does the work of enumerating. That's what we'll move on to next.

Understanding the Anatomy of an Enumerator

This is what the IEnumerator interface effectively looks like (it inherits a few functions from other interfaces, so a couple of these functions are here to satisfy the inheritance requirements):

```
public interface IEnumerator<T>
{
    object Current { get; }
    object IEnumerator.Current { get; }
    void Dispose();
    bool MoveNext();
    void Reset();
}
```

Each of these functions has a specific job to do, as described in Table 9-1.

Table 9-1. Component functions of IEnumerator

Function	Behavior	Returns
Current	Get the current data item.	The current item, or null if iteration hasn't started yet
IEnumerator.Current	Get the current data item. The same as Current, but included here from IEnumerator.	Same as Current
Dispose()	Break down everything in the IEnumerable to implement IEnumerator.	void
MoveNext()	Move to the next item.	true if another item is found, false if the enumeration process is complete
Reset()	Move back to the beginning of the dataset.	void

Most of the time, IEnumerable is simply enumerating over an array, in which case I'd imagine the implementation *probably* should be something vaguely like this:

```
public class ArrayEnumerable<T> : IEnumerator<T>
{
    public readonly T[] _data;
    public int pos = -1;
    public ArrayEnumerable(T[] data)
    {
        this._data = data;
    }

    private T GetCurrent() => this.pos > -1 ? _data[this.pos] : default;

    T IEnumerator<T>.Current => GetCurrent();

    object IEnumerator.Current => GetCurrent();

    public void Dispose()
    {
        //  Run!  Run for your life!
        // Run before the GC gets us all!
    }
    public bool MoveNext()
    {
        this.pos++;
        return this.pos < this._data.Length;
    }
    public void Reset()
    {
        this.pos = -1;
    }
}
```

I expect the real code by Microsoft is likely far more complicated—you'd hope there would be a lot more error handling and parameter checking. But this simple implementation gives you an idea of the sort of job the IEnumerator does.

Implementing Custom Enumerators

Knowing how the enumeration process works under the surface, you can see how it's possible to implement any behavior whatsoever that you'd like in an IEnumerable. I'll show you a few examples of how powerful this technique can be by creating an IEnumerable implementation that iterates through only every *other* item in an array by putting the following code in MoveNext():

```
public bool MoveNext()
{
    pos += 2;
    return this.pos < this._data.Length;
}

// This turns { 1, 2, 3, 4 }
// into { 2, 4 }
```

How about an `IEnumerable` that loops over every item twice, effectively creating a duplicate of each item when enumerating:

```
public bool IsCopy = false;
public bool MoveNext()
{
 if(this.IsCopy)
 {
  this.pos = this.pos + 1;
 }
 this.IsCopy = !this.IsCopy;

 return this.pos < this._data.Length
}

// This turns { 1, 2, 3 }
// into { 1, 1, 2, 2, 3, 3 }
```

Or an entire implementation that goes backward, starting with an enumerator outer wrapper:

```
public class BackwardsEnumerator<T> : IEnumerable<T>
{
    private readonly T[] data;

    public BackwardsEnumerator(IEnumerable<T> data)
    {
        this.data = data.ToArray();
    }

    public IEnumerator<T> GetEnumerator()
    {
        return new BackwardsArrayEnumerable<T>(this.data);
    }

    IEnumerator IEnumerable.GetEnumerator() => GetEnumerator();
}
```

And afterward, the actual `IEnumerable` that drives the backward motion:

```
public class BackwardsArrayEnumerable<T> : IEnumerator<T>
{
     public readonly T[] _data;

    public int pos;

    public BackwardsArrayEnumerable(T[] data)
    {
        this._data = data ?? new T[0];
        this.pos = this._data.Length;
    }

    T Current => (this._data != null && this._data.Length > 0 &&
```

```
        this.pos >= 0 && this.pos < this._data.Length)
            ? _data[pos] : default;

    object IEnumerator.Current => this.Current;

    T IEnumerator<T>.Current => this.Current;

    public void Dispose()
    {
        // Nothing to dispose
    }

    public bool MoveNext()
    {

        this.pos = this.pos - 1;
        return this.pos >= 0;
    }

    public void Reset()
    {
        this.pos = this._data.Length;
    }
}
```

The usage of this backward enumerable is pretty much exactly the same as a standard enumerable:

```
var data = new[] { 1, 2, 3, 4, 5, 6, 7, 8 };
var backwardsEnumerator = new BackwardsEnumerator<int>(data);
var list = new List<int>();
foreach(var d in backwardsEnumerator)
{
    list.Add(d);
}

// list = { 8, 7, 6, 5, 4, 3, 2, 1 }
```

Now that you've seen how easy it is to create your own IEnumerable with whatever custom behavior you want, conjuring up an IEnumerable that iterates indefinitely should be easy enough.

Indefinitely Looping Enumerables

Try saying this section title 10 times fast!

As you saw in the previous section, there's no special reason that an IEnumerable has to start at the beginning and loop to the end. We can make it behave in absolutely any way we care to.

Instead of an array, for this example we'll pass in a single state object of some kind, along with a bundle of code (i.e., a thunk, or Func delegate) for determining whether the loop should continue.

Working backward, the first thing we'll make is the IEnumerator. This is an entirely bespoke enumeration process, so we're not going to make any effort to make it generic in any way. The logic wouldn't make sense outside of a game state object:

```
public class SnakesAndLaddersEnumerator : IEnumerator<GameState>
{
    // I need this in case of a restart
    private GameState StartState;

    // old game state -> new game state
    private readonly Func<GameState, GameState> iterator;
    // some tricky logic required to ensure the final
    // game state is iterated.  Normal logic is that if
    // the MoveNext function returns false, then there isn't
    // anything pulled from Current, the loop simply terminates
    private bool stopIterating = false;

    public SnakesAndLaddersEnumerator(
        Func<GameState,
        GameState> iterator,
        GameState state)
    {
        this.StartState = state;
        this.Current = state;
        this.iterator = iterator;
    }

    public GameState Current { get; private set; }

    object IEnumerator.Current => Current;

    public void Dispose()
    {
        // Nothing to dispose
    }

    public bool MoveNext()
    {
        var newState = this.iterator(this.Current);
        // Not strictly functional here, but as always with
        // this topic, a compromise is needed
        this.Current = newState;

        // Have we completed the final iteration?  That's done after
        // reaching the end condition
        if (stopIterating)
            return false;
```

```
            var endConditionMet = this.Current.Players.Any(x => x.Position >= 100);
            var lastIteration = !this.stopIterating && endConditionMet;
            this.stopIterating = endConditionMet;
            return !this.stopIterating || lastIteration;
        }

        public void Reset()
        {
            // restore the initial state
            this.Current = this.StartState;
        }
    }
```

That's the hard bit done! We have an engine under the surface that'll allow us to iterate through successive states until we're finished—whatever we decide "finished" means.

The next item required is the IEnumerable to run the IEnumerator. That's pretty straightforward:

```
public class SnakesAndLaddersIterator : IEnumerable<GameState>
{
    private readonly GameState _startState;
    private readonly Func<GameState, GameState> _iterator;

    public SnakesAndLaddersIterator(
        GameState startState,
        Func<GameState,
        GameState> iterator)
    {
        this._startState = startState;
        this._iterator = iterator;
    }

    public IEnumerator<GameState> GetEnumerator() =>
        new SnakesAndLaddersEnumerator(this._iterator, this._startState);

    IEnumerator IEnumerable.GetEnumerator() => GetEnumerator();
}
```

Everything is now in place to carry out a custom iteration. We just need to define the custom logic and set up the iterator:

```
var state = new GameState
{
    CurrentPlayer = 1,
    Players = Enumerable.Range(1, noPlayers)
        .Select(x => (x, 1))
        .Select(x => new Player
        {
            Number = x.Item1,
            Position = x.Item2
        }),
```

```
        NumberOfPlayers = noPlayers
};

var update = (GameState g) =>
{
    var roll = die.Roll();

    var newState = g with
    {
        CurrentPlayer = roll == 6
            ? g.CurrentPlayer
            : g.CurrentPlayer == g.NumberOfPlayers
                ? 1
                : g.CurrentPlayer + 1,
        Players = g.Players.Select(x =>
            x.Number == g.CurrentPlayer
                ? UpdatePlayer(x, roll)
                : x
        ).ToArray()
    };

    return newState;
};

var salIterator = new SnakesAndLaddersIterator(state, update);
```

We have a couple of options for handling the iteration itself, and I'd like to take a little time out to discuss each of those options in more detail.

Using Indefinite Iterators

Strictly speaking, as a fully fledged iterator, any LINQ operation can be applied, as well as a standard foreach iteration.

Using foreach would probably be the simplest way to handle this iteration, but it wouldn't be strictly functional. It's up to you whether you want to compromise by adding a statement in a limited capacity, or want to seek out a more purely functional alternative. Implemented with a foreach, the code might look like this:

```
foreach(var g in salIterator)
{
// store the updated state outside of the loop.
 playerState = g;

 // Here you can do whatever logic you'd like to do
 // to message back to the player.  Write a message onto screen
 // or whatever is useful for them to be prompted to do another action
}

// At the end of the loop here, the player is now out of jail, and
// the game can continue with the updated version of playerState;
```

That code wouldn't give me too much cause for concern in production, honestly. But what we've done is negated all the work we've put into attempting to get rid of nonfunctional code from our codebase.

The other options use LINQ. As a fully fledged IEnumerable, our salIterator can have any LINQ operations applied to it. Which ones would be the best, though?

Select() would be an obvious starting place but might not behave entirely as you'd expect. Its usage is pretty much the same as any standard Select() list operation you've ever done before:

```
var gameStates = salIterator.Select(x => x);
```

The trick here is that we're treating gameIterator as an array, so Selecting from it will result in an array of game states. We'll basically have an array of every intermediate step the user has gone through, finishing with the final state in the last element.

The easy way to reduce this to simply the final state is to substitute Select() for Last():

```
var endState = var gameStates = salIterator.Last();
```

This assumes, of course, that you aren't interested in the intermediate steps. It might be that you want to compose a message to the user for each state update, in which case you might want to select and then provide a transformation:

```
var messages = salIterator.Select(x =>
    "Player " + x.CurrentPlayer + "'s turn." +
    "The current winner is: " +
    x.Players.Single(y => y.Number == x.Players.Max(z => z.Position))
);
```

That eradicates the actual game state, though, so Aggregate() might be a better option:

```
var stateAndMessages = (
    Messages: Enumerable.Empty<string>(),
    State: state
);

var result = salIterator.Aggregate(stateAndMessages, (agg, x) =>
{
    return (
        agg.Messages.Append("Player " + x.CurrentPlayer + "'s turn." +
                        "The current winner is: " +
                        x.Players.First(y =>
                            y.Position == x.Players.Max(z =>
                                z.Position)).Number),
        x
    );
});
```

The x in each iteration of the `Aggregate()` process is an updated version of the game state, and the code will carry on aggregating until the declared end condition is met. Each pass appends a message to the list, so what you finally get at the end is a tuple containing an array of strings, which are messages to pass to the player, and the final version of the game state.

Bear in mind that any use of LINQ statements that will terminate the iteration early in some manner—such as `First` or `Take`—will also prematurely end this iteration process, possibly in our instance with the player still in jail. Of course, this might be a behavior you want! For example, maybe you're restricting the player to just a couple of actions before moving on to another part of the game or to another player's turn. You could come up with all sorts of possibilities for the logic by playing with this technique.

Summary

You've learned how to implement indefinite iteration in C# using the `foreach` statement, which results in cleaner code with fewer possible side effects of execution.

It's not strictly possible to do this purely functionally. Several options are available, all of which carry some level of compromise to the functional paradigm. This is the nature of working in C#. Which option, if any, you wish to use is entirely a matter of personal choice and whatever of any constraints that apply to your project.

More often than not, I go with the trampolining option. It isn't as dangerous as recursion, nor as much work to implement as a custom iterator. As always with these things, your choice depends what you're trying to do. The requirements and constraints of your project will determine the best option.

Please be cautious with the use of recursion. It's a fast method of iteration that's purely functional, but if you aren't careful, it can lead to significant performance issues when it comes to memory usage.

In the next chapter, I'll show you a nice way to take advantage of pure functions to improve performance in your algorithms.

CHAPTER 10

Memoization

Using pure functions has more advantages than just producing predictable results. Granted, that's a good thing to have, but there's another way to use that behavior to our advantage.

Memoization is somewhat like caching, specifically like the `GetOrAdd()` function from the `MemoryCache()` class. Memoization takes a key value of some kind, and if that key is already present in the cache, it returns the object. If the key isn't present, you need to pass in a function that will generate the required value. Unlike with standard caching, you don't need to be concerned with cache invalidation or updating values already stored. Typically, memoization holds onto values for the duration of a larger calculation and then discards everything it has stored.

Memoization works to the exact same principle as standard caching, except its scope might not extend beyond a single unit of work, which might be simply a single calculation. It isn't a *replacement* for standard caching.

Memoization is useful in a multistep calculation that might be recursive, or involve the same calculations being performed multiple times for some reason. Maybe the best way to explain this is with an example.

Bacon Numbers

Have you ever wanted an entertaining way to waste an afternoon or two? Have a look into *Bacon numbers*. They're based on the idea that Kevin Bacon is the center of the acting universe, connecting all actors together. Like all roads lead to Rome, all actors somehow connect at some level to Bacon. An actor's Bacon number is the number of film connections you have to work through in order to reach Kevin Bacon. Let's work through a few examples:

Kevin Bacon

Easy. He has a Bacon number of 0, because he *is* the Big Bacon himself.

Tom Hanks

Bacon number of 1. He was with Bacon in one of my personal favorites, *Apollo 13*. Frequent Hanks collaborator Meg Ryan is also 1, because she appeared with Bacon in *In The Cut*.

David Tennant

Bacon number of 2. He appeared with Colin Firth in *St. Trinian's 2*. Colin Firth appeared in *Where the Truth Lies* with Bacon. That's two films before we find a connection, so a Bacon number of 2. Believe it or not, Marilyn Monroe also has a score of 2 because Bacon appeared in *JFK* with Jack Lemmon, who was also in *Some Like It Hot*.

Aamir Khan

This Bollywood superstar has a Bacon number of 3. He was with living legend Amitabh Bachchan in *Bombay Talkies*. Amitabh was in *The Great Gatsby* with Tobey McGuire. McGuire was in *Beyond All Boundaries* with Bacon.

My Bacon number is infinity! This is because I've never appeared in a film as an actor.[1] Also, the holder of the highest Bacon number I'm aware of is William Rufus Shafter, an American Civil War general who also appeared in a nonfiction film made in 1898, which still secures him a Bacon number. It's a whopping great 10!

Right, hopefully you understand the rules. Let's imagine we want to work out which of these actors has the lowest Bacon number programmatically. Our code looks like this:

```
var actors = new []
{
    "Tom Hanks",
    "Meg Ryan",
    "David Tennant",
    "Marilyn Monroe",
    "Aamir Khan"
};

var actorsWithBaconNumber = actors.Select(x => (a: x, b: GetBaconNumber(x)));

var report = string.Join("\r\n", actorsWithBaconNumber.Select(x =>
    x.a+ ": " + x.b);
```

---

1 I wouldn't say no, though. Anyone know a film director wanting to cast an aging, overweight, British tech-nerd? I probably couldn't play James Bond, but I'm willing to give it a go!

`GetBaconNumber()` could be calculated in many ways—most likely, by using a web API of film data of some kind. More advanced "shortest path" algorithms are out there, but for the sake of simplicity I'll say the process is something like this:

1. Get all of Kevin Bacon's films. Assign all actors in these films a Bacon number of 1. If the target actor (e.g., Tom Hanks) is among them, return an answer of 1. Otherwise, continue.

2. Take each of the actors from the previous step (excluding Bacon himself), get a list of all their films not already checked. Assign all actors from these films not already assigned a value of 2.

3. Continue in iterations, with each set of actors being assigned progressively higher values until we finally reach the target actor and return their number.

Since an API is working to calculate these numbers, every actor whose filmography we download, or every film whose cast list we download, all have a significant cost in processing time. Furthermore, an awful lot of overlap occurs between these actors and their films, so unless we step in and do something, we're going to be checking the same film multiple times.

One option is to create a state object to pass into an `Aggregate()` function. The process is an indefinite loop, so we'd also need to select one of the options for compromising on the functional principles and allowing the loop. The code might look something like this:

```
public int CalculateBaconNumber(string actor)
{

    var initialState = (
        checkedActors: new Dictionary<string, int>(),
        actorsToCheck: new[] { "Kevin Bacon" },
        baconNumber: 0
    );

    var answer = initialState.IterateUntil(
        x => x.checkedActors.ContainsKey(actor),
        acc => {
            var filmsToCheck =
            acc.actorsToCheck.SelectMany(GetAllActorsFilms);
            var newActorsFound = filmsToCheck.SelectMany(x => x.ActorList)
                .Distinct()
                .ToArray();

            return (
                acc.checkedActors.Concat(acc.actorsToCheck
                    .Where(x => !acc.checkedActors.ContainsKey(x))
                    .Select(x =>
                    new KeyValuePair<string, int>(x, acc.baconNumber)))
                    .ToArray()
```

```
        .ToDictionary(x => x.Key, x => x.Value),

    newActorsFound.SelectMany(GetAllActorsFilms)
        .SelectMany(x => x.ActorList).ToArray(),

    acc.baconNumber + 1
    );
});
return answer.checkedActors[actor];
}
```

 I've made up the web API for the sake of this example, so you won't be able to follow along at home, unless you make your own API first!

This code is fine but could be better. A lot of boilerplate code is concerned with tracking whether an actor has already been checked. For instance, the code contains a lot of uses of `Distinct`.

With memoization, we get a generic version of the check, like a cache, but it exists within the scope of the calculation we're performing and doesn't persist beyond it. If you do want the saved, calculated value to persist between calls to this function, `MemoryCache` may be a better choice.

We could create a memoized function to get a list of films that the actors listed previously have been in, like this:

```
var getAllActorsFilms = (String a) => this._filmGetter.GetAllActorsFilms(a);
var getAllFilmsMemoized = getAllActorsFilms.Memoize();

var kb1 = getAllFilmsMemoized("Kevin Bacon");
var kb2 = getAllFilmsMemoized("Kevin Bacon");
var kb3 = getAllFilmsMemoized("Kevin Bacon");
var kb4 = getAllFilmsMemoized("Kevin Bacon");
```

This calls the same function four times, and by rights it should have gone away to the film data repository and fetched a fresh copy of the data four times. In fact, the function fetched the data only a single time, when `kb1` was populated. Every time since then, a copy of the same data was returned.

Note also, by the way, that the memoized version and original version are on separate lines. That's a limitation of C#. You can't call an extension method on a function, only on a `Func` delegate, and the arrow function isn't a `Func` until it has been stored in a variable.

Some functional languages have out-of-the-box support for memoization, but F# doesn't, oddly enough.

This is an updated version of the Bacon number calculation, this time taking advantage of the memoization feature:

```
public int CalculateBaconNumber2(string actor)
{

    var initialState = (
        checkedActors: new Dictionary<string, int>(),
        actorsToCheck: new[] { "Kevin Bacon" },
        baconNumber: 0
    );

    var getActorsFilms = GetAllActorsFilms();
    var getActorsFilmsMem = getActorsFilms.Memoize();

    var answer = initialState.IterateUntil(
        x => x.checkedActors.ContainsKey(actor),
        acc => {
            var filmsToCheck = acc.actorsToCheck.SelectMany(getActorsFilmsMem);
            var newActorsFound = filmsToCheck.SelectMany(x => x.ActorList)
                .Distinct()
                .ToArray();

            return (
                acc.checkedActors.Concat(acc.actorsToCheck
                        .Where(x => !acc.checkedActors.ContainsKey(x))
                        .Select(x =>
                            new KeyValuePair<string, int>(x, acc.baconNumber)))
                    .ToArray()
                    .ToDictionary(x => x.Key, x => x.Value),

                newActorsFound.SelectMany(getActorsFilmsMem)
                    .SelectMany(x => x.ActorList).ToArray(),

                acc.baconNumber + 1
            );
        });
    return answer.checkedActors[actor];
}
```

The only difference here is that we've created a local version of the call to get film data from a remote resource, then memoized it, and thereafter referenced only the memoized version. Therefore, we're guaranteed no wasteful repeat requests for data.

Implementing Memoization in C#

Now that you understand some of the basics, this is how you'd make a memoization function for a simple, single parameter function:

```
public static Func<T1, TOut> Memoize<T1, TOut>(this Func<T1, TOut> @this)
{
    var dict = new Dictionary<T1, TOut>();
    return x =>
    {
        if (!dict.ContainsKey(x))
            dict.Add(x, @this(x));
        return dict[x];
    };
}
```

This version of memoize expects that the live data function has only a single parameter of any type. To expect more parameters, we'd need further Memoize() extension methods, like this:

```
public static Func<T1, T2, TOut> Memoize<T1, T2, TOut>(
    this Func<T1, T2, TOut> @this)
{
    var dict = new Dictionary<string, TOut>();
    return (x, y) =>
    {
        var key = $"{x},{y}";
        if (!dict.ContainsKey(key))
            dict.Add(key, @this(x, y));
        return dict[key];
    };
}
```

Now, to make this work, we assume that ToString() returns something meaningful, meaning that most likely it'll have to be a primitive type (like a string or int). The ToString() method on a class tends to simply return a description of the *type* of the class, not its properties.

If we absolutely have to memoize classes as parameters, some creativity is needed. The easiest way to keep it generic is probably to add parameters to the Memoize() function that require the developer to provide a custom ToString() function:

```
public static Func<T1, TOut> Memoize<T1, TOut>(
  this Func<T1, TOut> @this,
  Func<T1, string> keyGenerator)
{
    var dict = new Dictionary<string, TOut>();
    return x =>
    {
        var key = keyGenerator(x);
        if (!dict.ContainsKey(key))
```

```
            dict.Add(key, @this(x));
        return dict[key];
    };
}

public static Func<T1, T2, TOut> Memoize<T1, T2, TOut>(
 this Func<T1, T2, TOut> @this,
 Func<T1, T2, string> keyGenerator)
{
    var dict = new Dictionary<string, TOut>();
    return (x, y) =>
    {
        var key = keyGenerator(x, y);
        if (!dict.ContainsKey(key))
            dict.Add(key, @this(x, y));
        return dict[key];
    };
}
```

We might call it like this, in that case:

```
var getCastForFilm((Film x) => this.castRepo.GetCast(x.Filmid);
var getCastForFilmM = getCastForFilm.Memoize(x => x.Id.ToString());
```

This is possible only if you keep your functions *pure*. If there are side effects of any kind in your live Func, you might not necessarily get the results you expect (depending on what those side effects are).

Logging that you've called the API wouldn't be done with the cached version, but that's probably fine. Calling a secondary operation inside the function you're memoizing that you expect to be called every time is not only likely to be an example of poor coding practice, but also wouldn't happen when memoizing.

An example would be properties that were expected to be calculated uniquely in every instance of the generated class. If you wanted something like that, you'd probably have to split up the system domains a little more, so that the "get from API" function does literally just that, and another function and/or class handles the conversion of API data to something the rest of your application can understand.

In some cases, you might *want* the results to persist between calls to the Memoize() extension method. In that case, you'll also need to provide the Memoize() function with an instance of something like MemoryCache from the outside world.

If you really wanted, you could probably even write a version that uses a database to persist results between instances of the application running. That's probably defeating the whole purpose of what Memoize() is attempting to achieve, but the choice depends on just how resource intensive your live calls to the function you're memoizing are. I've come across functions that legitimately take half an hour to run;

perhaps you might want to memoize and persist those to storage. Alternatively, you might also want to look into a "proper" caching solution. As ever, it's up to you. This book and I, we're both nonprescriptive.

Summary

In this chapter, we looked at memoization and how to implement it. This lightweight alternative to caching can be used to drastically reduce the amount of time taken to complete a complex calculation with a lot of repetitive elements.

That's it for theory now! This isn't just the end of this chapter, but also of this part of the book.

Part I showed how to use functional ideas and out-of-the-box C# to improve your daily coding. Part II took a deeper dive into the theory behind FP and how to implement it with a little creative hacking about. Part III is a little more philosophical and will give you a few hints as to where to go next with what you've learned here with me.

Continue, if you dare, to enter Part III.

PART III

And Out the Other Side

That's it now. The hard part is all done. That's as much functional theory as I'm ever going to introduce in this book. If you want to look into that side of things further, you're going to need to consider learning category theory and/or a pure functional language like Haskell, or something along those lines.

Your journeyman days are over. You've learned all you'll need to be dangerous. Next is the slower path: more deliberate and ponderous toward becoming a master in your own right.

That path won't finish with this book. You'll need to go away and complete it yourself. For now, I can give you some ideas to consider and then take further on your own. Whether a true master even exists in the software development world is arguable, but I find it a nice horizon to aim for, even if I never ultimately reach it.

In the chapter that follows you'll look at performance considerations and the wider world of functional content around C#.

CHAPTER 11

Practical Functional C#

I'm not just a pretty face.[1] In addition to spending my days slogging at the virtual IT coalface each day, I've also been privileged enough to spend a lot of time over the years talking at various events on the subject of functional programming with C#. While at these talks, a few questions come up on a fairly regular basis.

The most common is "Why don't we just use F#?" See all the way back in "What About F#? Should I Be Learning F#?" on page 18 for my answer to that particular question. It comes up at just about every event I've ever spoken at, which is one of the reasons I gave such a detailed answer.

Oddly, the second most common question is to explain monads (which I did in Chapter 7). Hopefully, after getting to this point, you're something of an expert on that yourself now.

After these, the next most common question is about performance. There's a widespread belief that FP in C# is inefficient in production code compared with OOP. I'll spend the first section of this chapter talking about performance and whether it's an issue that you need to be concerned about before adopting functional C# in your everyday life—or, at least, your everyday life that involves .NET code. For me, there's a rather large overlap between those two things.

Functional C# and Performance

Let's continue now with a look at functional C# and performance. To do that, we're going to need a bit of code to use as a test subject, so we can compare imperative

---

1 OK, I'm not even that, but leave me my illusions, won't you!

code (i.e., the programming paradigm that OOP belongs to) to the various flavors of functional C#.

Now, I'm a big fan of the annual Advent of Code coding event (*https://adventof code.com*),[2] and the very first challenge ever published in its first event in 2015 is one I often link people to as a good example of how functional thinking can make a difference. Let's walk through that challenge.

The input is a string consisting strictly of the characters (and). These represent the movements of an elevator. A (represents a movement up a floor, and) represents a movement down a floor. We start on the ground floor, represented not by the letter *G* for "ground," but a 0, meaning we can work exclusively with an integer value to represent the current floor, with negative numbers representing floors beneath the ground. (Looking at some of the puzzle inputs, this particular building must have so many basement levels that it's in danger of making magma from the Earth's mantle a recurring problem. Never mind, though; it's a bit of fun, not an architectural blueprint.)

The challenge has two parts, which will serve perfectly for performance tests. The first is to run a series of instructions and calculate the final floor. The second is to work out which character of the input string gets you to floor –1 (the basement).

Here's an example for you. Given the input string ((()))))((((, we go up three floors (+3), then down five floors (–5), then finally up four floors (+4). The answer for this part the puzzle is the sum of all of these changes, so 3 – 5 + 4. The answer is 2, the floor the elevator finishes on after carrying out all the operations requested by the puzzle input.

To complete part 2, you need to determine which character of the input string is the one that first puts the elevator at floor –1. In Table 11-1, we can follow the sequence of instructions in turn.

Table 11-1. Instructions for the elevator and their resulting floors

Character	Instruction	Floor	Note
0	(	1	
1	(	2	
2	(	3	
3	)	2	
4	)	1	

---

2 Two coding challenges per day for 24 days leading up to Christmas. I've never managed to get further than about day 14 in real time, but they're fantastic puzzles, which I still continue to work on throughout the rest of the year.

Character	Instruction	Floor	Note
5	)	0	
6	)	−1	First reached floor −1 here!
7	)	−2	
8	(	−1	Reached it again here, but only the first time counts
9	(	0	
10	(	1	
11	(	2	

For part 2, the answer is 6: the seventh character is the first to put us on floor −1, but the array location is 6, because it's a zero-based array.

These two puzzles are great examples of both definite and indefinite loops, and the input provided by the puzzle is large enough (over 7,000 characters) that it'll cause the code to need to work for a bit—enough for me to gather some statistics.

If you care about spoilers, go ahead to the web page (*https://oreil.ly/uvtu-*) and solve the puzzle before continuing. Just know that if you use a functional approach, you can solve it in a single line!

 OK, here's a spoiler warning now: after this section, I'm launching into a full-on spoiler-heavy set of solutions to this eight-year-old puzzle.

Baseline: An Imperative Solution

Before delving into performance in the various functional solutions I have prepared, let's first explore how performance looks in an imperative solution. This is something of a scientific experiment, and to be a proper experiment, we need a *control*—a baseline to compare all the functional results to.

For performance measuring, I'm using Benchmark.NET with .NET 7. For those of you not familiar with this tool, it's similar in some ways to unit testing, except it'll compare the performance of several versions of the same code. It runs the same code many times, in order to get a mean of things like time taken to run and the amount of memory used.

The level of performance may vary among versions of .NET too if you try this yourself in something other than .NET 7, as performance improvements are added all the time by Microsoft.

The following are solutions to the two puzzles entirely using imperative-style coding:

```
// i.e., the definite loop
public int GetFinalFloorNumber(string input)
{
    var floor = 0;
    foreach(var i in input)
    {
        if(i == '(')
            floor++;
        else
            i--;
    }
    return floor;
}

// i.e., the indefinite loop
public int WhichCharacterEntersBasement(string input)
{
    var floor = 0;
    var charNo = 0;

    foreach(var i in input)
    {
        charNo++;
        if(i == '(')
            floor++;
        else
            floor--;

        if(floor == -1)
            return charNo;
    }
}
```

There might be better solutions, but this one will serve.

Performance Results

Now, these tests were performed for a 7,000-character input on my developer's laptop, so the actual numbers you might see when trying to replicate this experiment are likely to vary. The main point of the next few sections is to compare the results from the same test setup.

Imperative baseline results

Table 11-2 shows my results for this imperative solution.

Table 11-2. Object-oriented performance results

Loop type	Mean time taken	Time taken standard deviation	Memory allocated
Definite	10.59 µs[a]	0.108 µs	24 bytes
Indefinite	2.226 µs	0.0141 µs	24 bytes

[a] These are microseconds.

Despite the size of the task, the time taken is small indeed. Not too shabby. The indefinite loop is faster, but we'd expect that—it's not having to loop through the entire input string.

In the next sections, we're going to go through a few FP implementations of each loop type and see what difference it makes to performance.

Definite loop solutions

I did say that it was possible to solve this in a single line, didn't I? It's a fairly long line, but a single line nevertheless. Here's my line:

```
public int GetFinalFloorNumber(string input) =>
    input.Sum(x => x switch
    {
        '(' => 1,
        _ => -1
    });
```

I've added some newline characters to make the code readable, but it's still technically a single line!

This code is performing a Sum() aggregation method that adds either 1 or –1 at each iteration, based on the current character. Bear in mind that in C#, string is both a bit of text *and* an array, which is why we can apply LINQ operations to it like this. Table 11-3 shows the effect this has on performance.

Table 11-3. Sum() aggregation performance results

Solution	Mean time taken	Time taken standard deviation	Memory allocated
Imperative baseline	10.59 µs	0.108 µs	24 bytes
Sum aggregation	60.75 µs	0.38 µs	56 bytes

There's no avoiding that performance here is indeed worse. This is just out-of-the-box LINQ, so even using one of the Microsoft-provided tools, the code still doesn't run as quickly as the imperative version.

What do you think, should we throw in the towel now? Not likely! I have a few more things for us to try. How about if we separate out the conversion of char → int into two separate lines?

```
public int GetFinalFloorNumber(string input) =>
    input.Select(x => x == '(' ? 1 : -1).Sum();
```

Does this makes any difference? Let's examine Table 11-4 to find out.

Table 11-4. Select() then Sum() aggregation performance results

Solution	Mean time taken	Time taken standard deviation	Memory allocated
Imperative baseline	10.59 µs	0.108 µs	24 bytes
Select/sum aggregation	84.89 µs	0.38 µs	112 bytes

Well, that's a little worse. OK, how about converting to another data structure, like a dictionary, which has a fantastic reading speed:

```
public int GetFinalFloorNumber(string input)
{
    var grouped = input.GroupBy(x => x).ToDictionary(x => x.Key, x => x.Count());
    var answer = grouped['('] - grouped[')'];
    return answer;
}
```

This time, we're creating an IGrouping in which each possible char value is one Group within it. In our example, there will always be two Groups with a key of either (or). Once we have the groupings, we're deducting the size of one group from the other to get the final floor (i.e., deducting the total number of moves down from the total number of moves up).

As we can see in Table 11-5, not only is that even worse, but the amount of allocated memory is horrible.

Table 11-5. Group then insert dictionary performance results

Solution	Mean time taken	Time taken standard deviation	Memory allocated
Imperative baseline	10.59 µs	0.108 µs	24 bytes
Group/dictionary aggregation	93.86 µs	0.333 µs	33.18 kilobytes

I'd still like us to try an indefinite loop, and a few more things before I wrap up with my thoughts on what all this means. For now, I don't think this is as bad as it looks. Keep reading to see what I mean.

Indefinite loop solutions

Now we're going to try out a few solutions for the indefinite loop puzzle—i.e., which character of the input string is the first to bring us to floor –1. I can't say where that'll be, but we'll need to loop until the condition is met.

First, I've always heard that recursion in C# was a bad idea if you value your stack. Let's see just how bad things could be. This is a recursive solution to the problem:

```
public int WhichCharacterEntersBasement(string input)
{
    int GetBasementFloor(string s, int currentFloor = 0, int currentChar = 0) =>
        currentFloor == -1
            ? currentChar
            : GetBasementFloor(s[1..], s[0] ==
                '(' ? currentFloor + 1 : currentFloor - 1, currentChar + 1);

    return GetBasementFloor(input);

}
```

This code is nice, neat, and compact. Table 11-6 shows what the performance is like.

Table 11-6. Recursive loop performance results

Solution	Mean time taken	Time taken standard deviation	Memory allocated
Imperative baseline	2.226 µs	0.0141 µs	24 bytes
Recursive loop	1,030 ms	4.4733 µs	20.7 megabytes

That's honestly quite shocking. Note that those time results are in *milli*seconds, not *micro*seconds. That's nearly half a million times worse! The memory usage is also too large to be stored on a box of old floppy disks.

You now have the evidence before you, if it were needed, that recursion is a *really* bad idea in C#. Unless you're *very* sure of what you're doing, I'd tend to avoid it altogether.

What about nonrecursive functional solutions? Well, these are the ones that require a compromise of some sort. Let's start with the use of our IterateUntil() function from "Trampolining" on page 196. How does that affect performance?

This is our code:

```
public int WhichCharacterEntersBasement(string input)
{
    var startingInput = new FloorState
    {
        InputString = input,
        CurrentChar = 0,
        CurrentFloor = 0
    };

    var returnValue = startingInput.IterateUntil(x =>
     x with
    {
        CurrentChar = x.CurrentChar + 1,
        CurrentFloor = x.InputString[x.CurrentChar] ==
         '(' ? x.CurrentFloor + 1 : x.CurrentFloor - 1
    }
    , x => x.CurrentFloor == -1);
```

```
        return returnValue.CurrentChar;

    }

    public record FloorState
    {
        public string InputString { get; set; }
        public int CurrentFloor { get; set; }
        public int CurrentChar { get; set; }
    }
```

This time, we need something to track state with. We're trying a record type, since they've been provided to allow more functional code to be written. Table 11-7 shows the results.

Table 11-7. Trampolining performance results

Solution	Mean time taken	Time taken standard deviation	Memory allocated
Imperative baseline	2.226 μs	0.0141 μs	24 bytes
Trampolining	24.050 μs	0.3215 μs	55.6 kilobytes

Not so shocking this time, but still worse than the imperative version. Quite a large amount of memory is still being stored during the operation too.

How about if we were to swap record out for the previous functional-style structure Microsoft provided: the tuple. Would that improve performance? Let's take a look:

```
    public int WhichCharacterEntersBasement(string input)
    {
        var startingInput = (InputString: input, CurrentFloor: 0, CurrentChar: 0);

        var (_, _, currentChar) = startingInput.IterateUntil(x =>
        (
            x.InputString,
            x.InputString[x.CurrentChar] ==
             '(' ? x.CurrentFloor + 1 : x.CurrentFloor - 1,
            x.CurrentChar + 1
        ), x => x.CurrentFloor == -1);

        return currentChar;
    }
```

That's unfortunately not quite as friendly to look at—at least not if you're mostly an OOP developer. I adore the lovely syntactic sugar that record brings to us, but if performance is our goal, readability and maintainability may have to be sacrifices on its altar.

If you look at Table 11-8, you'll see the performance results.

Table 11-8. Trampolining with tuples performance results

Solution	Mean time taken	Time taken standard deviation	Memory allocated
Imperative baseline	2.226 µs	0.0141 µs	24 bytes
Trampolining with tuples	17.132 µs	0.0584 µs	24 bytes

That's substantially better. The time taken is still a little worse, but the amount of memory allocated is exactly the same!

The last test I want us to do is the custom IEnumerable option I demonstrated in "Custom Iterator" on page 200. Let's see how that compares to trying a ton of terrific trampolining tuples:

```
public class LiftEnumerable : IEnumerable<int>
{
    private readonly string _input;

    public LiftEnumerable(string input)
    {
        this._input = input;
    }

    public IEnumerator<int> GetEnumerator() => new LifeEnumerator(this._input);

    IEnumerator IEnumerable.GetEnumerator() => GetEnumerator();
}

public class LifeEnumerator : IEnumerator<int>
{
    private int _currentFloorNumber = 0;
    private int _currentCharacter = -1;
    private readonly string input;


    public LifeEnumerator(string input)
    {
        this.input = input;
    }

    public bool MoveNext()
    {
        var startingFloorNumber = this._currentFloorNumber;

        this._currentCharacter++;
        this._currentFloorNumber = startingFloorNumber == -1
            ? -1
            : this.input[this._currentCharacter]

        return startingFloorNumber != -1;
    }
```

```
    public void Reset()
    {
        this._currentCharacter= -1;
        this._currentFloorNumber = 0;
    }

    public int Current => this._currentCharacter + 1;

    object IEnumerator.Current => Current;


    public void Dispose()
    {
    }
}


// The actual code call
public int WhichCharacterEntersBasement(string input)
{
    var result = new LiftEnumerable(input).Select(x => x);
    return result.Last();
}
```

That's an awful lot of code, but is it any faster? See Table 11-9 to find out.

Table 11-9. Custom enumerable performance results

Solution	Mean time taken	Time taken standard deviation	Memory allocated
Imperative baseline	2.226 µs	0.0141 µs	24 bytes
Custom Enumerable	24.033 µs	0.1072 µs	136 bytes

The time taken is pretty much identical to the trampolining example with a record, but more data is allocated in this version. The results are not too bad and still nowhere near the calamity that is the recursive version.

Another option is to try to reference an F# project from a C# project (known as an *interop*) to have guaranteed functional code when C# really won't play along. Let's have a look at that.

Interop with F# performance

It's possible to write code in an F# project and reference it in C# as if it were just another .NET library. The process is fairly simple, and I'll walk you through it.

Create a new project in your Visual Studio solution, but instead of a C# library, select F# from the drop-down options.

You can reference the F# project in your C# code. Note that the code you've written won't be visible in C# unless you compile the F# project separately because F# uses a different compiler than that used by C#.

Since this is a C# book, I'm not going to go into how to write F#, but it's interesting to see how the performance would compare if we absolutely had to have a piece of entirely functional code without having to compromise with the limitations of functional C#.

In case you're curious, here is an F# solution to the problem—don't worry if you don't understand exactly how it works. I'm presenting it here as a curio rather than something you need to learn:[3]

```
module Advent =
    let calculateFinalFloor start input =
    input
        > Seq.fold (fun acc c -> match c
            with | '(' -> acc+1 | ')' -> acc-1 | _ -> acc) start


    let whichStepIsTheBasement start input =
    input
        |> Seq.scan (fun acc c -> match c with
            | '(' -> acc+1 | ')' -> acc-1 | _ -> acc) start
        |> Seq.findIndex(fun i -> i = -1)
```

This code is purely functional. Seq is the F# equivalent of IEnumerable, so some neat efficiency-saving features are at work here because of the lazy-loading nature of both of those types.

Given this is a C# book, I'm interested only in the performance effects on a C# project. F# handles these scenarios very efficiently in an F# project, but that's beyond the scope of this book. Let's look at the option available to interop F# code into C#.

What do I mean by this? Well, F# and C# both compile into the same .NET IL, meaning that once compiled, they not only look the same but can also reference each other. From a C# perspective, the F# code can appear available in C# code as a static function.

But what about the performance? Will the efficient nature of F# be countered somehow by being referenced over a C# channel? Let's have a look at Table 11-10 to see the results.

---

3 Thanks once again to F# guru Ian Russell for this code.

Table 11-10. F# interop performance results

Loop type	Solution	Mean time taken	Time taken standard deviation	Memory allocated
Definite	Imperative baseline	10.59 µs	0.108 µs	24 bytes
Definite	F# interop	63.63 µs	0.551 µs	326 bytes
Indefinite	Imperative baseline	2.226 µs	0.0141 µs	24 bytes
Indefinite	F# interop	32.873 µs	0.1002 µs	216 bytes

That's still worse, it turns out. It's not the worst of the options we've tried, but it's still not great. The indefinite loop example is 15 times worse than the original (control) imperative version. Even if you're happy with the performance hit going down this route will require learning F# first, and that's even further outside the scope of this book. At least you know F# is there in the future if you enjoy functional-style C# enough that you want to take it further still. You might need to make it an F#-only project if you want to enjoy the full benefits, however. As you can see here, performance issues arise when interoping with C#.

External factors and performance

Believe it or not, everything we've looked at so far is incidental in comparison to making any sort of interaction with the world outside your C# code. Let me show you what I mean.

In this next experiment, we'll modify both the original OOP baseline functions and the most efficient version of the FP solution, the one that used tuples. We'll set them not to accept any input strings, but instead to load the *same* data from a file stored in the local Windows filesystem. Functionally, we have the same input and same result, but a file operation is involved now.

What sort of difference could that make? Well, Table 11-11 just so happens to contain the answer.

Table 11-11. File process performance results

Loop type	Solution	Mean time taken	Time taken standard deviation	Memory allocated
Definite	Imperative baseline	10.59 µs	0.108 µs	24 bytes
Definite	Imperative with file	380.21 µs	15.187 µs	37.8 kilobytes
Definite	FP with file	450.28 µs	9.169 µs	37.9 kilobytes
Indefinite	Imperative baseline	2.226 µs	0.0141 µs	24 bytes
Indefinite	Imperative with file	326.006 µs	1.7735 µs	37.8 kilobytes
Indefinite	FP with file	366.010 µs	2.2281 µs	93.22 kilobytes

How about that? The functional solutions still take a little longer, but the proportion of difference is far less. When we compare the in-memory version of the FP solution with a definite loop using tuples to the imperative equivalent, the FP version takes about 8.5 times longer to complete. When we compare the two versions that include a file load, the proportional difference is only about 1.2 times slower—hardly that much more.

Imagine doing this if there were HTTP calls to web APIs or database connections established over a network? I can guarantee you that the time taken would be far worse than what we see here.

Join me, if you would, in the next section, where I'll put together my final thoughts on the conclusions we can draw from these experiments.

What Does All of This Mean?

It's an inescapable fact that functional C# is less efficient than well-written object-oriented code. That's just the way it is. Of course, poorly written suboptimal code in any language or paradigm will always find ways to be horribly inefficient.

We can also show that pure LINQ operations, kept as compact as possible, are the most effective of the functional features. If a state object of some kind is required, a tuple is currently the best choice. This assumes that performance is the most important goal of our code. Is it always? It depends entirely on what you're trying to achieve and who your customer is.

If you're planning to make an elaborate virtual reality application with high-definition 3D graphics, then honestly, you want to steer well away from functional solutions altogether. For projects like that, you'll need to squeeze every last bit of performance from your code that you possibly can and then some.

What about the rest of us? I've worked in a lot of companies and I would say that in nearly all of them, performance wasn't necessarily the most critical driver behind my development work. Mostly what I've worked on throughout my career is bespoke web applications used by internal employees carrying out some sort of business process as part of their daily workload. Whenever a requirement has been handed to me, getting it completed and released to production quickly is usually more important than spending time worrying about performance.

I've argued previously in this book that FP is easier to learn than OOP. Now, whether you agree with that or not, I hope by this point that I've at least convinced you that once you've taken the time to learn FP, putting an application together this way is faster than writing purely OOP-style code.

Even if there were issues with the app slowing down because of coding style, these days it's easy enough to pop onto Azure or AWS and click a button to add an extra virtual RAM chip to the virtual server, and the problem largely goes away. But what about the cost to the business for that nasty old RAM chip?

Well, what about it? Let me put it to you this way. If I'm right, and FP-style code really is more concise, more robust, and quicker to write than OOP-style code, that would mean we can get changes made and shipped to production quicker, and with a greater chance that everything will work the first time without errors. Given that fact, what would cost the company more? One extra virtual RAM chip, or the amount per hour that your time costs as you do all the extra development work and resolve the unnecessary bugs that would otherwise end up in production?

In any case, even though I've talked about the potential need for more RAM, would we necessarily even need it? In the experiments we've done in the previous sections of this chapter, we can see that although the functional solutions need more time than the object-oriented equivalent, the proportional difference once we invoke a file operation isn't really all that much. Hardly enough to start getting worried about.

Figure 11-1 shows the performance results of the two solutions that used files as input. The two sections of each pie chart represent the time required to load the file and the time required to process the data that was loaded.

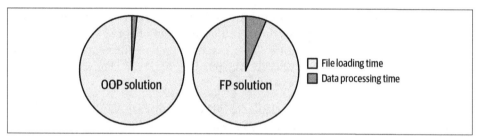

Figure 11-1. Comparing performance of tests with file operations

The difference doesn't look quite as bad when you see it in perspective, does it? Unless, that is, you really are working on a project that has financial consequences to every tiny loss in performance. This said, the stateless, side-effect-free nature of functional-style code strongly supports parallel processing. It might be easier to speed things up by standing up more instances of your application to get everything done quicker in a way that OOP tends not to support as well.

If you're less utterly, singularly focused on performance, and you'd be happier with nicer code that's easy to maintain, I'd suggest that any marginal loss in performance is a price worth paying to be able to write code in this style. Code spends whole orders of magnitude more time being read and maintained than it does being written in the first place. Having clearer, less error-prone code that you can end up with working within the functional paradigm is a very real benefit you can make use of.

As is always the case, it's up to you: Your personal coding preferences. The constraints of your working environment and the team you're part of. And, of course, whatever it is you're trying to develop. You're a grown-up,[4] and I can't possibly know the specific business drivers of your particular organization, so I'll leave you to decide for yourself.

For the second part of this chapter, I'm going to consider a few practical concerns you might have regarding functional C# in a production environment, and what my opinion is on each.

Functional C# Concerns and Questions

Right, no time to waste. Let's get cracking. First question, please!

How Functional Should I Make My Codebase?

One of the beauties of functional C# is that the functional content isn't part of a framework. You can choose how much you want to do functionally or not, and that sliding scale can move just about as far to either side as you want it to.

You can decide to make your entire codebase functional-style. Or restrict it to a single project. A single class. A single function. Or, if necessary, a single line. Mix functional and nonfunctional in the same function. It can be done. As an entirely personal preference, I probably wouldn't. But the point is you *can*, and there's no reason why you shouldn't.

I'm not a purist. I understand that sometimes in production all sorts of other concerns need to be considered beyond making the code exactly the way you want it.

You need to consider not just *where* you should be functional, but to what *extent*. Do you want to go all-out? Use partial application, monads, DUs, and the rest of it. Or you might feel like just using an awful lot of LINQ to replace `while` loops. That's fine too—whatever you feel comfortable with. You don't need to feel like a traitor to the cause.

Another consideration is the level of FP your colleagues are comfortable with. Do consider that however beautiful your functional code may be, it still has to be maintained by the team. I'd argue that monads aren't really all that hard to understand, but you still need to convince everyone to learn how to use them before they'll be ready to support code containing them—even if it might be in their best interests. You can lead a horse to water, and all that.

As I'm always saying, at the end of the day, the question you have to ask yourself is "What am I trying to achieve?" Once you've answered that truthfully, your decision-making process should be relatively easy.

---

4 Probably. Fair play to you if you aren't and you've read this far. You'll do well in life!

You could always leave a few copies of this book lying around the office. See what happens. I don't know how long after the publication date you're reading this, but there's even a chance that I may still be around. Feel free to get folks to reach out to me with questions.

How Should I Structure a Functional C# Solution?

You should structure a functional C# solution in classes and folders, largely the same as an existing OOP C# project. Strictly speaking, classes are *not* a functional concept. If you look at F# projects, they don't necessarily have classes at all.

You can contain all your code in modules, but they aren't really the same thing. They're convenient ways for F# developers to group code. Modules are more like a C# namespace. There's no functional meaning to a module.

In C#, on the other hand, there *have* to be classes. There's no way around it, so that will still have to be a thing you do.

In pure functional-style C#, you could make every class and function static. If you did that, I feel sure you're going to run into practical problems somewhere, especially when you have to try to interact with a nonfunctional class from NuGet or one of the built-in Microsoft classes.

Lack of dependency injection would also make unit testing far harder. Languages like Haskell get around this by using monads of various kinds. In C#, I'd say make your life easy and just use standard classes and an inversion-of-control (IoC) container, as hopefully you already have been.

A happy medium you could try is the Functional Core, Imperative Shell architectural model. Have all dependency injection carried out in the imperative outer layers; then the functional inner layers can be developed to have all dependencies passed in as parameters.

How Do I Share My Functional Methods Among Applications?

I maintain a set of functional libraries that are full of classes and extension methods, and these provide all my implementations of the monads, DUs, and other useful extension methods I want to use in my code. I usually have a separate project in the solution called *Common*, where I place anything generic like that. That way, the project can all sit somewhere in the codebase where I can use it, but I don't necessarily have to look at it again while I'm getting on with my work.

The contents of my Common project are copied from solution to solution for the time being. At some point at work, we're planning to set up our own local instance of NuGet, and when we do so, we'll probably have the Common project set up as a consumable NuGet package. That'll make it easy to distribute bug fixes, improvements, and new features. For now, copying over every time mostly works.

Did You Order This Pizza?

Erm, I'm not sure. That looks like it has got anchovies, so it's probably not for me. I asked for a meat feast. Let me just check with Liam; I think it might be his. Give me five seconds, I'll be right back.

How Do I Convince My Teammates to Do This Too?

Good question. When you work out how to do this consistently, let me know how you managed it.

I've been giving talks on this subject for a long time now, and reactions to FP seem to fall into one of a few categories:

- OMG! This is the holy grail of development! I want moooooore!
- Great ideas. I don't want to commit to the whole functional paradigm, but I'm going to take a few bits that are especially cool away with me.
- This is vaguely interesting, but I think I'll carry on working the way I always have, thanks.
- This is the worst. Boo!

I couldn't give you any real statistics on how many people fall into each camp, but my feeling is it's roughly a small number in the first and last group, and the vast majority in the other two in the middle.

That being the case, it's our job as FP advocates to try to convince others of the benefit to changing their ways. Bear in mind, most human beings are creatures of habit who don't really want to make huge changes to their daily lives like that, unless there's a good reason.

The way to convince others also depends on where you work and what your project constraints are. If you're creating mobile applications where every bit of memory is crucial, or a 3D graphics system for a virtual reality device and can't afford even the tiniest bit of inefficiency in your code, then you probably will find FP quite a hard sell.

If, however, you don't do those things, then there may well be a possibility you can convince everyone by talking about the benefits. Just don't become an FP bore. At some point, it may become obvious there's no traction with everyone else. Then it's best to hold off and hope there's a chance you can win the long game by attrition, rather than via a big, bold frontal attack.

The benefits I'd focus on, in roughly descending order, are as follows:

Reliability

Because functional-style applications are developed around the idea of consistent, predictable results with no side effects, they tend to be more robust and to consequently fail less. FP also massively enables unit testing. So by following this paradigm, you'll end up with a higher-quality product that fails less. This will save the company a whole load of money in time that would otherwise be required to resolve bugs in production.

Development speed

It's usually quicker and easier to write code using the functional paradigm (once you're familiar with it, that is!), and enhancements tend to be especially easy because of the way that functional code is structured and tends to have fewer bugs. I'd talk about the amount of time and money that will be saved in the initial development effort, and in time no longer required following release to squash as many bugs as you might otherwise have to with OOP.

Domain-driven design

Although it's not a stated goal of the paradigm, functional-style code tends to align well with DDD-style architecture, at least in comparison with OOP. If your team is interested in DDD, it's perhaps worth mentioning that FP is a good fit in that case.

Microsoft support

It's a stated goal of the .NET team to support the functional paradigm. Talk about how this style of programming isn't abusing .NET; it's actually *using* it the way it was intended (mostly).

Easy to learn

I hope you feel that way now, after getting to this point in the book. I don't believe that FP is all that hard to learn, at least not once you dispense with all the formal definitions and scary-sounding terminology. In fact, adopting FP requires *less* to learn than a new developer faces in learning the object-oriented paradigm. Far more theory needs to be learned to fully master the OOP paradigm than FP. If you find OOP easier to grasp, you may be an experienced developer, well grounded in OOP after many years of experience. I don't believe it takes as long to become proficient to the same extent with FP as it does with OOP. I'd reassure everyone that the learning overhead isn't all that big.

Pick and choose

Mention also that you can adopt as much or as little of the paradigm as you want. You don't need to throw away your old codebase and move to an entirely different one. You can start small by refactoring a single function or even just a single *piece* of a larger function, and you don't even have to use monads (although I think you might get great results if you do!).

It's not new!

It might finally be worth talking about how old the functional paradigm is. Many companies may be reluctant to adopt a new, trendy technology that hasn't proven it'll stay around long enough to be worth the investment. That's a reasonable concern, but FP was first used as a software development concept in the 1960s, and its roots go back to the late 1800s. It's already been proven a million times over in production environments.

I really *wouldn't* necessarily start talking right away about monads, DUs, currying, or anything like that. Keep your points of discussion as familiar as you can.

Aside from talking about it yourself, there's always this book and many more other good books on the subject. There's a section coming up shortly in which I'll recommend the ones I like the most.

Is It Worth Including F# Projects in My Solution?

Whether you include F# projects is up to you. Performance-wise, there's no real issue with it I'm aware of.

The best usage might be to consider using F# for the deeper, rules-based parts of your codebase—for example, the functions that convert data from one form to another based on a set of business requirements. F# is likely to make those parts neater, more robust, and more efficient. Your code will also be a whole ton more functional than anything C# can do, if that's what you're after.

The only thing I'd consider is whether your team is willing to support F#. If so, great. Go for it. If not, get together with the team and have a discussion. That sort of decision needs to be made by everyone.

If your team isn't comfortable with F#, you can at least take some comfort in the fact that most of the functional paradigm is still here in C#.

Will Functional Coding Solve All My Problems?

FP is unlikely to improve your poker game, read you a bedtime story, or make you cups of coffee when you're in need. It certainly will provide you with a higher-quality codebase that's easier to live with once it has been released to your production environment, will give you fewer live issues, and will be easier for new members of the team to learn when they join.

It's still possible for someone who's determined to, to write bad code, or to be lazy one day and make a mistake. Nothing on this planet can stop that from happening.[5] Well, besides the usual methods of enforcing automated testing, code reviews, and manual quality checks—the sorts of things that have mostly been around since the beginning of development as an industry.

Functional-style coding will facilitate *spotting* problems, however. Its concise style makes it easy to tell at a glance what a function *does* and whether it's doing what its name suggests.

Functional also—as stated earlier in this chapter—won't be the *most* efficient solution to your coding requirement, but it's near enough that unless absolute peak performance matters to you, it's likely to be just fine.

None of this will help with any of your usual project management issues either. Issues with unclear requirements are between you and whichever business analyst you believe in.

FP will make you cool, though. Kids might even give you the thumbs-up in the street as you pass. Such is the street cred of FP. True fact.

Connery, Moore, or Craig?

None of the above, I'm a big fan of Timothy Dalton. He deserved more attention.

How Do I Think Through a Problem Functionally?

There isn't one way think through a problem functionally any more than there's *one* way to develop a piece of software. If it helps, though, I'll briefly describe my process.

I would start by thinking through the *logical* steps of the code you're trying to write. Try splitting it into the steps you'd describe if you were talking through your work with someone else: "First I'd do X, then I'd do Y, then Z." This isn't a way you can work especially well with object-oriented-style code, but it's the best way to split up functional code.

---

5 Probably nothing off it either, but who knows.

I'd then write each piece of functional code based on those steps.

Wherever possible as well, I'd consider making whatever you're working on an IEnumerable of some kind, whether that be of primitives, complex objects, or Func delegates. FP is often at its most potent when you're running list-based operations, as in T-SQL.

I would advise against making chains of functions too long. You want opportunities when you're developing to be able to examine the previous steps of a complex calculation, to make sure everything is working the way you expect. Splitting up long chains of functions also gives you chances to apply meaningful names to what you store at each stage of the process.

FP supports unit testing very well, so I'd also suggest breaking the entire process into as many smaller functions as you can, and then make sure you've tested each one as thoroughly as possible. If you have the advantage of being able to break the steps up logically, use it to the best effect you can.

What If There's No Way to Make a Bit of Code as High-Performant as I'd Like with Functional-Style Code?

Dude, there are no rules. Make that bit imperative. Have a look at articles like those written by Steve Gordon (*https://oreil.ly/mLFRu*) on how to write high-performance C#. At the end of the day, you have to be pragmatic. I love functional-style code. It has an awful lot of benefit to bring to a project, but if there's one business-critical function somewhere that is run thousands of times a second and needs every last drop of performance that can be had—do it in the way that makes the best sense. I won't tell on you.

Summary

This chapter was a game of two halves.

In the first, we considered the myth of poorly performing functional code, and hopefully busted it to some extent. We saw that it's a real phenomenon, but the difference is insignificant compared to any amount of I/O in your code.

In the second half, we considered some of the more esoteric, philosophical issues of FP in the industrial setting.

FP will return in ~~You Only Live Twice~~ Chapter 12, in which I'll present options you have for doing FP by using third-party packages from NuGet.

Existing Functional Programming Libraries in NuGet

It may, or more likely may *not*, surprise you to learn that I'm not the first person in the world to advocate for functional C#. Far from it. Quite a lot of people have done so before me, many of whom have even created handy libraries you can use to write functional-style code without making it all yourself.

Over the course of this chapter, I'll talk about each of the libraries that exist in NuGet to provide functional features, how to use them, and what I think of them. Just be aware I didn't make any of them. I just wrote this book.

A quick note first about the use of NuGet libraries like these. These aren't necessarily the product of a big company that's paying its employees to produce a shippable product to customers. Many of them are the work of passionate, talented developers who are doing this work in their spare time. This has both advantages and disadvantages if you're considering using these packages in a production environment.

The big advantage is that you'll honestly tend to get a better product in many cases than a company might manage. With no work politics, concerns over the needs of certain high-paying customers, paying staff or arbitrary deadlines, you can often get an amazing product fueled by pure passion.

The downside is that there's no guarantee that these libraries will always be supported. Real life gets in the way sometimes, in ways that are unavoidable and impossible to predict. A one-person operation providing amazing work for us to use in C# might find themselves thinking again about the amount of work they do when they find themselves with a new addition to the family, an exciting new job that requires more of their available time, or even a lottery ticket that comes up as a winner on some sort of mega roll-over jackpot, giving them enough money to buy a private island in the tropics. The code might well continue to run for many years, but sooner or later a change may come to a new release of .NET five years from now that makes the library less than usable.

I'm not saying anything of that sort *will* happen, but bear it in mind when deciding whether to integrate a package's features into your codebase. Have a look at the relevant GitHub pages and the level of support the package is getting. Try to determine whether it has some form of corporate sponsorship, or at least whether an active team of people is supporting the product and a community exists around them.

Open source projects that die can even be resurrected if there's enough community support. Another advantage of being open source is that you can take the source code yourself, and maintain your own version in the event of there being no further official support.

To put things in perspective, Vue.js started life as a one-man open source operation. It's now used extensively in production around the world.

I can't ultimately advise you on whether you should choose an open source project from NuGet or create your own functional tools. That's a decision that has to be made by you, your team (if there is one), and your organization (if you belong to one), and must be done bearing in mind the unique constraints of whatever project you're working on.

I've tried my best to select projects in this chapter that are well supported, and owned by people who care about their product and the community. The open source world changes rapidly, however, so I'd still advise performing your own investigation to ensure that nothing has changed since I wrote this.

OneOf

The OneOf library (*https://oreil.ly/JxPSy*) is owned by Harry McIntyre. It seems to be one of the better-known functional libraries out there, and folks I've talked to have recommended this one more than any other.

Its stated intention is to provide "F#-like" DUs in C#. To give them a test run, I've redeveloped all my code samples from Chapter 6 using OneOf to see how it compares.

First, the `CustomerOffering` union type looks like this:

```
var customerOffering = new OneOf<Holiday, HolidayWithMeals, DayTrip>();
```

Note here that there is no abstract base class. With this library, all the DUs we create are of the type OneOf<T, T, T> or however many types we attach to the union.[1] This makes it easier to declare unions on the fly, without needing to create the additional code infrastructure required by my method.

Since there's no abstract base class, however, it's necessary instead to use the built-in OneOf Match() function to collapse the union down to a concrete type. This is how our sample from Chapter 6 determining which format method to call would look:

```
public string formatCustomerOffering(
    OneOf<Holiday, HolidayWithMeals, DayTrip> c) =>
    c.Match(
        x => this.formatHoliday(x),
        x => formatHolidayWithMean(x),
        x => formatDayTrip(x)
    );
```

This code is nice and neat, but you should bear a few points in mind when comparing it to our version:

- There's no default match, as when using a switch expression, so every single member type of the union has to have a switch expression matched. This may not be a problem if we want to ensure that every possible member of the union has a specific handler.

- Use of the switch expression when keyword to examine the values of the properties of the type we're examining isn't possible. That logic would have to be written into the Match function somehow.

- Each match type has to have the same return value, unless you convert to yet another union type! This may not be an issue if you're constructing some sort of feedback message to the end user, however.

To get a concrete, real object out of the union type, we can use a set of functions to check the real type and then convert it over:

```
var offering = GetCustomerOffering();
if(offering.IsT0)
{
    var holiday = offering.AsT0;
    // do something with the holiday type
}
if(offering.IsT1)
{
    var holidayWithMeals = offering.AsT1;
    // do something with the HolidayWithMeals type
}
```

---

1 Up to a maximum of 32, in actual fact.

```
if(offering.IsT2)
{
    var dayTrip = offering.AsT2;
    // do something with the DayTrip type
}
```

Note that this is being handled generically, so the types are simply referred to as T1, T2, etc. The order they're listed in the definition of the DU determines which number corresponds to which type.

This library has a whole load of built-in classes too, which are there to use in unions. They have names like Some, None, Yes, No, and Maybe. Despite the names, these can't be used to create a Something<T> class as we did in Chapter 7; they're just handy types to use when there is no return value and we'd like to return something descriptive to the outside world.

To create a true Maybe with OneOf, we'd need to define our own:

```
public class Something<T>
{
    public T Value { get; set; }
}


public OneOf<Something<Holiday>,None> GetHoliday() { }
```

The None class here is out of the OneOf library. It's only purpose is to signify that no data was found, so it's perfectly usable here. No Bind() or Map() functions are associated with the OneOf classes, which are purely to be used as DUs; it's not possible to use an instance of OneOf as a monad.

Nothing is stopping you from writing your own Bind() to extend a OneOf DU into a true monad, however:

```
public static OneOf<Something<TOut>, None> Bind<TIn, TOut>(
  this OneOf<Something<TIn>, None> @this,
  Func<TIn, TOut> f)
{
    if (!@this.IsT0) return new None();
    var sth = @this.AsT0;
    var returnValue = f(sth.Value);
    return new Something<TOut>
    {
        Value = returnValue
    };
}
```

OneOf is certainly a nice, easy-to-use, lightweight library. If you feel that the loss in flexibility compared to creating your own custom unions is acceptable, it's a worthwhile addition to your codebase. I'd certainly have no issues if someone asked to include it on a project I was working on.

One thing to bear in mind is that you can create DUs like a Maybe with OneOf, but you can't make it a monad—there are no implementations of the Map() or Bind() functions. If you really want the monad functionality, you might need to look into other libraries or make your own.

LanguageExt

Owned by Paul Louth, and found in NuGet as LanguageExt.Core, this library is an attempt to implement as much of the functional paradigm as is possible in C#.

LanguageExt (*https://oreil.ly/beFuq*) is a very large library of classes, static functions, and other features. I can't hope to describe all of it here, as that would probably fill an entire chapter! I'll restrict myself to just presenting the features that match functional content I've covered here already, and hopefully give a flavor of how LanguageExt is to use.

Before I begin, most of the functions and types required are part of a large partial class called Prelude. It might be worth adding this line to your global using statements file:

```
using static LanguageExt.Prelude;
```

Once that's done, it should be possible to construct most monads and other structures with a simple function call.

Option

Maybes are available in LanguageExt, though they're called Options. Another difference in approach is that for instantiating objects of that kind, static methods are defined for the purpose.

This is what my MakeGreeting() function looks like in LanguageExt:

```
public static Option<string> MakeGreeting(int employeeId) =>
    employeeId.Bind(empRepo.GetById)
        .Map(x => "Hello " + x.Salutation + " " + x.Name);
```

There are a few things to explain here. Strictly speaking, there is a difference between Map() and Bind(). They're often used interchangeably, but there is a difference.

Bind() takes a normal C# object or primitive and passes it to a function that returns an "elevated" value—i.e., instead of an int, it returns Maybe<int> or something of that sort.

Map() attaches to an "elevated" value (e.g., Maybe<int>) and allows you to pass the value inside it to another function without having to worry about unwrapping the elevated value. This is pretty much the same as the Bind() function used in Chapter 7.

In the preceding code sample, we start with a non-elevated `int` and use `Bind()` to pass it to the employee repository, which returns a type of `Maybe<Employee>`. The `Map()` function that follows just sees the `Employee` object that *may* have been returned by the `GetById()` function. In a process going on under the surface, `Maybe<int>` is unwrapped to `int`; then, once the arrow function we've passed in has executed, its `string` return value is wrapped into a `Maybe<string>`.

It doesn't help that `Map()` is also used in some programming languages like JavaScript to describe the sort of operation that's applied to arrays like `Select()` that operate element by element. `Map()` is also used in Jimmy Bogard's AutoMapper library (*https://automapper.org*), which is another reason to carefully consider using the term in C#. The term `Map` is heavily overloaded in the programming world, which is why I tend to shy away from it.

You can't use `null`, incidentally, with LanguageExt. It uses its own `None` type to denote the lack of a solid return value. This way, returning "nothing" is a choice made by the developer, rather than relying on the built-in default value of a type.

You might define functions by using `Some` and `None` like this:

```
public Option<Employee> GetById(int id)
{
    try
    {
        var emp = this.DbConnection.GetFromDb(id);
        return emp == null
            ? Option<Employee>.None
            : Option<Employee>.Some(emp);
    }
    catch(Exception e)
    {
        return Option<Employee>.None
    }
}
```

Collapsing an `Option` to a real value doesn't appear to be possible with the use of a C# `switch` expression. Instead, LanguageExt requires the use of a `Match()` function, to which we pass in two arrow functions—one to be executed in the event of `Some`, and the other in the event of `None`:

```
var result = empRepo.GetById(10);
var message = result.Match(s => "Hi there, " + s.Name,
    () => "I don't know who you are, but Hi all the same");
```

LanguageExt also contains a rich set of functions that can be applied to elevated values like `Maybe`. Here are a few examples:

Iter()

A kind of Tap() to perform a read-only action in the event of the Option currently being a Some. Slightly more descriptive alternatives are also available: ifSome() and IfNone().

MatchUnsafe()

Like a normal Match(), but also allows null to be returned, in the event that it matters to you.

Fold()

An aggregation function that is like Aggregate() in LINQ but that is aware of the Option and won't try to operate on None types.

Filter()

Like Where() in LINQ, but aware of the Option type.

Either

The Either monad is available in LanguageExt as well. Its typical usage of this is to have the left as the "unhappy" path, containing error details, but in fact you can do anything you'd like with the two forms. This effectively means you can use it as a DU as well.

Here's a LanguageExt version of the name-formatting function from Chapter 6:

```
public string formatName(Either<ChineseName, BritishName> n) =>
    n.Match(
        bn => bn.Honorific + " " + bn.FirstName + " " +
            string.Join(" ", bn.MiddleNames) + " " + bn.LastName,
        cn => cn.FamilyName + " " + cn.GivenName + " " +
            cn.Honorific + " \"" + cn.CourtesyName + "\"");
```

Note also that when using this method, there's no need for an inheritance connection to exist between the two classes, although the only way to use a switch expression would be if we referenced the classes as simply Object, since there's nothing else tying them together, but then the LanguageExt Match() function is a replacement for the switch statement. The library has no built-in support for matching on properties and subproperties without switch expressions, though.

As with all things, whether to use a library like LanguageExt depends on what you're trying to accomplish and the constraints of your project.

Memoization

LanguageExt has a class and a set of extension methods to implement memoization. Unfortunately, only Func delegates with either a single parameter or no parameters at all can be memoized, so you may have to write your own extension method for LanguageExt itself if you have memoized functions with multiple parameters.

This is our Bacon number example from Chapter 10 with LanguageExt swapped in for our version. As you can see, it's pretty much a straight replacement:

```
var getCastForFilm((Film x) => this.castRepo.GetCast(x.Filmid);
var getCastForFilmM = getCastForFilm.Memo(x => x.Id.ToString());
```

Here's a simple example to prove this implementation of memoization works in principle. We're using xUnit for the unit-test framework and Fluent Assertions to provide assertions:

```
[Fact]
public void memoized_functions_should_not_call_again_with_the_same_parameter()
{
    var timesCalled = 0;
    var add10 = (int x) => { timesCalled++; return x * 10; };
    var add10M = add10.Memo();

    add10M(1);
    add10M(2);
    add10M(1);

    timesCalled.Should().Be(2);
}
```

In the preceding example, add10M() is called three times, but the add10 delegate that sits behind it is called only twice, because the value returned by a parameter value of 1 is cached, and the stale cached version is returned instead.

I added a bit of code inside the add10() function to record the number calls to it. It's really super nonfunctional, but don't hold it against me. I wouldn't do that sort of thing in production!

Reader

The implementation of Reader in LanguageExt is probably slightly neater than ours. LanguageExt uses a delegate type to allow a function to be directly converted into a Reader, and an object containing a ton of helper functions called Prelude that we can make a global static, making it a little easier than our version (see Chapter 7) with extension methods:

```
using static LanguageExt.Prelude;

var reader = Reader<int, int>(e => e * 100)
    .Map(x => x / 50)
    .Map(x => x.ToString());

var result = reader.Run(100);
```

As you can see, the use of the LanguageExt implementation of the Reader monad is similar to our version, but with a few nice touches to make it a little easier on the eyes.

State

The last feature of LanguageExt I want to present (there are many more, I'm just sticking to what I see as the main ones) is the State monad (see Chapter 7 for our version).

This monad has a little more boilerplate as compared to ours, but it's largely the same:

```
var result1 = State<int, int>(x => (10, x))
    .Bind(x => State<int, int>(s => (x * s, s)))
    .Bind(x => State<int, int>(s => (x - s, s)))
    .Bind(x => State<int, int>(s => (x, s - 5)))
    .Bind(x => State<int, int>(s => (x / 5, s)));

var (finalValue, finalState, _) = result1(10);
// finalValue = 18
// finalState = 5
```

That'll do with LanguageExt features for now. Hopefully, this whistle-stop tour has given you an idea of its capabilities.

LanguageExt Wrap-up

Overall, LanguageExt is a deep, rich functional library with pretty much all the features you're likely to want in order to implement as much of the functional paradigm as is possible in C#.

I'm also only scratching the surface in terms of the features available in LanguageExt. There are also, among others, libraries included for fluent assertions in unit testing and more besides.

Should you use LanguageExt in production? That's entirely up to you. I don't find it's much effort to implement the functional paradigm in C#, with only a few lines of code required in most cases. That also means I can stick to whatever style of syntax suits me best. As a consequence, I don't use LanguageExt myself, but having said that, there's no special reason *not* to. It's a lovely, well-designed library.

Consider also the consequences of adopting such a large, extensive library of features across your codebase. I'm hoping it's around for many years to come, as it appears to be popular, but in case it ever isn't one day, that may cause a real problem if you rely on it heavily.

Either way, it's up to you, and your own personal risk/benefit ratio calculation. Let me know how you get on if you do use it!

Functional.Maybe

The Functional.Maybe library (*https://oreil.ly/cLgZ4*) is currently maintained by Andrey Tsvetkov, based on a now-abandoned project called Data.Maybe by William Casarin.

This project is a fairly lightweight implementation of the `Maybe` and `Either` monads, and may well be of interest if those are the only bits of the functional paradigm you're wanting to inject into your codebase.

Rather than implementing the `Maybe` monad as a DU via an abstract base class, this library implements it as a `readonly` struct with a `bool` property that can be used to determine whether there is a value inside the `Maybe`.

Here's an implementation of a Fahrenheit-to-Celsius temperature conversion function using Functional.Maybe:

```
public string FarenheitToCelsius(decimal input) =>
input.ToMaybe()
    .Select(x => x - 32)
    .Select(x => x * 5)
    .Select(x => x / 9)
    .Select(x => Math.Round(x, 2))
    .Select(x => x.ToString())
    .Value;
```

To better tie in with the existing .NET LINQ syntax, the `Bind()` function is called `Select()` here. Whether this is a confusing overload of an existing term or a comforting use of a familiar term is a decision I leave to you.

This is how you'd use the `Maybe` as the return type from a function that gets data from an external source—to represent the uncertainty of any data being received back:

```
public Maybe<Employee> GetById(int id)
{
    try
    {
        var e =  this.DbConnection.GetFromDb(id);
        return e.ToMaybe();
    }
    catch (Exception e)
    {
        return Maybe<Employee>.Nothing;
    }
}
```

The code is pretty straightforward. You don't necessarily have to use the `ToMaybe()` function; `Maybe<T>` has a constructor, but I find this syntax cleaner.

This method doesn't use inheritance, and there is no `Match()` extension method, so the way to move from the `Maybe` to a real, concrete value is to check for a value and then return whatever you want based on it:

```
var e = this.EmployeeRepo.GetById(24601);
var message = e.HasValue
    ? "Hello " + e.Value.Name
    : "I don't believe we've met, have we?";
```

A few extra bits of functional theory are included with the version of `Maybe` in this library. A `Tap()` function is also available, here called `Do()`. The `Do()` function executes only if the source `Maybe` has a value, so it's the equivalent of my `OnSomething()` function:

```
var taxData = this.EmployeeRepo.GetById(24601)
    .Do(x => this.logger.LogInfo("got employee " + x.Id)
    .Select(x => this.payrollRepo.GetTaxInfo(x.TaxId));
    .Do(x => "Got his tax too!");
```

In addition, a nifty `Or()` function acts like an alt combinator (see "Alt Combinator" on page 108), but with the monad flow feature integrated into it.

One big difference from our version is that the parameter set has no `params` list of functions and also requires that every function provided to the alt combinator has no parameters and returns a `Maybe` type. The James Bond function from Chapter 5 might work, provided each lookup function returns something like a `Maybe<SecretAgent>`, like this:

```
var jbId = "007";
var jamesBond = this.hotelService.ScanGuestsForSpies(jbId)
    .Or(() => this.airportService.CheckPassengersForSpies(jbId))
    .Or(() => this.barService.CheckGutterForDrunkSpies(jbId));

if(jamesBond.HasValue)
    this.deathTrapService.CauseHorribleDeath(jamesBond);
```

This code requires a few extra hoops to jump through, but it's still usable.

Also worthy of mention is that the library comes with an extension method for one of my favorite C# features: the dictionary. Instead of trying to get a key, you can get a `Maybe` from it instead. I like this idea very much.

CSharpFunctionalExtensions

The CSharpFunctionalExtensions library (*https://oreil.ly/SLDAr*) is maintained by Vladimir Khorikov as an extension of his Pluralsight course "Applying Functional Principles in C# 6" (*https://oreil.ly/nBkno*).

The name of the course aside, as of the time of writing, the library supports all versions of .NET up to .NET 6.0, and updates have occurred within the last few months, so it would appear that Khorikov is keeping up with the latest .NET developments. My experiments with the library were all with .NET 7.0, in any case, and everything worked just fine.

Maybe

I tried the same Maybe-driven MakeGreeting function that I've used elsewhere in this chapter, but CSharpFunctionalExtensions supports only Maybes with nullable data types, so an int simply wasn't possible as a parameter value.

The easy fix is to make the employeeId variable nullable. Alternative solutions could have included making a complex parameter class with potentially many parameters or making the int a Maybe<int> instead. This will do for the purposes of demonstration, though.

Here's the code we'd end up with:

```
public static Maybe<string> MakeGreeting(int? employeeId) =>
    employeeId.AsMaybe().Map(empRepo.GetById)
        .Map(x => "Hello " + x.Salutation + " " + x.Name);
```

As with many other libraries I've looked at, there's no option to use a switch expression to collapse the Maybe down to a concrete value; instead, some built-in helper functions allow us to do the job:

```
var martyMcFly = MakeGreeting(1985);
var messageToUser = martyMcFly.HasValue
    ? martyMcFly.Value
    : "Intruder Alert!";
```

Alternatively, we can use a Match() function:

```
var martyMcFly = MakeGreeting(1985);
var messageToUser = martyMcFly.Match(x => "Success: " + x,
    () => "Intruder Alert!");
```

Nothing really is wrong with this. There are only two possible values, so it's a perfectly decent way of handling the Something/Nothing scenario.

It has built-in features for handling async functions as well, and some functions for applying logical operations to the contents of the Maybe, like this:

```
public static Maybe<string> MakeMessage(int? employeeId) =>
    employeeId.AsMaybe().Map(empRepo.GetById)
        .Where(x => !x.Interests.Contains("Homer Simpson"))
        .Map(x => "Welcome, " + x.Name + "!")
            .Or(() => "This is the No Homers Club, be off with you!!");
```

I quite like the Where() and Or() methods, and I can't promise I won't be using a version of them in my own code at some point!

Result

Result is similar in some ways to the Either monad I mentioned back in Chapter 7. Like a Something, it holds a value, but beyond that, it can also exist in one of two forms: Success or Failure. The difference between this and the Maybe is that either way it holds the value.

The two classes in this union type are used for information purposes—do we consider this operation a success or not. The library contains a set of fluent-style functions we can use to define whether we think the end result should be a success.

Here's an example:

```
public static Maybe<string> MakeMessage(int? employeeId) =>
    employeeId.AsMaybe()
        .Map(empRepo.GetById)
        .ToResult("Could not find the employee")
        .Ensure(x => x.Interests.Contains("Doctor Who"), "You don't like DW!")
        .Ensure(x => x.Name != "Homer Simpson",
        "I keep telling you Homer, this is our tree house!")
        .Tap(x => Logger.LogInformation("Processing " + x.Name))
        .Finally(
        x => x.IsSuccess
        ? "Welcome to the No Homers Club, " + x.Value.Name
            : "Couldn't sign up " + x.Value.Name + ": " + x.Error);
```

The Ensure() function here will return a Result<T> that's a Success if its parameter function returns true; otherwise, it's a Failure.

As with a Maybe, once a result is in the Failure state, any subsequent Ensure() calls will not be executed.

The Finally() function will be executed at the end, regardless of Success or Failure, and can be used to collapse Result into a real value.

Fluent Assertions

One of my favorite libraries in NuGet is Fluent Assertions. It's used to write asserts for unit tests that are something closer to natural language. Not just that, but it's an incredibly rich library, containing all sorts of nifty assert types to make the job of writing unit tests easier.

CSharpFunctionalExtensions can also be further extended with another library: CSharpFunctionalExtensions.FluentAssertions, which adds more asserts to Fluent Assertions, specifically for use with this functional library. If you've decided to use CSharpFunctionalExtensions, I'd make sure you include that library as well.

CSharpFunctionalExtensions Wrap-up

The CSharpFunctionalExtensions library isn't as definitive as LanguageExt; it contains only two structures. However, the design of those structures is really quite lovely. The expressive function names and the ability to use a fluent-style interface to write a detailed piece of functionality make this library well worth your consideration.

The F# Programming Language

Oh, come on. You're just being silly now!

This said, it's not a NuGet package, but you *can* reference .NET projects written in F# from C# projects, so...yes, I *suppose* so. This topic is well outside the scope of this book, however.

Summary

Quite a few libraries are available already in NuGet if you want the initial creation of functional structures handled for you. These range from the fully comprehensive (LanguageExt) to those that just supply a few functional features each (OneOf, Functional.Maybe, etc.).

Whether you want to use some, all, or none of these libraries is entirely up to you.

Using none of them will mean you'll have to develop your own functional classes and extension methods. This is a little more work, but means you won't be dependent upon a third-party library, and you'll be able to customize your classes and methods to work however you'd like.

Using a library will save you that effort, but force you to work to the style required by that library. You'll also be dependent on that library's development team to continue to produce updates.

As with all decisions, you need to consider the risks and benefits, weigh them, and see which way the scales tilt.

I can't advise you on this, but I'll be honest—I don't use a library. I have my own custom functional library that I port between projects—either in part or in its entirety, depending on what I need to do. Having said that, there's nothing wrong with using one. The libraries I've listed in this chapter are excellent pieces of work, and no doubt will be invaluable to you if you choose to use them.

In the next chapter, I'm going to put everything together into a game you can write and play yourself—entirely in functional-style C#. Have fun!

CHAPTER 13

The Martian Trail

Well folks, our time together is coming to an end shortly. I hope you're finding this book as rewarding to read as I did to write. Since it's nearly the proverbial last day of school, I thought we could have a bit of fun to put everything together. This way, I can show you an example of how a complete functional C# application might look.

When I was young, in the days when we still traveled to school on dinosaurs and had mammoth steak for lunch, I learned to program from a series of books on BASIC.[1] These Usborne Publishing books had titles like *Computer Battlegames* and contained the source code to games you could enter into the computer yourself. They're all available on the Usborne website (*https://oreil.ly/FpZkr*) if you're interested. They usually had a sci-fi theme but turned out to be entirely text based and nothing whatsoever like the painted action scene that accompanied them. In that vein, I present to you my own contribution to that rather obscure genre.

I've taken inspiration from the 1975 version of *Oregon Trail* by Don Rawitsch, Bill Heinemann, and Paul Dillenberger in HP Time-Shared BASIC. This is just inspired by it, however; none of the original code or text has been used here.

Story

The year is 2147, and humanity has finally reached the planet Mars. Not only have we traveled there, but settlement of the red planet is well underway. New cities, outposts, and trading posts are starting to spring up everywhere.

---

1 BASIC stands for Beginner's All-purpose Symbolic Instruction Code, a programming language popular in the '70s and '80s and now only really interesting to hobbyists like myself.

You and your family are among the latest batch of settlers to set down at the main travel terminus, which is located in the colossal impact crater known as Hellas Basin. Travel time from Earth to Mars is far faster than it was back in the old days, but it's still a matter of weeks. You spent all that time planning your route from Hellas Basin to your plot of land up in Amazonis Planitia, which will involve a crossing of Tharsis Rise along the way. It's going to be a long, difficult, and dangerous journey.

Not only is Mars a harsh environment, requiring everyone to wear atmosphere suits the entire time you're on the surface, but also it turns out there absolutely *are* Martians. Writers from the 20th century who took space exploration far less seriously than they should have portrayed Martians as small, green-skinned creatures with no hair and antennae coming out of theirs heads. As it turns out, that's *precisely* what they look like. Who'd have thought it?

Most Martians are fairly affable and don't mind trading with the incoming Earthlings. Humanity could learn a lot from those folks. But some aren't keen on what they see as trespassers on their land, and those are the ones to look out for on the trail ahead.

For gathering food on the journey (it'll last weeks, and you can't carry that much with you), you'll have the chance to hunt a type of native Martian fauna: Vrolids. They're short, stocky, and purple, and smell bad but taste good.

For earning money, you can attempt to corner a herd of wild Lophroll, whose long, luxuriant fur is perfect for coats, or '70s prog-rock style wigs for amateur guitarists and flutists. Prog rock had a resurgence in popularity in 2145, and there are even now alters to rock gods Ian Anderson and Steve Hackett on Earth's capital city.[2] Finally, you'll periodically be able to trade with outposts along the route for supplies, if you make it that far!

It's going to take weeks of hard traveling by hover barge to get where you need to be—over 16,000 kilometers away! Best of luck!

Technical Detail

We'll need a few things to make our game of Martian travel and survival come to life.

First, we'll need a central game engine, as shown in Figure 13-1. I'm keeping life simple and making this entirely text based in a console app. You can always adapt it however you'd like in your own version and create a graphic interface of some kind. Graphics aren't a specific feature of the functional paradigm, so I'm considering them outside the scope of this book.

---

2 Would you believe, so much arguing arose over where to make the capital that after nearly 500 vetoes, it turned out to be British seaside resort Bognor Regis by default. Now political debates can be done on the beach with an ice-cream cone.

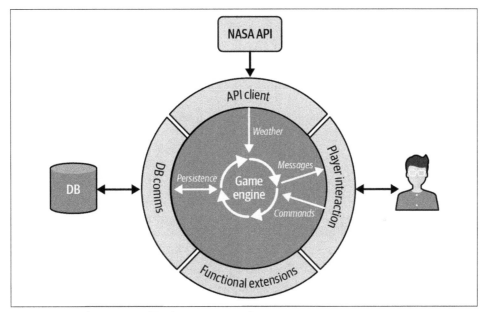

Figure 13-1. The Martian Trail game engine design

The game engine itself will be an indefinite loop of some kind. It will prompt the player for a command and then return that command to be processed.

Many small modules will hang off the central game engine, doing all sorts of bits of work based on the command entered.

That's the central, entirely functional, part of the system. Around it is the nonfunctional shell that provides some essential nonfunctional extension methods and communications with the outside world.

A few external interactions occur in this game. These include a database to allow the player to save their progress, which I'll simplify to a flat file to reduce the number of necessary steps, and the NASA web API to look up details of current conditions on Mars. It'd be fun to make it a little more accurate.

The game starts with a setup sequence in which the player spends money on the following:

Batteries
    For holding solar power. The more batteries you have, the more distance you can travel in a day.

Food
    If you don't know what this is, I'm not sure how you've made it past infancy!

Laser charges
> For powering laser guns, naturally.

Atmosphere suits
> Needed for surviving out on the inhospitable Martian surface.

Medipacks
> Standard Kornbluth medical supply packs can cure nearly anything. They come in little black bags.

Terran credits
> Easily exchangeable for the local currency of your choice. No one is sure what the Martians use for money. Perhaps they're too civilized to need it!

Once the initial inventory is set up, the turn sequence consists of the following:

1. Check for special statuses and prompt the player to do something.

2. Display the actions for the current turn and record the player's choice, which can include trading, hunting for food, hunting for Lophroll furs to sell, or just continuing on with the journey.

3. Update the number of kilometers traveled and food eaten.

4. Determine which random events occur and inform the player of the results.

5. Clean up and make everything ready for the next stop.

This carries on until the player has traveled more than 16,000 km, meaning they've reached Amazonis Planitia, or an end game condition has occurred (i.e., the death of the player's character).

Creating the Game

In the sections that follow, I'll talk you through the process of creating the game with as many notes as possible to help understand my thought process and how I architect it. I'm not going to spell out every single step, but a complete copy of the source code is available in my GitHub account (*https://oreil.ly/PxHQv*).

The Solution

Before we start, we need to set up a solution and subprojects.

Create a new Solution of type Console Application and call it *MartianTrail*. This will be our game itself.

You'll need a unit test project as well, called MartianTrail.Tests. I prefer xUnit. As a matter of personal preference, I usually install the following NuGet dependencies to the test project: Fluent Assertions, Moq, AutoFixture, and AutoFixture.AutoMoq. These aren't necessary, so I'll leave those up to you.

Communications

As we start building out the game, the first thing we need is the ability for the player and game to communicate. For this, create a new folder called *UserInteraction*, and in it a new code file containing a couple of DUs that represent interactions with the player and the possible consequences.

These are as follows:

UserInteraction
> Information provided by the user via the console. This information has these possible states:

> IntegerInput
>> The player entered a numeric value. We can use this for determining which choice from a selection the player made, or validating amounts of money spent.

> TextInput
>> The player entered text that wasn't numeric.

> EmptyInput
>> The player just pressed the Enter key without any input. This is a form of error state.

> UserInputError
>> An exception was raised from the console.

Operation
> An interaction with the user in which we aren't expecting any data back. This occurs in situations such as writing a message to the console, but not expecting anything to be typed back. Here are its possible states:

> Success
>> The operation completed without error.

> Failure
>> The operation resulted in an exception being thrown. The exception is captured in this object.

Details of how to implement these unions, along with a ConsoleShim and User Interaction client class can be found in Chapter 6.

Now that we're able to swap data two ways between the game and player, we need something to say.

Want to Learn How to Play?

The first task of the game upon loading is to ask the player whether they'd like instructions on how to play.

For that, we need to combine our existing abilities to take input from the player and to send messages, and have the function that results from the combination also return a calculated Boolean value that will determine whether the message should be sent. This removes the need to have `if` statements in the purely functional area of the codebase.

Add these two functions to both the `IPlayerInteraction` interface and the `Player Interaction` class that implements it:

```
public Operation WriteMessage(params string[] prompt) =>
    console.WriteLine(prompt);

public Operation WriteMessageConditional(
    bool condition,
    params string[] prompt) =>
    condition
        ? WriteMessage(prompt)
        : new Success();
```

Now, back in the root of the project, we can create a new folder called *Instruction* that contains an interface called `IDisplayInstructions` and its implementation `DisplayInstructions.cs`. These represent the operation to ask the player if they want instructions on how to play, and the message that's written to screen if they do.

The interface is as simple as it gets. We don't necessarily care how the operation went, so a `void` return type is fine:

```
public interface IDisplayInstructions
{
    void DisplayInstructions();
}
```

I'm not going to present the whole of the code for the `DisplayInstructions` class here, because the instructions are fairly lengthy. Instead, I'll show a few choice extracts.

First, a `UserInteraction` instance needs to be injected via the constructor, to allow us to test it, as well as to provide a method for communication with the player:

```
private readonly IPlayerInteraction userInteraction;

public DisplayInstructions(IPlayerInteraction userInteraction)
```

```
{
    this.userInteraction = userInteraction;
}
```

For determining whether the user has said some variation on *yes*, a collection-based approach tends to keep things simple:

```
void IDisplayInstructions.DisplayInstructions()
{
    var displayInstructionsAnswer = this.userInteraction.GetInput(
      "Would you like to learn how to play this game?");

    var positiveResponses = new []
    {
        "YES",
        "Y",
        "YEAH",
        "SURE",
        "WHY NOT"
    }

    var displayInstructions = displayInstructionsAnswer switch
    {
        TextInput ti when positiveResponses.contains(ti.TextFromUser.ToUpper() =>
          true,
        _ => false
    };

    this.userInteraction.WriteMessageConditional(displayInstructions,
          "Martian Trail - Instructions"
          string.Empty,
          "Welcome to the Planet Mars, brave explorer.  Here are the",
          "things you need to know in order to survive here, on your new",
          "homeworld..."
          // Insert the rest of the instructions here...
        );
}
```

Now that the player hopefully knows what they're doing, the next step is to give them their initial bank balance and ask them to buy things for the journey ahead.

We could put that `positiveResponses` logic into a shared class somewhere, but as it happens there isn't anywhere else in this codebase that needs to know whether a response was positive, so that logic can simply sit here by itself.

The Inventory Setup

Writing a function to set up the player's Inventory is going to call for a series of wheels within wheels. We require not only a loop to move from inventory item to item, but also a loop within each item to validate the player's input. In addition, a bit of overarching logic determines whether the player has overspent.

We're going to move from inventory item to item, and in each case ask the player what they'd like to spend on it. If their choice is invalid, we'll ask them to try again until we get an answer we like.

The player has a total of 1,000 Terran credits to play with.[3] The only rules for each iteration of the inventory selection are that the spending must be 0 or more, and that it can't be greater than the current number of credits remaining.

At the end of the entire sequence, we'll prompt the player with a list of their choices, and ask whether they're happy. If they are, we can move on. Otherwise, it's time to loop back to the beginning and try the whole thing again.

The GameState object will have a section for inventory, but this section has its own metadata (a bool that records whether the player is happy with their selection) which is of no use later, so let's create a state record specifically for this section:

```
public record InventorySelectionState
{
    public int NumberOfBatteries { get; set; }
    public int Food { get; set; }
    public int LaserCharges { get; set; }
    public int AtmosphereSuits { get; set; }
    public int MediPacks { get; set; }
    public int Credits { get; set; }
    public bool PlayerIsHappyWithSelection { get; set; }
}
```

We'll also need a cross-application domain version that doesn't contain the additional metadata and can be passed around between modules:

```
public record InventoryState
{
    public int NumberOfBatteries { get; set; }
    public int Food { get; set; }
    public int LaserCharges { get; set; }
    public int AtmosphereSuits { get; set; }
    public int MediPacks { get; set; }
    public int Credits { get; set; }
}
```

The next step is to set up an indefinite loop that is looking for a happy player to allow the loop to complete. Strictly speaking, the concept of classes isn't a thing in FP, but in the C# world, we have a few choices.

If you want to go down the more purely functional route, create a static class called InventorySelection and have a static function within that to return an Inventory record. This will be done only after the final selections have been made.

---

3 "Terra" is the Latin word for "the Earth." A lot of old sci-fi stories call us "Terrans" and I rather like it!

This isn't conducive to good unit testing, though. It'd need all sorts of User Interaction mock setups to be created for every unit test that touches the main game module. It's less purely functional, but given this is C#, I'd rather continue to use classes and interfaces so that we can more easily provide mocks during unit tests.

The interface for the inventory selection module looks like this:

```
public interface IInventorySelection
{
  InventoryState SelectInitialInventory(IPlayerInteraction playerInteraction);
}
```

Next, put the InventorySelectionState record, this interface, and its implementation all together in a folder called *InventorySelection* in the project. This way, we're keeping everything grouped together logically.

This approach also allows the InventorySelectionState to be expanded later, if we think of some other metadata we want to throw in after improving the game, but the cross-domain version InventoryState can stay as it is, not needing to know what's happened internally within this module.

Create a new class in the *InventorySelection* folder called SelectInitialInventory Client, which should implement IInventorySelection.

To represent the outcome of each attempt by the player to select a usable value for the current inventory item, let's create a DU to represent every eventuality:

```
public InventoryState SelectInitialInventory(IPlayerInteraction pInteract)
{
    throw new NotImplementedException();
}

public abstract class InventorySelectionResult { }

public class InventorySelectionInvalidInput { }

public class InventorySelectionValueTooLow { }

public class InventorySelectionValueTooHigh { }

public class InventorySelectionValid
{
    public int QuantitySelected { get; set; }
    public int UpdatedCreditsAmount { get; set; }
}
```

We've defined this within the SelectInitialInventoryClient class, since it'll never be used anywhere else. I wouldn't blame you for wanting to use less verbose class names, but I like my code to be descriptive.

To save effort, we can create a generic function to handle all the inventory selections. We'd just need to pass it the parts of the logic that would change every time:

- The name of the inventory item
- The place within `InventorySelectionState` to update
- The cost in credits of the items being bought

It might look something like this:

```
private InventorySelectionState MakeInventorySelection(
    IPlayerInteraction playerInteraction,
    InventorySelectionState oldState,
    string name,
    int costPerItem,
    Func<int, InventorySelectionState, InventorySelectionState> updateFunc)
{
    var numberAffordable = oldState.Credits / costPerItem;
    var validateUserChoice = (int x) => x >= 0 && x <= numberAffordable;

        var userAttempt = playerInteraction.GetInput(
        name + " Selection.  They cost " +
        costPerItem + "per item.  How many would you like? " +
         " You can't afford more than " +
         numberAffordable);

    var validUserInput = userAttempt.IterateUntil(
        x =>
        {
            var userMessage = userAttempt switch
            {
                IntegerInput i when i.IntegerFromUser < 0 =>
                 "That was less than zero",
                IntegerInput i when
                 (i.IntegerFromUser * costPerItem) > oldState.Credits =>
                  "You can't accord that many!",
                IntegerInput _ => "Thank you",
                EmptyInput => "You have to enter a value",
                TextInput => "That wasn't an integer value",
                UserInputError e => "An error occurred: " +
                 e.ExceptionRaised.Message
            };

            playerInteraction.WriteMessage(userMessage);

            return x is IntegerInput ii && validateUserChoice(ii.IntegerFromUser)
                ? x
                : playerInteraction.GetInput("Please try again...");
        }, x => x is IntegerInput ii && validateUserChoice(ii.IntegerFromUser));

    var numberOfItemsBought = (validUserInput as IntegerInput).IntegerFromUser;
```

```
    var updatedInventory = updateFunc(numberOfItemsBought, oldState) with
    {
        Credits = oldState.Credits - (numberOfItemsBought * costPerItem)
    };

    return updatedInventory;
}
```

Let's consider for a few minutes what this function is doing.

First, we're including *everything* it needs in the parameters list to keep it pure. If you want, you could have the constructor to this class contain the IPlayerInteraction instance, and reference that as a property of the class. It would save a bit of code noise, and there's nothing wrong with doing it that way. I'll leave the choice to you.

Next, we're making an initial attempt at getting the player's choice, and then iterating on that indefinitely until we're certain it's a valid choice. We've held the logic to validate the number of items bought as a Func delegate, so we can reference it multiple times without repeating the same code.

Inside the indefinite iteration, we're determining exactly what was entered by the player, determining what to say back to them, and then choosing whether to iterate again.

Figure 13-2 shows what this process looks like in diagram form.

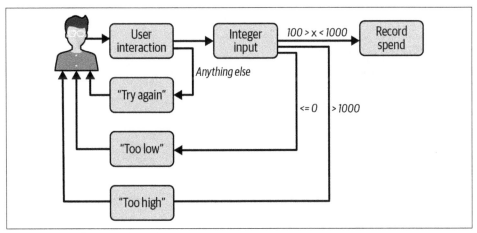

Figure 13-2. The initial purchases process

An interesting phenomenon to note: Visual Studio will complain about the casting of validUserInput into an IntegerInput as a possible null reference exception, even though there is nothing else it could ever logically be. I'd guess that Visual Studio simply can't see deeply enough into the code to understand that no null value is possible. The compiler warning can be ignored safely in this instance.

Sadly, so far as I'm aware, it's not currently possible to have lambda expressions in tuples as of .NET 7, so we can create a quick struct to wrap the inventory configurations instead:

```
public struct InventoryConfiguration
{
    public string Name { get; set; }
    public int CostPerItem { get; set; }
    public Func<int, InventorySelectionState, InventorySelectionState>
    UpdateFunc { get; set; }

    public InventoryConfiguration(
     string name,
     int costPerItem,
     Func<int, InventorySelectionState, InventorySelectionState> updateFunc)
    {
        Name = name;
        CostPerItem = costPerItem;
        UpdateFunc = updateFunc;
    }

}
```

This is how I created the inventory configurations. The prices I've chosen here are a little arbitrary. Feel free to tinker around with them if you want to try developing this game yourself:

```
private readonly IEnumerable<InventoryConfiguration> _inventorySelections = new[]
{
    new InventoryConfiguration("Batteries", 50, (q, oldState) =>
        oldState with { NumberOfBatteries = q}),
    new InventoryConfiguration("Food Packs", 10, (q, oldState) =>
        oldState with { Food = q}),
    new InventoryConfiguration("Laser Charges ", 40, (q, oldState) =>
        oldState with { LaserCharges = q}),
    new InventoryConfiguration("Atmosphere Suits", 15, (q, oldState) =>
        oldState with { AtmosphereSuits = q}),
    new InventoryConfiguration("MediPacks", 30, (q, oldState) =>
        oldState with { MediPacks = q})
};
```

I'm aware it's probably not all that much work to do something clever with reflection and remove this entire array with a few lines of code, but I'm not sure what the benefit is going to be. The code is unlikely to be updated often, if at all, and reflection has a performance cost, as well as potentially giving rise to problems if things don't match up at runtime.

Here's a function to display the current state of the inventory:

```
private void DisplayInventory(IPlayerInteraction playerInteraction,
  InventorySelectionState state) =>
    playerInteraction.WriteMessage(
```

```
        "Batteries: " + state.NumberOfBatteries,
        "Food Packs: " + state.Food,
        "Laser Charges: " + state.LaserCharges,
        "Atmosphere Suits: " + state.AtmosphereSuits,
        "MediPacks: " + state.MediPacks,
        "Remaining Credits: " + state.Credits
    );
```

We'll use this here and there so the player can make informed choices.

Here's how we'd code a request to the player to confirm whether they're happy with the selection of inventory purchases:

```
private InventorySelectionState UpdateUserIsHappyStatus(
  IPlayerInteraction playerInteraction,
    InventorySelectionState oldState)
{
    var yes = new[]
    {
        "Y",
        "YES",
        "YEP",
        "WHY NOT",
    };

    var no = new[]
    {
        "N",
        "NO",
        "NOPE",
        "ARE YOU JOKING??!??",
    };

    this.DisplayInventory(playerInteraction, oldState);

    bool GetPlayerResponse(string message)
    {
        var playerResponse = playerInteraction.GetInput(message);
        var validatedPlayerResponse = playerResponse switch
        {
            TextInput ti when yes.Contains(ti.TextFromUser.ToUpper()) => true,
            TextInput ti when no.Contains(ti.TextFromUser.ToUpper()) => false,
            _ => GetPlayerResponse("Sorry, could you try again?")
        };
        return validatedPlayerResponse;
    };

    return (oldState with
    {
        PlayerIsHappyWithSelection = GetPlayerResponse(
          "Are you happy with these purchases?")
    }).Map(x => x with
    {
```

```
        Credits = x.PlayerIsHappyWithSelection ? x.Credits : 1000
    });
}
```

Note the use of a recursive function here. It was the simpler choice in this situation, and there are unlikely to be that many wrong attempts at entering some variation on yes or no, so it's a fairly safe thing to use here.

Finally, we need to make a public implementation of the `SelectInitialInventory()` function that puts everything together:

```
public InventoryState SelectInitialInventory(IPlayerInteraction playerInteract)
{
    var initialState = new InventorySelectionState
    {
        Credits = 1000
    };

    var finalState = initialState.IterateUntil(x =>
            this._inventorySelections.Aggregate(x, (acc, y) =>
                    this.MakeInventorySelection(
                        playerInteract, acc, y.Name, y.CostPerItem, y.UpdateFunc)
                ).Map(y => this.UpdateUserIsHappyStatus(playerInteract, y))
            , x => x.PlayerIsHappyWithSelection);

    var returnValue = new InventoryState
    {
        NumberOfBatteries = finalState.NumberOfBatteries,
        Food = finalState.Food,
        LaserCharges = finalState.LaserCharges,
        AtmosphereSuits = finalState.AtmosphereSuits,
        MediPacks = finalState.MediPacks,
        Credits = finalState.Credits
    };
    return returnValue;
}
```

All done. We now have all the code required to request the player to select how many of each item of inventory they want, along with various bits of validation logic. An overarching loop will allow the player to validate their entire set of choices and decide whether to move on to playing the game.

If you want to give this code a test run quickly now, try changing your *program.cs* file to the following:

```
using MartianTrail.InventorySelection;
using MartianTrail.PlayerInteraction;

var inventory = new SelectInitialInventoryClient();
inventory.SelectInitialInventory(new PlayerInteractionClient(new ConsoleShim()));
```

This will create the class that will create the initial inventory for the player, and also pass in all the real implementations of the interfaces it depends on.

This game is small and simple enough that there's no real point in creating an IoC container—unless you really want to. It's your code!

The Game Loop

Now that we have some of the basic structure set, the first thing needed for an actual playable game is a basic loop that represents the player's turn. These turns consist of a message from the game, prompting the player to make a choice, and the player's choice and its consequences.

We need an indefinite loop that continues until the game has ended, one way or another. For that, we'll also need a GameState record. Let's create it now with a couple of properties:

```
public record GameState
{
    public bool PlayerIsDead { get; set; }
    public bool ReachedDestination { get; set; }
}
```

To drive the indefinite loop, use the IterateUntil() extension method from Chapter 9, which we can place in a file called *FunctionalExtensions.cs*.

Finally, for the loop, we want to keep the code nice and neat when we're defining the flow of the game turn, so let's also create an extension method to continue the progress of the turn that will internalize the logic that checks to see whether the game has ended. It's a technique inspired by the Bind() function attached to some monads:

```
public static GameState ContinueTurn(
    this GameState @this,
    Func<GameState, GameState> f) =>
    @this.ReachedDestination || @this.PlayerIsDead
        ? @this
        : f(@this);
```

This means we can chain together many functions that create new instances of the GameState record, but we won't be required to make a check after every update to see whether the game has ended already. This will act somewhat like a two-state Maybe monad and not execute any functions provided in the event of the game ending.

Each game module after this point takes the form of a function that takes the current instance of the GameState record and returns a new, modified GameState to replace it with.

In fact, it's easy enough to create a generic interface that represents any given phase of the game. So that's just what we'll do:

```
public interface IGamePhase
{
    GameState DoPhase(IPlayerInteraction playerInteraction, GameState oldState);
}
```

Consequently, the entirety of the loop that powers the game engine can now be written in a fairly simple bit of code:

```
public class Game
{
    public GameState Play(
     GameState initialState,
     IPlayerInteraction playerInteraction,
     params IGamePhase[] gamePhases)
    {
        var gp = gamePhases.ToArray();

        var finalState = initialState.IterateUntil(x =>
            gp.Aggregate(x, (acc, y) =>
             acc.ContinueTurn( z => y.DoPhase(playerInteraction, z))),
            x => x.PlayerIsDead || x.ReachedDestination
        );

        return finalState;
    }
}
```

This class takes the initial state, and a list of all the phases of the game that will update that state. We use `Aggregate()` to apply the phases one after the other. Note the use of the `ContinueTurn()` extension method. This has the monad-like short-circuit built in that'll stop future phases from being executed after the game has already ended.

This indefinite loop will continue to run the turn sequence again and again until either the player dies or the final destination of the expedition is reached. Either would trigger the end of the game.

Let's define a few game phases now. Then the last job will be to reference the `Game` class in *program.cs* and pass it all the phases we've defined.

Creating a weather report

I'm British, and as I've said previously, there's nothing more British than discussing the weather, which is exactly what I'll begin this game with, even if we are now on Mars. I'd do it by getting some real Martian data. Give this a sense of authenticity. We can do that by creating a web API call to NASA's Mars API. Since that's a call to an external system, we'll also need to wrap that in a `Maybe`, since any manner of things can go wrong. See Chapter 7 for more details on how to implement a `Maybe` monad in C#.

This is a super simple implementation of a set of classes to provide a mechanism to download data from a web API endpoint. Feel free to make this as complicated as you like, but I'm keeping it simple since this is just an example, not a chapter on web communication.

First, we need a shim class for the built-in `HttpClient` class, which has no usable interface to inject into dependent classes:

```
public interface IHttpClient
{
    Task<HttpResponseMessage> GetAsync(string url);
}

public class HttpClientShim : IHttpClient
{
    private readonly HttpClient _httpClient;

    public HttpClientShim(HttpClient httpClient)
    {
        _httpClient = httpClient;
    }

    public Task<HttpResponseMessage> GetAsync(string url) =>
        _httpClient.GetAsync(url);
}
```

We're still using the built-in `HttpResponseMessage` for now, but if you want to do this, you'll probably need to provide your own shim implementation of each of the subclasses.

Here's a class that uses `async` bind calls to various `HttpClient` methods to convert ultimately from a URI to usable data:

```
public interface IFetchWebApiData
{
    Task<Maybe<T>> FetchData<T>(string url);
}

public async Task<Maybe<T>> FetchData<T>(string url)
{
    try
    {
        var response = await this._httpClient.GetAsync(url);
        Maybe<string> data = response.IsSuccessStatusCode
            ? new Something<string>(await response.Content.ReadAsStringAsync())
            : new Nothing<string>();

        var contentStream = await data.BindAsync(x =>
            response.Content.ReadAsStreamAsync());
```

```
            var returnValue = await contentStream.BindAsync(x =>
              JsonSerializer.DeserializeAsync<T>(x));
            return returnValue;
        }
        catch (Exception e)
        {
            return new Error<T>(e);
        }
    }
```

Now that we got that, we can make a call to the NASA Mars API to display the current weather on Mars. The Martian day is measured in *sols*, which is the amount of time required for Mars to rotate once on its axis. It's just short of 40 minutes longer than an Earth day. There are 668 sols in a Martian year (that's how long it takes for Mars to complete an orbit around the sun).

The NASA API call returns a set of historical data for the current sol, and a large number of sols previous to it. We're going to treat each day as a sol, so we'll start with the lowest sol on record, then count up by one on each turn, using an integer field in the game state object to keep track of the player's location.

The weather information should give a bit of real Martian flavor to our game, as well as providing a practical example of the use of the Maybe monad in real code.

First, we need a class to store the NASA data. The API contains a lot more than this, but this code is restricted to just the data items we're interested in:

```
public class NasaMarsData
{
    public IEnumerable<NasaSolData> soles { get; set; }
}

public class NasaSolData
{
    public string id { get; set; }
    public string sol { get; set; }
    public string max_temp { get; set; }
    public string min_temp { get; set; }
    public string local_uv_irradiance_index { get; set; }

}
```

Create a folder called *GamePhases* to store all these code classes we're about to make.

This is the code to display today's Martian weather:

```
public class DisplayMartianWeather : IGamePhase
{
    private readonly IFetchWebApiData _webApiClient;

    public DisplayMartianWeather(IFetchWebApiData webApiClient)
    {
```

```
        _webApiClient = webApiClient;
    }

    private string FormatMarsData(NasaSolData sol) =>
        "Mars Sol " + sol.sol + Environment.NewLine +
        "\tMin Temp: " + sol.min_temp + Environment.NewLine +
        "\tMax Temp: " + sol.max_temp + Environment.NewLine +
        "\tUV Irradiance Index: " + sol.local_uv_irradiance_index +
         Environment.NewLine;


    public GameState DoPhase(
        IPlayerInteraction playerInteraction,
        GameState oldState)
    {

    // I'm calling Result here, which forces this to be synchronous.
    // This isn't a web app, there is only a single user, so I'm not
    // really very concerned.
        var data =
            this._webApiClient.FetchData<NasaMarsData>(
            "https://mars.nasa.gov/rss/api/?" +
            "feed=weather&category=msl&feedtype=json")
             .Result;

        var currentSolData = data.Bind(x => oldState.CurrentSol == 0
            ? x.soles.MaxBy(y => int.Parse(y.sol))
            : x.soles.SingleOrDefault(y =>
                y.sol == oldState.CurrentSol.ToString())
        );

        var formattedData = currentSolData.Bind(FormatMarsData);

        var message = formattedData switch
        {
            Something<string> s => s.Value,
            _ => string.Empty
        };

        playerInteraction.WriteMessage(message);

        return oldState with
        {
            CurrentSol = currentSolData is Something<NasaSolData> s1
            ? int.Parse(s1.Value.sol) + 1
             : 0
        };
    }
}
```

The point of this code is to grab the data from NASA, which contains a list of recent sols and their respective weather reports. If we've already determined the current sol and stored it in GameState, we use that sol; otherwise, we use the oldest sol in the dataset.

If we were doing this for real, we'd probably also implement a caching system to prevent the need to fetch a fresh dataset from NASA every turn. I'll leave you to work out how to include that, since it's not really what this book is about.

The first step of the game is now finished. Next up is to decide which actions are available and to ask the player to select what they want to do.

Choosing what to do this turn

In our version of Mars, there are two possible areas to explore: relatively settled areas with buildings and fortifications, and wilderness (where anything is possible). Different choices will be available to the player, depending on whether they're in wilderness or near a settlement.

There's a roughly 33% chance that the current turn takes place near a settlement, and a 66% chance it's in the wilderness. All sorts of enhancements are possible; the probabilities could vary depending on which region of Mars the player is passing through. Let's keep it simple for now, though.

The first thing we need is the capability to select something randomly from a list of possibilities. We can't use the built-in .NET Random class, as that would mean adding unpredictable side effects into our functions, rendering them impure. Instead, we'll need to inject a dependency of some kind.

A purer language like Haskell does these jobs with one of its number of available monads. In a hybrid language like C#, I don't see any issue with simply using OOP-style dependency injection and adding in another shim class with an interface:

```
public interface IRandomNumberGenerator
{
    int BetweenZeroAnd(int input);
}

public class RandomNumberGenerator : IRandomNumberGenerator
{
    public int BetweenZeroAnd(int input) =>
        new Random().Next(0, input);
}
```

Injecting this, we can create a new class to handle the selection of available actions.

First, create an enum of actions, because these will be used now to make a selection, and then later again to make calculations on how far the player has traveled in this sol:

```
public enum PlayerActions
{
    Unavailable,
    TradeAtOutpost,
    HuntForFood,
    HuntForFurs,
    PushOn
}
```

The next step is to scaffold out a new game phase for selecting an action:

```
public class SelectAction : IGamePhase
{
    private readonly IRandomNumberGenerator _rnd;
    private readonly IPlayerInteraction _playerInteraction;


    public SelectAction(
        IRandomNumberGenerator rnd,
        IPlayerInteraction playerInteraction)
    {
        _rnd = rnd;
        _playerInteraction = playerInteraction;
    }

    public GameState DoPhase(
        IPlayerInteraction playerInteraction,
        GameState oldState)
    {
        // TODO
    }
}
```

The DoPhase() function here will be used to select which actions are available and which the player wants to perform.

I've decided to make the choices all based on more probability curves, with hunting actions being more likely to be available in the wilderness, and trading actions being more likely near settlements.

Bearing in mind that FP is structured more like the individual steps required to solve a mathematical problem, with no if statements or variables changed after they're created, we can write out this section as a series of Boolean flags:

```
var isWilderness = this._rnd.BetweenZeroAnd(100) > 33;
var isTradingOutpost = this._rnd.BetweenZeroAnd(100) > (isWilderness ? 90 : 10);
var isHuntingArea = this._rnd.BetweenZeroAnd(100) > (isWilderness ? 10 : 20);

var canHuntForFurs = isHuntingArea && this._rnd.BetweenZeroAnd(100) > (33);
var canHuntForFood = isHuntingArea && this._rnd.BetweenZeroAnd(100) > (33);
```

To be able to make lists of options in messages to the player, we need an array of everything that's possible to do this sol. I don't fancy having nested `if` statements to append into a list, so we need to do this in one. My solution is to have each of the available options with a ternary-style `if`, which either stores the option or an "unavailable" state, which we can use to filter by:

```
var options = new[]
    {
        isTradingOutpost
            ? PlayerActions.TradeAtOutpost
            : PlayerActions.Unavailable,
        canHuntForFood ? PlayerActions.HuntForFood : PlayerActions.Unavailable,
        canHuntForFurs ? PlayerActions.HuntForFurs : PlayerActions.Unavailable,
        PlayerActions.PushOn
    }.Where(x => x != PlayerActions.Unavailable)
    .Select((x, i) => (
        Action: x,
        ChoiceNumber: i + 1
    )).ToArray();
```

We've finished by selecting the list of available choices into a tuple, with the array index value used to give the user an integer to select options by. The advantage of doing it this way is that both the options and integer values associated with them are generated at runtime. This approach facilitates customizing the action list in any way, while still having a dynamically generated list of options (each with an integer ID) presented to the player.

We do need to actually send the message to the player, along with a bit of preamble, which we can do with a `string.join()` and a `Concat()`, which is a LINQ method that merges two arrays into a single array:

```
var messageToPlayer = string.Join(Environment.NewLine,
    new[]
    {
        "The area you are passing through is " + (isWilderness
        ? " wilderness"
        : "a small settlement"),
        "Here are your options for what you can do:"
    }.Concat(
        options.Select(x => "\t" + x.ChoiceNumber + " - " + x.Action switch
        {
            PlayerActions.TradeAtOutpost => "Trade at the nearby outpost",
            PlayerActions.HuntForFood => "Hunt for food",
            PlayerActions.HuntForFurs => "Hunt for Lophroll furs to sell later",
            PlayerActions.PushOn => "Just push on to travel faster"
        })
    )
);

this._playerInteraction.WriteMessage(messageToPlayer);
```

It's also necessary to ask the player what they want, and to validate that input with an indefinite loop to ensure they've entered something correct:

```
var playerChoice = this._playerInteraction.GetInput(
    "What would you like to do? ");
var validatedPlayerChoice = playerChoice.IterateUntil(
    x => this._playerInteraction.GetInput(
    "That's not a valid choice.  Please try again."),
    x => x is IntegerInput i && options.Any(y =>
    y.ChoiceNumber == i.IntegerFromUser));

var playerChoiceInt = (validatedPlayerChoice as IntegerInput).IntegerFromUser;
var actionToDo = options.Single(
 x => x.ChoiceNumber == playerChoiceInt).Action;
```

Finally, now that we have a validated player action in an enum type variable, we can apply it by selecting from a list of private functions in this class (which we'll create shortly):

```
Func<GameState, GameState> actionFunc = actionToDo switch
{
    PlayerActions.TradeAtOutpost => DoTrading,
    PlayerActions.HuntForFood => DoHuntingForFood,
    PlayerActions.HuntForFurs => DoHuntingForFurs,
    PlayerActions.PushOn => DoPushOn
};

var updatedState = actionFunc(oldState);

return updatedState with
{
  UserActionSelectedThisTurn = actionToDo
};
```

Let's start with the easiest: push on without doing anything. Honestly, that means that nothing is done, so no state change occurs (but mileage will be calculated differently later):

```
private GameState DoPushOn(GameState state) => state;
```

We'll handle the Hunting options in one go. For that, we need a way to represent the difficulty of hunting. My answer is to prompt the player with four randomly selected letters that they need to type in order. Their accuracy and the speed with which they type are then used as a multiplication factor to determine success.

That success factor is then used to modify the player's inventory. Better success means more gains and fewer losses.

The random letter mini-game is one that's likely to come up repeatedly whenever things like this happen, so we'll make that a module of its own, separate from the game phases. Place it in a folder called *MiniGame*.

Here's the interface:

```
namespace MartianTrail.MiniGame
{
    public interface IPlayMiniGame
    {
        decimal PlayMiniGameForSuccessFactor();
    }
}
```

And here's an implementation, which takes an IRandomNumberGenerator and IPlayerInteraction in its constructor, as well as another new shim, this time for DateTime.Now:

```
public interface ITimeService
{
    DateTime Now();
}

public class TimeService : ITimeService
{
    public DateTime Now() => DateTime.Now;
}
```

The MiniGame class has a single public function that generates the four random letters and then rates the player between 1 and 0 on two factors:

Text accuracy

Was each character accurately entered? The player earns 25% for each correct character. A score of 0 results if the length of text entered was wrong, or it wasn't text. An error on the console results in a retry.

Time accuracy

This starts at 1 and then reduces by 10% (0.1) for each additional second the player takes.

These two factors are then multiplied together. Here are two versions of the calculation.

Say the player is prompted to enter the text CXTD, and does so with 100% accuracy in 4 seconds. That would be a text accuracy of 1, and a time accuracy of $1 - (0.1 \times 4)$, which is 0.6. Multiplying 1×0.6 gives a final accuracy of 0.6.

On the other hand, say the player is prompted to enter the text EFSU but incorrectly enters EFSY in 3 seconds. That would be a text accuracy of 0.75 (calculated from $0.25 \times$ the 3 correct letters) and a time accuracy of 0.7 (calculated from $1 - (0.1 \times 3)$), giving a final accuracy of 0.525 (calculated by multiplying the two factors, 0.75×0.7).

As a final example, if the player panics and simply presses the Enter key instead of any text, they'd get a text accuracy of 0, and it wouldn't matter how much time they took, because the two factors are multiplied together and anything multiplied by 0 is also 0:

```
private static decimal RateAccuracy(string expected, string actual)
{
    var charByCharComparison = expected.Zip(actual,
        (x, y) => char.ToUpper(x) == char.ToUpper(y));
    var numberCorrect = charByCharComparison.Sum(x => x ? 1 : 0);
    var accuracyScore = (decimal)numberCorrect / 4;
    return accuracyScore;
}

public decimal PlayMiniGameForSuccessFactor()
{
    // I don't care what the user enters, I'm just getting them ready to
    // play.
    _ = this._playerInteraction.GetInput(
        "Get ready, the mini-game is about to begin.",
        "Press enter to begin....");

    var lettersToSelect = Enumerable.Repeat(0, 4)
        .Select(_ => this._rnd.BetweenZeroAnd(25))
        .Select(x => (char)('A' + x))
        .ToArray();

    var textToSelect = string.Join("", lettersToSelect);

    var timeStart = this._timeService.Now();

    var userAttempt = this._playerInteraction.GetInput(
        "Please enter the following as accurately as you can: " +
        textToSelect);

    var nonErrorInput = userAttempt is not UserInputError
        ? userAttempt
        : userAttempt.IterateUntil(
        x => this._playerInteraction.GetInput(
            "Please enter the following as accurately as you can: " +
            textToSelect),
        x => x is not UserInputError
    );

    var timeEnd = this._timeService.Now();

    var textAccuracy =
        nonErrorInput is TextInput { TextFromUser.Length: 4 } ti
            ? RateAccuracy(textToSelect, ti.TextFromUser)
            : 0M;

    var timeTaken = (timeEnd - timeStart).TotalSeconds;
```

```
    var timeAccuracy = 1M - (0.1M * (decimal)timeTaken);

    return textAccuracy * timeAccuracy;
}
```

With this all done, we can now inject an instance of the `MiniGameClient` into our `SelectAction` game phase class and use it for determining whether the player was able to hunt successfully. Then, based on that accuracy, the number of laser charges needs to be reduced, and the number of one of the inventory items needs to be increased.

Here's the hunting for food mini-game. I won't bother adding the furs version here, as it's effectively the same but with a different inventory item to update and different flavor text. You can still check out the full source code on my GitHub site (*https://oreil.ly/PxHQv*).

```
private GameState DoHuntingForFood(GameState state)
{
    this._playerInteraction.WriteMessage("You're hunting Vrolids for food.",
        "For that you'll have to play the mini-game...");

    var accuracy = this._playMiniGame.PlayMiniGameForSuccessFactor();

    var message = accuracy switch
    {
        >= 0.9M => new[]
        {
            "Great shot!  You brought down a whole load of the things!",
            "Vrolid burgers are on you today!"
        },
        0 => new[]
        {
            "You missed.  Were you taking a nap?"
        },
        _ => new []
        {
            "Not a bad shot",
            "You brought down at least a couple",
            "Don't go too crazy eating tonight"
        }
    };

    this._playerInteraction.WriteMessage(message);

    var laserChargesUsed = 50 * (1 - accuracy);
    var foodGained = 100 * accuracy;

    return state with
    {
        Inventory = state.Inventory with
        {
```

```
            LaserCharges = state.Inventory.LaserCharges - (int)laserChargesUsed,
            Food = state.Inventory.Food + (int)foodGained
        }
    };
}
```

I'll skip trading for now too. It's basically the same idea as the initial choice of actions. List a set of things the player can do: buy food, laser packs, batteries, etc., or else sell something they already have. Based on the selection made, update the inventory. Use an indefinite loop to keep presenting the player with things to do in the outpost until the player selects the "Leave the trading outpost" option.

Updating progress

This phase of the game doesn't involve any user choices. It's the phase that updates the game state based on the current supplies and conditions affecting the player.

Keeping the code fairly simple for now, it looks like this:

```
public GameState DoPhase(
    IPlayerInteraction playerInteraction,
    GameState oldState)
{
    playerInteraction.WriteMessage("End of Sol " + oldState.CurrentSol);
    var distanceTraveled = oldState.Inventory.NumberOfBatteries *
        (oldState.UserActionSelectedThisTurn == PlayerActions.PushOn ? 100 : 50);

    var batteriesUsedUp = this._rnd.BetweenZeroAnd(4);

    var foodUsedUp = this._rnd.BetweenZeroAnd(5) * 20;

    var newState = oldState with
    {
        DistanceTraveled = oldState.DistanceTraveled + distanceTraveled,
        Inventory = oldState.Inventory with
        {
            NumberOfBatteries = (oldState.Inventory.NumberOfBatteries -
              batteriesUsedUp)
                .Map(x => x >= 0 ? x : 0),
            Food = (oldState.Inventory.Food - foodUsedUp)
                .Map(x => x >= 0 ? x : 0)
        }
    };

    playerInteraction.WriteMessage("You have traveled " + distanceTraveled +
        " this Sol.",
    "That's a total distance of " + newState.DistanceTraveled);

    playerInteraction.WriteMessageConditional(batteriesUsedUp > 0,
        "You have " + newState.Inventory.NumberOfBatteries + " remaining");

    playerInteraction.WriteMessageConditional(foodUsedUp > 0,
```

```
        "You have " + newState.Inventory.Food + " remaining");

    return newState;
}
```

This is where it made a difference if the player stopped to do something or just rushed ahead. They're also burning up food and battery packs, which is why hunting, selling goods, and buying replacement supplies is essential to win the game.

Summary

I haven't given you code for a lot of the game. That's largely because it's fairly repetitive, and I just wanted to include pieces illustrating any interesting additional bits of functional structure. You can either visit my GitHub page (*https://oreil.ly/PxHQv*) to see the current version of the code, or you could be really daring and finish it yourself.

The main piece that's left is a random-event-generator module. All that essentially consists of is a call to the random-number generator and then selecting a function out of a long list, triggering a random event that affects the player.

This is where you can really let your imagination go wild! Here are a few ideas for positive events:

- The player finds a crashed speeder that has a stash of credits inside.
- A stampede of Vrolids occurs. Distance traveled is reduced, but there's extra food to be had! Perhaps a round of a mini-game can control how much of an effect this has.
- The player encounters some settlers having a yard sale. They're selling off their old batteries and atmosphere suits extremely cheaply.
- Friendly Martians appear and guide the player to a food source.

Here are a few ideas for negative events:

- Sand storm! Atmosphere suits are needed to survive. A number are used up. If the player is out of atmosphere suits, they die, lost to the storm.
- Dangerous predators attack during the night. Perhaps a mini-game is needed to fend them off. Failure of the player to defend themselves means death, as does running out of laser charges!

- Bandits are on the trail. They need to be fought off if any laser charges remain, or given all the credits the player has left.
- The player falls ill with some sort of awful, and slightly embarrassing, Martian illness. Medical supplies should be used, or the player dies.

Hopefully, this has given you plenty to go on and many ideas to try out. Feel free to add as many of your own as you can think of.

This game also could be expanded in plenty of ways. The Martian landscape could even be split into areas, with some having higher and lower probabilities of certain events occurring. This can be as complicated or as simple as you like.

The rest of it, though, I leave to you. It only remains for me to wish you a safe journey and happy trails ahead!

CHAPTER 14

Conclusion

It's the end of the book, party time! Right, everyone, let's get ready. I want the dancing girls over *there*, the dancing boys over *there* and...

Oh, just got a note from Mr. O'Reilly. We don't have the money for the big Broadway-style spectacular finish.

OK, what *do* we have. Right, there's my recorder, that'll do. Everyone likes the recorder, don't they? OK, and a *one* and a *two* and a...

Sorry, folks. I've just been reminded of what happened to all the milk in the house last time I played recorder. I suppose we'll just have to make do with a few thoughts from me to go home with. Such is life...

What Kind of Day Has It Been?

Joking aside, I hope you've enjoyed this book. It's taken me a fair bit of time to write, and as you can tell, I've put a lot of myself into it.

I've tried to keep the tone light throughout for a couple of reasons. First, so many dry (but nevertheless excellent) computing books are out there that I'm sure the market can handle *one* that isn't.[1] Second, FP itself has so many sites, articles, and books that focus on formal definitions that even I find nearly unreadable that I wanted to show that it doesn't have to be that way.

Over the course of this book, I've tried to take a shallow sloping path from out-of-the-box C# all the way to something that F# developers would find somewhat

---

1 This and *Mr. Bunny's Big Cup o' Java* by Carlton Egremont III (Addison-Wesley Professional), which I'm reliably informed really *is* the silliest computer book ever written. I almost wish I were a Java developer myself so I could read it!

familiar. Hopefully, none of it was too painful, and I hope you had a bit of fun along the way!

C# is, and will always remain, a hybrid language. It's unlikely to allow pure functional code ever to be written, and that's not a complaint. It's just the reality of the situation.

You have a few options for where to go from here, if you're still interested in continuing your functional journey beyond the scope of this book. Let me talk you through a few of those now.

Where Do I Go from Here?

You could continue your journey in many ways from here. I'll list them roughly in order from things that you'll find familiar to things that will require more learning from you to appreciate.

More Functional C#

It would be bizarrely remiss of me not to again mention Enrico Buonanno's fantastic book *Functional Programming in C#*, 2nd edition (Manning). It's one of the best programming books I've ever read. If you've started into FP here with me, Buonanno's book is the best place to continue.

He goes a little deeper into functional theory than I do and covers further ground that I've not gone into. Compared to my book, this one is a fine wine—worth savoring slowly and fully.

The most useful thing you can do, though, is to practice. Learning is mostly about repeating the same thing over and over again until you can do it without thinking. The best way to grow as a functional programmer is to worry less about learning theory and more about writing code.

As I've shown in this book, you don't have to implement the entire paradigm. Start with whatever you're comfortable with and go from there. Dip back into some of the available books once in a while for ideas of new techniques to try.

I advise bringing up the subject with your team at work, however. The material from the first few chapters of this book is all fairly noncontroversial, but it might raise eyebrows if you start throwing monads into your code unexpectedly. Or not. Depends on your team. Having a conversion first will at least avoid the awkward situation of someone objecting to functional-style coding *after* you've already filled a codebase with it, necessitating a long, expensive, tedious removal process.

After reading further into functional C# and practicing enough to become an expert, your next step would be to pick up a new language.

Learn F#

F# is the obvious next step for a functional C# developer. It's a .NET language and interops easily with C#, which means you can mix the code in your solution between the two languages, if that's what you want.

Many good sources are available for learning F#. I'd probably start with Scott Wlaschin's superlative website F# For Fun and Profit (*https://oreil.ly/r8uvQ*).

Ian Russell's ebook *Essential F#* (*https://oreil.ly/hxY9w*) costs *nothing* beyond whatever amount you'd like to pass his way. Ian has helped a great deal with proofreading and validating the content for this book, so I'm greatly indebted to him. Say hi to him for me, would you?

I rather like Isaac Abraham's book *Get Programming with F#* (Manning), which I also found quite easygoing.

Pure Functional Languages

If you've learned F# and are still hungry for more, the next step is to pick up one of the purer functional languages. No interop is possible between these and the .NET Framework, so how useful these would be in your .NET day job is questionable.

If you go to the extent of learning one of these languages, such as Elm or Haskell, your goal is going to be either of the following:

- To learn a purer form of the functional paradigm, with an idea of returning to .NET with new ideas for how to write code.
- To start an alternative career path away from .NET. There's a good chance this would have to be with an organization other than the one you're currently working for, unless they're very open-minded indeed.
- To satisfy pure intellectual curiosity. Learning is fun. That's why I'm still here in this industry two decades after leaving higher education.

I'll leave it to you to decide if you want to do this. For reference, however, I'm not interested in learning another language. I couldn't even tell you which to choose.

If it's of any use, though, the only source consistently recommended to me over the years is Miran Lipovača's website and book *Learn You a Haskell for Great Good!* (No Starch Press) (*https://oreil.ly/8V8CS*). That's probably as good as anywhere to start your new journey.

What About You?

Me? Well, it's time for this much 'nighted showman to wend his weary way onward—Punch and Judy show, puppets and tricks all packed up and carried on my back. If you want to keep in touch, you can find me on my website (*http://www.thecode painter.co.uk*) or at various software development meetups and conferences (mostly around Europe, but not exclusively). If you should run into me, leave me not yet cold and dark. Feel free to say hi. I might even share a round or two of beer!

Looking at the clock, there's still time for one last trick.

See here, nothing up this sleeve. Feel free to take a peek. Not that close, though! Cheeky. Nothing up *this* sleeve, either. Yet I shall vanish before your very eyes.

Are you watching carefully? Here I go…

Now you see me.

Index

goto command for trampolining, 198

H

Hanks, Tom, 209
Haskell
    Haskell Brooks Curry, 179
    as pure functional language, 17
Heinemann, Bill, 257
higher-order functions
    about, 4, 97-98
        flavors of, 97
        properties, 98
    alt combinator, 108
    chaining functions, 104-106
        Tap() to inspect at any point, 114
    composing complex functions, 109-112
    currying and, 184
    delegate types, 4
    enumerables updated, 121-123
    fork combinator, 106-108
    functional programming property, 4
        functions of functional programming, 4
        LINQ implementation, 32
    null handling, 119-121
    problem report showing need for, 98-101
        copy-paste and unit-test coverage,
            100-101
        thunks, 101-104
    thunks, 101-104
        doughnut functions, 102
    transducers, 112
    try/catch blocks, 115-119
history of functional programming, 1, 14, 179
Hoare, Tony, 72, 119
holiday package travel agency system
    discriminated unions version, 127-129
    object-oriented version, 125-127
Hugener-Olsen, Kim, 73
hypotenuse of triangle via Fork(), 107

I

IDbConnection via Reader monad, 165-168
    mock IDbConnection unit tests, 168
IDE and compiler option for nullable reference
    types, 70-72
Identity functor, 164
Identity monads, 174
IEnumerable
    custom enumerations, 89-92

custom iterator, 200
    custom enumerators implemented, 201
    enumerator anatomy, 200
    IEnumerable as pointer, 200
    indefinitely looping enumerables,
        203-206
film query code
    functional, 31
    nonfunctional, 30
Funcs to customize, 78
Maybe DU return type, 144
    Map() versus Bind(), 153
Seq as F# equivalent, 229
Snakes and Ladders via recursion, 194
thinking through a problem functionally,
    239
updating an enumerable, 121-123
IEnumerator, 200
    custom enumerators implemented, 201
IL (see Intermediate Language)
immutability
    functional programming property, 3
        LINQ implementation, 32
    making your code immutable, 46-48
        C# not enforcing immutability, 48
    read-only structs, 65
    recursion example, 10
imperative programming paradigm, 2
    baking a cake, 13
    functional code including, 239
    iterator value in Select(), 39
    List with foreach to be avoided, 38
    performance of OOP versus functional C#,
        231
indefinite iterators, 206-208
indefinite loops
    about, 191
    custom iterator, 200-208
    goto command, 198
    indefinite iterators used, 206-208
    Martian Trail game, 259
        game loop, 271-284
    recursion for, 194-196
    Snakes and Ladders game
        about, 191-194
        Dictionary of Snakes and Ladders on
            board, 192
        indefinitely iterating IEnumerable,
            200-208

Maybe DU with State monad, 170
user input error trapping and logging
without, 139
Tsvetkov, Andrey, 250
tuples, 55
old C# use KeyValuePair, 84
Reader monad for database connection,
165-168
mock IDbConnection unit tests, 168
State monads, 168-170
error handling with Maybe DU, 170
for state objects, 231
two dots (..) in switch expression, 63

U

unary functions, 187
unit tests (see testing)
Unless() executing Action only if false, 120
Usborne Publishing game source code, 257
user input for Oregon Trail via discriminated
unions, 136-139

V

validator code example, 79-81
variables
debugging via intermediate variables, 52,
152
Func delegates
about, 78
Funcs in enumerables, 78

pattern matching in old versions of C#,
81-85
validator code example, 79-81
higher-order functions passed as, 4
delegate types, 4
immutability of functional programming, 3
making your code immutable, 46-48
recursion example, 10
names serving as comments, 52
Visual Studio
currying and function type, 186
debug tools and Bind(), 152
F# code referenced in C#, 228-230
performance, 229
void return type
Action delegates, 4
methods, 5

W

warnings in IDE and compiler option for nullable reference types, 70-72
web page for this book, xvi
website for author, 290
where to go from here
learn F#, 289
more functional C#, 288
Where() and transducers, 112
with (keyword of record types), 68
Wlaschin, Scott, 74, 151, 289

About the Author

Simon J. Painter has been developing professionally for far, far too long now (well, since 2005) and has worked with every version of .NET ever released (including Compact Framework—remember that?) in around a dozen industries. In addition to his day job, he appears regularly at user groups and conferences to give talks on functional programming and general .NET topics. Simon has been a coding enthusiast since he was old enough to read his dad's copy of the Sinclair ZX Spectrum BASIC handbook. Besides code, he loves playing music, cryptic crosswords, *Fighting Fantasy* gamebooks, and far more coffee than is likely to be healthy for him. He lives in a small town in the UK with his wife and children.

Colophon

The animal on the cover of *Functional Programming with C#* is the eastern coyote (*Canis latrans* var.), also known as the coywolf.

One of 19 subspecies of coyote inhabiting the Americas, the eastern coyote is actually a hybrid of eastern wolf (*C. lycaon*), coyote (*Canis latrans*), and domestic dog, and is thus larger than the typical western coyote, weighing an average of 45–55 lb. It also holds a more extensive territorial home range and is present throughout the eastern United States and Canada, from Newfoundland and Labrador to Georgia.

Eastern coyotes are opportunistic omnivores and will feed on whatever is available and easy to kill or scavenge, from grasshoppers to moose. They typically live and hunt in small family units (consisting of an adult breeding pair and pups), though anyone privileged enough to have overheard a group howl at night might think them pack hunters like their wolf relatives: coyotes can raise quite a cacophony (*https://oreil.ly/IGHUv*) when they want to!

With a rising global population trend, coyotes are not currently considered threatened from a conversation point of view. Many of the animals on O'Reilly covers are endangered; all of them are important to the world.

The cover illustration is by Karen Montgomery, based on an antique line engraving from Lydekker's *Royal Natural History*. The cover fonts are Gilroy Semibold and Guardian Sans. The text font is Adobe Minion Pro; the heading font is Adobe Myriad Condensed; and the code font is Dalton Maag's Ubuntu Mono.

Go on, shoo!

And now you don't. You're still here? It's over. Isn't your family missing you? Go, spend some time with them!